D1070417

Colección Támesis

SERIE A: MONOGRAFÍAS, 359

NEW READINGS OF SILVINA OCAMPO

BEYOND FANTASY

NEW READINGS OF SILVINA OCAMPO

BEYOND FANTASY

Edited by

PATRICIA N. KLINGENBERG

and

FERNANDA ZULLO-RUIZ

TAMESIS

First published 2016
Tamesis, Woodbridge

ISBN 978 1 85566 308 4

Tamesis is an imprint of Boydell & Brewer Ltd
PO Box 9, Woodbridge, Suffolk IP12 3DF, UK
and of Boydell & Brewer Inc.
668 Mt. Hope Avenue, Rochester NY 14620–2731, USA
website: www.boydellandbrewer.com

The publisher has no responsibility for the continued existence or accuracy of URLs for
external or third-party internet websites referred to in this book, and does not guarantee
that any content on such websites is, or will remain, accurate or appropriate

A CIP record for this title is available
from the British Library

Typeset by
www.thewordservice.com

Contents

Illustrations

The editors, contributors, and publishers are grateful to all the institutions and
persons listed for permission to reproduce the materials in which they hold
copyright. Every effort has been made to trace the copyright holders; apologies
are offered for any omission, and the publishers will be pleased to add any
necessary acknowledgment in subsequent editions.

Contributors

Marjorie Agosín is Luella Lamer Slaner Professor of Latin American Studies at Wellesley College. Among her academic and creative publications are several articles on Silvina Ocampo. Her recent publications include a memoire, *Of Earth and Sea* (2009), and an edited collection of essays entitled *Inhabiting Memory: Essays on Memory and Human Rights* (2011).

Daniel Balderston, Mellon Professor of Hispanic Languages and Literatures at the University of Pittsburgh, is also the director of the Borges Center and editor of *Variaciones Borges*. His numerous publications include the first article on Silvina Ocampo published in the United States and an anthology of her stories in English translation, *Leopoldina's Dream* (1988). A much revised and expanded version of the latter is his *Thus Were Their Faces* (2015).

Patricia N. Klingenberg is Professor of Latin American Literature at Miami University, Oxford, Ohio. She has published numerous articles on Silvina Ocampo's short stories and is the author of *Fantasies of the Feminine* (1999). Recently she edited a collection of short stories entitled: *Silvina Ocampo: Cuentos de la 'nena terrible'* (2013).

Fiona J. Mackintosh is a senior lecturer at the University of Edinburgh. Her research on Silvina Ocampo has concentrated on poetry and translations. In addition, she is author of *Childhood in the Works of Silvina Ocampo and Alejandra Pizarnik* (2003) and co-editor of *Arbol de Alejandra: Pizarnik Reassessed* (2007).

Andrea Ostrov, Professor of Latin American Literature at the Universidad de Buenos Aires and researcher at CONICET, has published numerous articles on Latin American writers, including several on Silvina Ocampo. She is the author of *El género al bies: Cuerpo, género y escritura en cinco narradoras latinoamericanas* (2004) and editor of *Alejandra Pizarnik/León Ostrov: Cartas* (2012).

Ashley Hope Pérez is a graduate of Indiana University where she wrote a dissertation on cruelty in Latin American fiction. She is now Assistant Professor of Comparative Studies at The Ohio State University. She is author of several academic articles as well as of works of fiction including her novel, *Out of Darkness* (2015).

Judith Podlubne is Professor of Literature at the Universidad Nacional de Rosario where she directs the Maestría en Literatura Argentina. She has published important articles on Silvina Ocampo and recently authored *Escritores de* Sur: *Los inicios literarios de José Bianco y Silvina Ocampo* (2012).

Giulia Poggi is Professor of Spanish Literature at the University of Pisa. Her published articles cover a wide variety of authors of the Hispanic world, including several which study Ocampo's stories as they recast classic fairy tales in modern contexts and often with absurdist or surrealist subversions of contemporary logic.

María Julia Rossi is a recent graduate of the University of Pittsburgh and is an Assistant Professor at John Jay College, CUNY. Her research focuses on translation among the *Sur* writers and on the theme of servants in Latin American fiction.

Noemí Ulla, a writer of novels and short stories, was also a pioneer of studies of Silvina Ocampo and her literary circle. She was a researcher of the CONICET of the Universidad de Buenos Aires and author of a book-length interview with Silvina Ocampo, *Encuentros con Silvina Ocampo* (1982), as well as *Identidad rioplatense* (1990), *Invenciones a dos voces* (1992), and *La insurrección literaria* (1996). She was also the editor of *Silvina Ocampo: Una escritora oculta* (1999), and *Poesía inédita y dispersa* (2001), among other titles. She died on May 22, 2016.

Fernanda Zullo-Ruiz is Associate Professor of Spanish at Hanover College in Hanover, Indiana. Her research includes contemporary Latin American cinema as well as the works of Silvina Ocampo.

Acknowledgments

We would like to thank the Department of Spanish and Portuguese of Miami University and the Faculty Development Committee of Hanover College for material support. Deeply appreciated are Charles Ganelin's generous gifts of his time and expertise.

Patricia Klingenberg: I would like to dedicate this book in fond memory of Thomas C. Meehan, who introduced me to Silvina Ocampo in the first place and to Noemí Ulla who died during the final preparations of this manuscript.

Fernanda Zullo-Ruiz: I am grateful for the camaraderie and motivation of the Hanover Research Group and my Spanish colleagues who deserve many thanks for their consistent help and friendship. Through their example, on this project and others, Dan Balderston and Patricia Klingenberg have taught me how to be mentors in the truest sense. Their generosity, kindness, and friendship mean a great deal to me.

My parents, Angelo Zullo and Mirta Ruiz, were my first teachers and loving friends. They postponed their dreams so that I could pursue mine. Saying a mere thank you feels inadequate, but I will start there. A special thank you to my beloved daughter, Maris Buckwalter-Zullo. Your bravery, intelligence, and kindness inspire me every day. I hope to be like you when I grow up. And finally, my utmost gratitude to my best friend, stimulating colleague, and favorite interlocutor, James Buckwalter-Arias. He has proven to be my best reader (of people and books!) and loyal partner.

Introduction

Reading Silvina Ocampo

PATRICIA N. KLINGENBERG AND FERNANDA ZULLO-RUIZ

Silvina Ocampo has been described as having practiced the art of hiding in plain view. She remained a shadowy presence within the literary group which included her sister Victoria, the founder of *Sur*, Jorge Luis Borges, its most famous contributor, José Bianco, *Sur*'s director, and Adolfo Bioy Casares, *enfant terrible* and Silvina's husband, to name just the obvious connections. Once described as Argentina's most underrated writer (King, "Victoria" 18), Silvina Ocampo has more recently received a heightened level of attention from many different quarters. For instance, after many years all her works are back in print and a new critical book on her early work argues for her key position among the writers of *Sur*'s literary elite. As this book was being prepared for publication two new translations of her works into English have been published in the United States, and a book-length biography and numerous film and theater adaptations are appearing in Argentina and elsewhere.[1] These are excellent developments for those of us interested in her work, and make the current volume especially timely as it seeks to look both forward and back, at what has been written about and what still remains unstudied and unheralded in this remarkable writer's extensive oeuvre.

Noemí Ulla, the scholar who pioneered the systematic study of Ocampo's works, pointed out (*Escritora oculta*) that Ocampo was not studied at the Universidad de Buenos Aires until the late 1980s. Indeed, Patricia Klingenberg's 1981 dissertation, written at the University of Illinois, was, to our knowledge, the first in any language. The belated aspect of critical work on Ocampo has persisted even to the present. Part of the answer to why this has been so lies

---

[1]   A series of posthumous publications, discussed below, have appeared, beginning in 2006 and all of Ocampo's important poetry and stories have been issued in complete works format (Emecé) or as separate editions in recent years. Judith Podlubne's *Escritores de Sur* (2012) is the most detailed analysis of Ocampo's relationship to the *Sur* circle to date. Translations of Ocampo's short stories by Daniel Balderston and poetry by Jason Weiss, together with the biography by Mariana Enriquez, are listed in the Works Cited.

with the author herself: she refused to follow what Matilde Sánchez has described as the "career" of the literary author: attending awards ceremonies, serving on panels, granting interviews, and so forth. Silvina Ocampo refused absolutely to discuss her adult life, wrote no account of herself and her opinions, and deliberately allowed confusion to circulate around her, permitting, for instance, errors as basic as her date of birth to persist without correction, and famously signing books written by Silvina Bullrich for people who mistook her for a writer she despised. The shy, sly smile which comes through the photographs of the various gatherings taken of *Sur*'s glittering galaxy of stars can now be appreciated as indicating the conscious choices she was making, to remain aloof, even secretive, like one of her fictional characters. A second compelling reason for Ocampo's relative obscurity arises from the chaos into which her affairs fell following her death in 1993. Her estate was rolled into Bioy's and became part of litigation among the heirs upon his death in 1999. As late as 2014, the destiny of the personal library she shared with Bioy (and on many occasions with Borges) remained uncertain: more than four hundred boxes of books, many with notations by these authors, are in precarious storage as the National Library, the heirs, and other collectors dispute their ultimate fate.[2] The primary difficulties of her legacy, of course, involve the texts themselves, and this will be the focus of our efforts here.

Biographical Note

Silvina Ocampo was the youngest of six daughters born to one of Argentina's wealthy families. Her sister Victoria, the eldest, inherited the bulk of the family fortune and used it to found and support *Sur*, the literary magazine published from 1931 to the late 1970s, a publication of enormous cultural influence in Argentina and throughout Latin America.[3] Silvina first imagined herself as an artist, and studied in Paris with two famous precursors of surrealism, Fernand Léger and Giorgio de Chirico. On her return to Buenos Aires in the late 1920s she met Jorge Luis Borges through his sister Norah, a fellow artist; in the early 1930s she met and fell in love with Adolfo Bioy Casares and in that same period she gradually turned her attention to writing. Borges, Bioy, and Silvina Ocampo would join Victoria in the nurturing of the *Sur* literary project but, as John King pointed out, they formed a kind of subgroup who never fully embraced Victoria's enthusiasms.

---

[2]   An article in *Clarín* details the current condition of the books in the former Bioy-Ocampo library; the books are in boxes, unprotected from deterioration, and unavailable to scholars: http://www.revistaenie.clarin.com/literatura/biblioteca-maestros-cajas-deposito-alquiler_0_1212479151.html (accessed 25 April 2016).
[3]   Readers unfamiliar with *Sur* are urged to consult John King's invaluable study, *Sur: A Study of the Argentine Literary Journal and its Role in the Development of a Culture 1931–1970.*

1. Ocampo sisters on the steps of the family estate near San Isidro, c.1911. Victoria (reclining) and (l. to r.) Alejandro Leloir, Pancha Ocampo, Clara Ocampo, a cousin Saenz Valiente, Rosa Ocampo, and Silvina Ocampo (with arm around pet goat).

Silvina Ocampo's first literary work appeared in *Sur* in 1936, a short story that was included the following year in a volume of twenty-eight stories entitled *Viaje olvidado*, itself published by *Sur*'s book publishing house. On the occasion of this literary debut Victoria wrote a review of Silvina's book, which offered some scathing words of criticism and extensive advice. Forty years later, Silvina quoted nearly word for word several passages of this review as part of an interview with Noemí Ulla (*Encuentros*), an indication of how wounding this episode was for her. It would be ten years before she published short stories again.

In 1940 she married Bioy Casares in a small ceremony in which Borges was one of the witnesses. The same year Bioy published *La invención de Morel*, his most famous novel, and the three friends together published what would become a foundational volume, *La antología de la literatura fantástica*, which inaugurated Borges as a short story writer by including his "Tlön, Uqbar, Orbis Tertius." In the 1940s Silvina Ocampo published four volumes of poetry plus a detective novel with her husband, the only time they would collaborate directly.[4] In 1948

---

4   Other collaborations include two fairly unfamiliar plays: *Los traidores* (1956), co-authored with Juan Rodolfo Wilcock, and *La lluvia de fuego*, co-authored with Juan José Hernández, unpublished in Spanish, though published posthumously in French as *La pluie de feu* (1997). See Hernández's discussion of the writing process with Ocampo and why he was inadvertently uncredited: http://www.lanacion.com.ar/214576-la-obra-de-teatro-que-escribimos-con-silvina-ocampo (accessed 25 April 2016).

a new collection of short fiction, *Autobiografía de Irene*, appeared. For the rest of her life she would continue to write both fiction and poetry, eventually producing seven volumes of short fiction for adults and several additional ones for children. Her seven volumes of poetry were awarded the Premio Municipal in 1942 for *Enumeración de la patria*, a second place in 1954 for *Los nombres*, and the Premio Nacional in 1962 for *Lo amargo por dulce*. Ironically, her poetry, so highly rewarded during her life, has remained the least studied of her creative endeavors, excepting perhaps her plays and her works for children.

Silvina Ocampo wrote no memoir in the traditional sense, and in interviews throughout her life she refused resolutely to discuss her private life, famously omitting any mention of dates, and firmly placing questions about her husband off limits. Bioy Casares wrote several volumes of memoirs, which are listed in the Works Cited. In addition there are published biographies of both Victoria Ocampo and Bioy Casares, still better-known figures, which we have not listed since they are remarkably reticent on the subject of Silvina either as person or as author. Important sources for biographical information include the book-length interview of Silvina Ocampo by Noemí Ulla, originally published in 1982 (reissued and revised in 2003). *Encuentros con Silvina Ocampo* is rich in detail about Silvina's reminiscences about her childhood, which inform her fiction; her reflections on the practice of poetic vs. prose writing; and her attitudes generally about the imagination. Since the publication of Ulla's interview new information has become available in a memoir by Jovita Iglesias, the long-time housekeeper of Silvina Ocampo and Adolfo Bioy Casares, entitled *Los Bioy*. This is the best picture so far of the private life of the couple. It is especially useful in that it takes up their story around 1949, at a time when Ocampo herself was completely silent about personal events. Jovita is sympathetic, intelligent, and insightful; her evident affection for both of her subjects allows readers to see close up that the marriage between them was a real and loving one, despite its differences from conventional arrangements. Silvina Ocampo and Adolfo Bioy Casares forged a partnership which, in emotional terms, seems to have sustained them both in important ways for the fifty-plus years of their marriage.

Obviously, many gaps in Ocampo's biography still exist. It would be invaluable to have an account of the Paris years of the 1920s when her perceived failure as an artist was clearly an important experience. The combination of Ocampo's determined silence and the awkwardness of Bioy's written memoirs suggests that both were complicit in maintaining a wall of privacy around their personal arrangements. This tactic has not prevented speculation and rumor from swirling around them. In the years before her death in 1993 Silvina Ocampo suffered from dementia; she died in December, and in January of 1994, not even a month later, her daughter Marta was killed in an automobile accident. Bioy, devastated by the double loss, died himself five years later. Despite their fifty-year marriage, they are buried separately in the Recoleta cemetery, Bioy with his family and Ocampo (unmarked) with hers.

Early Critical Reception

As Silvina Ocampo's publications appeared they were reviewed regularly in the pages of *Sur*, first by her sister Victoria, as mentioned above, and subsequently by Ezequiel Martínez Estrada, Rosa Chacel, and Eduardo González Lanuza, among others. Their first comments regarding her short stories note the importance of the child's narrative perspective and of child characters, the marked presence of ordinary objects, and an interest in dream states, the fantastic, and horror. Her poetry is identified by the erudition of its historical and mythological references and its adherence to strict metrical forms. The publication of *La furia y otros cuentos* in 1959 merited a double review in which Eugenio Guasta describes the first notes of humor, the extreme brevity of many of these stories, and the combination of innocence and horror reminiscent of fairy tales. Mario A. Lancelloti, for his part, describes their poetic tone, and the author's interest in Buenos Aires which she describes with humor in an unlikely combination with the supernatural. The publication of *Las invitadas* in 1961 inspired a review by Lancelotti in which he uses the word *cruel* for the first time, a word that recurs in criticism of this author. Alejandra Pizarnik's review in *Sur* addressed the first anthology of Ocampo's stories, selected and introduced by José Bianco. Her review downplays the presence of the fantastic and stresses instead the ambiguity of Ocampo's tales. For many years the only lengthy article on Ocampo's poetry was the one by Helena Percas of 1954. Necessarily at that time her comments referred only to Ocampo's first three volumes. Percas compares *Enumeración de la patria* (1942) to the works of Leopoldo Lugones in order to underline the originality of Ocampo's "enumerative" rather than descriptive mode, and willingness to include the unlovely along with more traditionally beautiful items in her lists. As per Victoria's criticism of her prose, Percas notices the intrusion of English usage, specifically the preference for *con* [with] where Spanish would prefer *de*. Unlike Victoria, Percas sees this as part of Ocampo's originality. Her reflections on *Espacios métricos* (1945) include a comparison of Ocampo's poem entitled "Autobiografía de Irene" with the short story of the same title which had been published the previous year in *Sur*. Both works, she argues, illustrate Ocampo's relationship to reality: "La realidad objetiva es el pretexto de otra realidad mucho más viva y actual, ... la realidad de la imaginación que juega con los acontecimientos, los recuerdos, los objetos, y que nos los devuelve recreados" ("La original expresión" 289) [Objective reality is the pretext for another much more lively and current reality ... the reality of imagination that plays with events, memories, objects, and which returns them to us recreated].[5] As do commentators on the fiction, Percas notices the contrasting styles of her language, which includes "vocabulario corriente y prosaico" [ordinary and prosaic vocabulary] and "este otro, elegante y culto" [this other one, elegant and cultured] (294).

In 1966 and 1970 two anthologies of Ocampo's stories were collected by José Bianco and Edgardo Cozarinsky. Both provided extensive essays of introduction which offer the first serious study of the entirety of her fiction to that point. Bianco speaks about her use of fantastic devices that play with time and space, such as clairvoyance and metamorphosis; he addresses for the first time the sexual content of many of the stories. Cozarinsky describes the importance of everyday objects through their association with the sacred invested in humble beings. He suggests that the minutely described atmosphere, which resembles realism, is constantly subverted by fantastic elements. If Lancelloti had seen elements of Goya and Bosch in Ocampo's stories, an unspecified allusion to the grotesque (and to painting), Cozarinsky compares them to those of near contemporaries such as Franz Kafka, Katherine Mansfield, Isak Dinesen, Henry James, and James Joyce. Both Bianco and Cozarinsky noticed the odd combination of tones, the childlike with the poetic and highly literary, the innocent and the crude. Important full-length articles began to appear in the late 1960s by Enrique Pezzoni, Sylvia Molloy, Rosario Castellanos, and Blas Matamoro which fill in the details of the paradoxical quality of the stories and the odd mixture of styles. Even though Silvina Ocampo continued to publish major works, Matamoro's 1975 book chapter on her remained the most complete study of her work for many years.

In the 1970s not only did Ocampo publish a new volume of stories, *Los días de la noche* (1970), and a major volume of poetry, *Amarillo celeste* (1972), but also a series of works for children: three stories published separately, *El caballo alado* (1972), *El cofre volante* (1974), and *El tobogán* (1975); a volume of stories "for all ages" entitled *La naranja maravillosa: Cuentos para chicos grandes y grandes chicos* (1977); and a volume of poetry, *Canto escolar* (1979). These latter, to date, have received no real attention from critics. The translation of Ocampo's stories into French for the publishing house Gallimard, *Fait divers...* (1974), included a prolog by Borges and an introduction by Italo Calvino. Daniel Balderston's English translations of thirty-two of Ocampo's stories, *Leopoldina's Dream* (1988), were preceded by an introduction written in English by Silvina

---

5   Percas also quotes the line "Yo sólo recordaba el porvenir" [I only remembered the future], written fifteen years before the publication of Elena Garro's novel *Los recuerdos del porvenir*. For more on the complicated relationship between Elena Garro, Octavio Paz, and the Bioys, see Klingenberg, "A Life" 120–25.

Ocampo and a translation from the French of Borges's introduction to the Gallimard volume. Until recently this was the only English-language version of her work, and has been long out of print. In the 1980s the last of the author's original work published in her lifetime, *Y así sucesivamente* (1987) and *Cornelia frente al espejo* (1988), were issued by Tusquets.

The critical articles of this period can be counted on two hands: Giulia Poggi's 1978 essay identifying the fairy-tale underpinning of Ocampo's stories; Balderston's proposal of an aesthetic of cruelty in her work; Klingenberg's studies of feminine doubles, violence, and subjectivity; Barbara Aponte and Helena Araújo's studies of "El pecado mortal" [The mortal sin]. All of Ocampo's works were by then out of print and available only in academic libraries. The late 1990s brought a surge of critical interest in her work with important monographs appearing nearly simultaneously.[6] Those writers from around the world had been working in isolation from one another with little opportunity to assimilate new critical approaches from each other. The first essay of this volume offers an annotated bibliography of critical works from this period in an effort to understand the complex ways those critics intersected with and perhaps contradicted each other. In addition to a new critical interest in Ocampo through the 1990s, there was a publishing effort to bring her works back into print. Emecé began to offer both individual collections, crucially *Viaje olvidado* (1998), and volumes of complete works (*Cuentos completos* of 1999 and *Poesía completa* 2002). Sudamericana embarked on a multi-volume project to bring unpublished pieces into print. These posthumous pieces, mentioned above, are discussed in more detail next.

Posthumous Publications

First among the recently published titles is a compilation of poetry organized by Noemí Ulla (*Poesía inédita y dispersa*). A series of others, organized by Ernesto Montequin, also began to emerge, starting in 2006. Montequin has provided useful additional information about the condition of the various manuscripts and about the working process deduced from them. In prologs to the various volumes, which include a new compilation of short stories, a novel, a journal, and a memoir, Montequin has included details about how and where each manuscript was found, in part to situate each in its chronological order and to suggest its level of completion. Frequently, he says, Ocampo would write ideas in pen or pencil on random pieces of paper: envelopes, recipes, bills. Her

---

6   The list includes Graciela Tomassini (Argentina, 1995), Annick Mangin (France, 1996), Belinda Corbacho (France, 1998), and Klingenberg (U.S.A., 1999), with a book of essays edited by Ulla (*Escritora oculta*, 1999).

secretary of fifty years, Elena Ivulich, would type these so that the author could then make changes; she then would pass these along to Bioy who would make corrections and suggestions from which Silvina would again write a modified version. Often, according to Montequin, all of these versions were kept together in drawers and file folders. His depiction of Silvina's papers shows how important Bioy was to her work, a remarkable situation given that the evidence suggests (see, for instance, articles by Martínez de Richter and Astutti, discussed in the following chapter) that she often did not agree with him. What we find in these pieces is a continuation of themes and techniques already visible in her published volumes. In some cases these throw light on Ocampo's known material. It can be concluded that Ocampo knew how to select her work for publication: in general the items she left in the drawer are those that reveal too much, that fail to maintain the delicate ambiguity she prized and that her readers have long appreciated. That said, these often flat-footed versions do help to confirm some of the mysteries that have tantalized critics.

Of all the posthumous works, *Invenciones del recuerdo* (2006), a book-length autobiography in verse, is the most significant. Written and rewritten over many years – the author evidently began and destroyed various attempts in prose – it was a project with which she was never satisfied. Although we cannot know what form the author might ultimately have chosen, it is important to have this version come to light, especially since Ocampo wrote no other account of her life. This narrative poem is as close as we are likely to get to a first-person telling of her story in her own words. Montequin relates in his introduction a few facts about Ocampo's life as it is known from other sources, and confirms that the poeticized narrative matches these in most details. These situational elements appear in the poem and establish its autobiographical nature despite its third-person voice. The descriptions of her parents are more detailed than in any of her other evocations of them; she describes events surrounding the death of her sister Clara; her fraught relationship with one of the household servants; her love of animals; her first experiences with drawing; her puzzlement over her ability to predict the future. Ocampo said on more than one occasion that the experiences of childhood were the most intense and emotional of her life: here we revisit this familiar territory, now expressed explicitly as the author's truth.

Montequin describes *Ejércitos de la oscuridad* (2008) as a kind of diary, but without an ordered chronology. It is a series of fragments, deliberately disconnected. Montequin suggests that it was a kind of evening meditation for the author (Ocampo, *Ejércitos* 9). It is divided into four large sections written at different moments of her long life. One of the sections was written in a notebook given to her by Alejandra Pizarnik around the end of the 1960s. However, Montequin says that the friendship between the two poets does not seem to serve as an organizing principle since its contents are similarly loose ideas ("ideas sueltas") as in the others. Ocampo's readers will recognize the originality of these fragments and their humor: "A la vanidad le crece papada y a la modestia joroba" (20) [Vanity grows a double chin while modesty a hunched back]; "la bondad es el último subterfugio de las personas perversas" (21) [goodness is the ultimate subterfuge of perverse people]. One of the longer pieces can be recognized as the germ of a notorious story, "Las vestiduras peligrosas" [Dangerous dresses]. The author concludes that her husband thinks it is obscene or that it will seem pornographic in print. This cannot be helped, Ocampo writes in her journal, "Si un recién nacido tiene cola de cerdo o cuernos de ciervo o cara de enano, la madre llora pero no puede impedirlo" (99) [If a newborn has the tail of a pig or deer's horns or the face of a dwarf, the mother cries but cannot prevent it]. These posthumous works fill in the portrait of the author whose labor was even more constant and varied than had been imagined.

New Readings

Several of us who attended a conference dedicated to Silvina Ocampo in Buenos Aires in 2003, the year that marked the centenary of her birth, remarked on the need to offer new readings of Ocampo's works, since over the years the same stories had attracted the interest of many critics. The title of the current volume was born at that time. The second and equally notable aspect of the conference and the volume that emerged from it (Domínguez and Mancini) is that few of the contributors reflect a reading of each other. We have tried here to move beyond the most often-studied of her stories, and also to recognize and engage the different voices that have emerged regarding Ocampo's work. The contributors were asked to reflect on the work of others and not just to speak out of an imagined void. As a result, the chapters discuss the complex participation and resistance that Silvina Ocampo offered to her immediate literary circle; they analyze neglected aspects of her complete creative work, her poetry, her translations, and prose works either newly published or long overlooked; and they draw on critical approaches from a wide range of literary theories.

In the first essay of this volume, "Silvina Ocampo for the Twenty-First Century: A Review of Recent Criticism," Patricia Klingenberg provides a retrospective reading of assessments of the author: she begins with a consideration of the first book-length studies of Ocampo's short stories which all appeared at the end of the 1990s and then provides summaries of significant analyses up to the present. This long view reveals some of the critical threads which have shaped our understanding of this writer. All of the monographs of the late 1990s continued to concentrate on the stories, but sought to flesh out comments made more briefly by earlier critics. For instance, early reviews mentioned what Eduardo González Lanuza called "ese no sé qué inasible pero tan irreductiblemente femenino" [that ungraspable yet so irreducibly feminine something] of her stories, but systematic analysis from a feminist perspective would appear in these longer critical works. From the beginning, critics mentioned the peculiarity of Ocampo's style, and recent studies have worked to clarify her use of regional dialect and popular sayings, and her insistent narrative ambiguity. Gradually a body of comparative approaches has emerged, with essays that read Silvina with Victoria (Heker, Astutti), with Cortázar (Ulla), with Borges and Bioy (Speranza), and with Bianco (Podlubne). Only recently have studies focused on extended analysis of single stories, the poetry, or on Ocampo's endeavors as a translator of works from both French and English. In her recent monograph Judith Podlubne initiated a re-evaluation of Silvina Ocampo's place within her literary generation, which has already begun to reframe critical understanding of Ocampo's conscious decision-making as a writer.

The study of Ocampo's narratives continues in the present volume with a concentration, not on the plots, but on the voices of the narration. Andrea Ostrov's essay, "Re-reading *Autobiografía de Irene:* Writing and its Double in the Narrative of Silvina Ocampo," takes up one of the least studied works of Ocampo's oeuvre. The general consensus among scholars has been that *Autobiografía de Irene* (1948) represents a serious detour in Ocampo's evolution as a writer wherein she modified her style and thematics to better match those of her contemporaries, particularly Borges. Ostrov agrees with that assessment, suggesting that Ocampo took seriously the early criticism of her first compilation of stories, and strove to accommodate her style and subject matter to the prevailing taste. What Ostrov also shows is the continued originality of Ocampo's voice, despite her evident wish to bend her creative talents to a prescribed direction. Ostrov analyzes each of the five stories in terms of the meaning and problem of representation per se; what she finds is a constant association of language with duplicity and death. Re-reading them from this perspective makes the stories new again, and (re-)establishes Ocampo's unique talent even within an early stage of intense criticism.

Judith Podlubne continues in this vein with her essay, "*Sur* in the 1960s: Toward a New Critical Sensibility," making the claim that Silvina Ocampo from 1948 onward wrote with the understanding that her stories were deliberately conceived against the grain of her close associates and companions. They were neither the spiritual, "humanistic" efforts of a superior soul, as preferred by one group among *Sur*'s leadership, particularly her sister Victoria and Eduardo Mallea, nor were they the aesthetically perfected, well-wrought plots of Borges and especially Bioy. Others have observed that Ocampo puts almost too much faith in her reader, providing few internal clues as to how the often disparate elements of her stories are to be reconciled. Rather than attempt such a reconciliation, Podlubne demonstrates in detail the ways in which Ocampo avoids settling into any firm conclusion; her stories suggest several possible readings without favoring any single version. The interest inspired by these narratives is the indecipherable location of the narrative voice, rather than a decoding of what happened. The group of young critics working at *Sur* in the 1960s were the first to see this original element of Ocampo's fiction and used these insights, according to Podlubne, to fabricate a new critical method.

Ashley Hope Pérez's essay, "Reading Cruelty in Silvina Ocampo's Short Fiction: Theme, Style, and Narrative Resistance," argues that this very ambiguity, so prized by Ocampo, contributes to the reader's sense of the narrative's cruelty. Pérez provides a detailed overview of how critics have read and attempted to "explain away" the cruelty in Ocampo's stories, thus giving it a less threatening interpretation. She refutes these claims and asserts that Ocampo is actually deploying different strategies to frustrate readers' expectations for stable meaning, thus making the cruelty unassimilable. The interpretative burden resides with the reader since Ocampo's stories do not allow for neat and easy resolutions. Like Podlubne, Pérez locates the sense of cruelty in the narrative voice more than in the events of the plot, thereby refocusing attention on the style and tone of the narratives. By shifting the sense of cruelty to the narrative voice, Ocampo consistently blocks the reader's empathy, thereby creating resistant texts that stress their own artificiality and alterity.

In "Eros and Its Archetypes in Silvina Ocampo's Later Stories," Giulia Poggi concentrates her analysis on Ocampo's last published volume, *Cornelia frente al espejo* (1988). She analyzes the ways in which Ocampo incorporates classic fairy tales or folk motifs. While this is a practice Poggi has commented on in earlier articles, here she associates the process with postmodern tactics involving parody and collage, and an echo of the violence and cruelty observed in the previous chapters by Podlubne and Pérez. Poggi argues that in contrast with earlier stories which pair Snow White with the evil queen, female incarnations of good and evil eternally in violent rivalry, the late stories take a more singular and intimate view of female subjectivity, much more centered on the erotic. This is an unexpectedly rich approach to what are otherwise extremely puzzling stories. Poggi compares Ocampo's use of this material to that of contemporary women writers elsewhere, such as Angela Carter's "The Bloody Chamber." She is able to bring this analysis to bear on a wide range of stories included in the 1988 volume, convincingly proving that the classic fairy tale is central to Ocampo's purpose, rather than a detail.

In turning to Ocampo's poetry, we have translated an earlier study by Noemí Ulla, "In Memory of Silvina Ocampo," originally written to mark Ocampo's death. Noemí Ulla was the recognized pioneer of serious study of Ocampo's work, as well as being a creative writer of short stories and novels in her own right. This and her personal friendship with the author permitted her a unique perspective and allowed her to trace Ocampo's intimate, coded autobiographical references within her poetry. The poems speak about the author's parents, her sisters, her love of nature and the arts, her friendship and collegial dialogs, often about poetry, with Borges, and her theories of love. As Ulla had argued elsewhere (*Invenciones*), Ocampo's works, both in poetry and prose, indirectly map out a critique of the conventions of courtly love and invent new ways of being and of being in the other. The essay speaks of Ocampo's poetry in its entirety, providing a perfect bridge to the remainder of our volume.

Fiona Mackintosh has established herself as a pioneer in the consideration of elements of Ocampo's oeuvre beyond the realm of the short story. She has discussed the intersection of visual elements and poetry in Ocampo's collaboration with Norah Borges, and has worked extensively on Ocampo's interest in translation. Her essay, "Classical Reference in Silvina Ocampo's Poetry," continues these efforts to illuminate the poetic works of the author by relating the threads of classical mythology in both the poetry and prose. Ocampo's practice of translating English and French poets prodded her to incorporate references and motifs whose influence produces, in Mackintosh's words, a "classical feel" in both form and content. More specifically, the tension between old world and new is most evident in the poetry where the author often expresses her sense of being torn between two cultures. Mackintosh argues that in the poetry, the references to classical mythology clearly seek to "relocate the muse relative to her own New World position." The most frequent reference to classical literature is to Ovid's *Metamorphosis*, a consistent touchstone for Ocampo. Mackintosh concludes her essay with a study of the theme of Narcissus, whose focus on mirroring and identity enriches an understanding of Ocampo's insistence on doubles, eroticism, and death.

In "Silvina Ocampo and Translation," María Julia Rossi undertakes a study of Ocampo's work as a translator of poetry, recognizing that Ocampo considered the art of translation as itself a creative endeavor. The author's translations of various poets, but especially of Emily Dickinson, illustrate her interest in the process and also her dedication over many years to the exercise of translation. Drawing on the work of Fiona Mackintosh and others, Rossi begins with a general comparison of Ocampo's translations of Dickinson into Spanish with those made by others: she concludes that Ocampo's linguistic choices consistently opt for an emphasis on the emotional and intimate quality of Dickinson's verse, often reducing its metaphysical or philosophical overtones. Though Dickinson was clearly her most sustained interest, Ocampo also worked on other authors and in other genres. As the list grows it becomes truly remarkable that this aspect of Ocampo's work has been so little noted by scholars. Rossi dedicates the larger part of her chapter to yet another aspect of Ocampo's creative energy, a poem written originally in English. It was published under the pseudonym

"George Selwyn" and subsequently translated into Spanish by Ocampo; one of her short stories later uses the name of her pseudonymous author for the title character. The relationships among poem, translation, and story are a fascinating example of Ocampo's skill and humor.

One of the great themes of Ocampo's stories is children, a topic addressed by many of her scholarly admirers; the related theme of mothering, however, has been less often considered. The essay by Fernanda Zullo-Ruiz, "The Gender-Bending Mother of 'Santa Teodora,'" reads one poem in detail in order to demonstrate the complex play of gender at the heart of Ocampo's entire body of work. "Santa Teodora" appeared in *Breve santoral* (1984), a volume of poems and images prepared in collaboration with Norah Borges. This sonnet (con)fuses gender identity and sexuality in motherhood: the speaker in the poem is a woman masquerading as a man who is accused of raping and impregnating a young woman. Zullo-Ruiz explores how the voice and experience of the main character offer a reworking of the virginal, saintly, Madonna-like conceptualization of motherhood while simultaneously forcing a re-evaluation of the conflictive paternal role. Teodora's very existence in this poem, her overlapping identities and roles, combined with the ambiguity regarding her predicament force the reader to question the stability of meaning regarding gender, sexuality, and traditional parenting roles in a patriarchal context.

Daniel Balderston's comparative analysis of Silvina Ocampo and Alejandra Pizarnik, "Illicit Domains: Homage to Silvina Ocampo in Alejandra Pizarnik's Works," starts with a brief summation of their personal relationship as revealed in Pizarnik's diary and correspondence. The personal, intense identification of Pizarnik with Ocampo is obvious from these documents, and can be read in the poetry as well. Ocampo's professional importance to Pizarnik began with her review of Ocampo's *El pecado mortal*, the anthology of stories prepared by José Bianco, entitled "Dominios ilícitos," which appeared in *Sur* in 1968. Bianco's introduction to the volume and Pizarnik's review were two of the first serious studies of Ocampo's work to that date. Subsequently, several of Pizarnik's poems named Ocampo directly: Balderston offers an extensive comparative reading of "A un poema acerca del agua, de Silvina Ocampo" [On a poem about water by Silvina Ocampo], a poem that remained unpublished during Pizarnik's life. Balderston speculates that the particular Ocampo poem glossed is "Para el agua" [For water] from her *Amarillo celeste* (1972). Balderston draws from his comparison not only an illumination of the works of both poets but of their relationship to Octavio Paz. This essay offers an example of the work that still lies ahead for scholars, to further study the way Ocampo influenced writers of the following generations.

One of those writers of the subsequent generation provides a meditation which stands as a kind of conclusion to our volume. Marjorie Agosín reflects on the ways she has read and understood Silvina Ocampo, and in doing so, brings together many of the threads we have worked with as critics. As we explore in this volume the mechanisms at play in Ocampo's work, we discover traces of this extraordinary woman herself. Not only does this volume offer critical readings from different generations and nations, but it also reveals an intellectual map of Ocampo's readings of others. That is, we start to see her constant and consistent dialogue with *Sur* writers, either as a response to or reaction against them (Ostrov and Podlubne), with classical mythology and folktales (Mackintosh and Poggi,), and with other literary authors such as Ovid and Dickinson (Mackintosh and Rossi). In essence, we discover her dialogue with other texts. This volume, at its core, celebrates the richness of Silvina Ocampo the writer; and just as importantly, it celebrates the richness of Silvina Ocampo the reader and translator.

For Future Reference

Ocampo's poetry and stories have inspired many adaptations over the years – in music, cinema, and theater – and they, combined with her biography, continue to fuel new works. For instance, the Argentine composer Alberto Ginastera set to music Ocampo's poem "Enumeración de la patria" (1942) in his celebrated *Las horas de una estancia, Op. 11* (1943), for voice and piano. To date, nobody has explored the interplay between the written word and the accompanying musical score or the genesis of this project. Similarly, several of Ocampo's short stories have been adapted for both the big and small screen. The first of her stories to receive a filmic treatment was "El impostor": Alejandro Maci, María Luisa Bemberg's assistant, took over direction of the film *El impostor* (1997) following Bemberg's death in 1995. In 2000 the INCAA (The National Institute of Cinema and Audiovisual Arts) sponsored a contest for filmic adaptations of Argentine literary texts; Lilián Morello's script for "El vestido de terciopelo" was one of twelve chosen to become a telefilm and was broadcast in 2001 on the state-sponsored channel, Canal 7. *Cornelia frente al espejo* (2012), directed by Daniel Rosenfeld, is the latest reworking of an Ocampo short story for the cinema, and since its debut at the MALBA (The Latin American Art Museum of Buenos Aires) in 2012, it has been screened at other cultural venues in Argentina. All of these films owe an obvious debt to Ocampo's written texts, and we look forward to comprehensive studies of how these works were translated to the screen, incorporating or eschewing many of Ocampo's themes or stylistic choices.

In theater, the relatively recent discovery of Ocampo's posthumous piece (co-written with Hernández) *La lluvia de fuego* could offer scholars still another insight into this brilliant writer's literary work and writing process. One could perceive Ocampo's voice, through excerpted writings or fictionalized representations of her life, in the theater in the 2000s. The play *Cortamosondulamos* (2002) was based on her stories and *Divagaciones* (by Inés Saavedra and María Marta Guitart, 2004) on her poetry. In 2009 *Invenciones*, a play written by Alejandro Maci (based on poems and stories by Ocampo as well as a journalistic interview with her), debuted in Buenos Aires. The following year, *Mujeres terribles* by Marisé Monteiro and Virginia Uriarte, a piece inspired by the personal and professional relationship between Silvina Ocampo and Alejandra Pizarnik, ran at the Centro Cultural San Martín in Buenos Aires. And in 2013 three plays based loosely on her works were on stage: two of them, *Reliquia* (Julia Nardozza, Carlos Peláez, and Valeria Pierabella) and *Todo disfraz repugna a quien lo lleva* (Alfredo Martín and Grupo Hipocampo), used her stories as inspiration; the third, *Dirán que fue la noche* (Alfredo Martín), incorporated one of her poems as well as those of other Argentine women poets into the musical format. Clearly, proof of Ocampo's enduring legacy – not as Bioy's wife, Borges's friend, or Victoria's sister, but as one of the greatest Argentine writers of the twentieth century – is her growing influence on the many and varied forms of cultural life. Carlos Rapolla, the Argentine theater director, reminds us that "Silvina es un ícono de nuestra cultura. Que en la actualidad haya en cartelera una 'movida Ocampo' habla de su vigencia y de su poder de seducción, que actúa como un imán para cualquier director de teatro o cine" [Silvina is an icon in our culture. That at present there is an "Ocampo movement" in theater speaks to her relevance and her powers of seduction that work like a magnet on any director of theater or cinema] (quoted in Sabatés).

However, focusing solely on adaptations of Silvina Ocampo's works for cinema offers a myopic view of her impact on the seventh art. To Ocampo cognoscenti who watch a Lucrecia Martel film, it becomes apparent that this director not only read Ocampo, but learned a great deal from her. Interestingly, it was Martel who directed the television documentary on Ocampo for Canal 7 entitled *Silvina Ocampo: las dependencias* (1999), written by Graciela Speranza and Adriana Mancini. Martel's feature films *La ciénaga* (2000), *La niña santa* (2004), and *La mujer sin cabeza* (2007) have many points of contact with Ocampo's works. Laurence Mullaly's article, "Silvina en el espejo de Lucrecia: Ocampo-Martel, regards croisés entre cinéma et littérature," begins to trace various stylistic connections between the two artists, though much more remains to be explored in terms of their mutual interest in ambiguity, child protagonists, and violence. It is our hope that this volume will spur others to engage in the effort to uncover the unexpected reach of Silvina Ocampo's legacy.

1

Silvina Ocampo for the Twenty-first Century:
A Review of Recent Criticism

Patricia N. Klingenberg

A modest surge in scholarly interest, especially in the past decade, has meant that in some quarters Silvina Ocampo is now considered a canonical writer, while in others she remains virtually unknown. This uneven knowledge even among specialists in Latin American literature inspires the present review of publications whose purpose is to provide a history of recent criticism on the author which will bring this volume's reader up to date. The need for such a review reflects the multiple languages in which the literary analyses were written and the obscurity of the publication outlets, often small presses with low distribution, proceedings of conferences, local university operations, etc. This chapter begins with a discussion of five books that appeared nearly simultaneously in the late 1990s, the first book-length studies of Ocampo's work. A second section considers articles of the same period; the final section includes books and articles that have appeared in the last decade, beginning in 2003. The summaries are arranged in roughly chronological order for the purpose of providing a sense of the evolution of thought through the last two decades. The selection of the specific essays for detailed commentary necessarily reflects my own interests and bias, but the bibliography included at the end should assist further reflection or independent investigation.

Books at the End of the 1990s

At the end of the 1990s the first book-length studies of Silvina Ocampo's short stories began to appear nearly simultaneously. Noemí Ulla's *Invenciones a dos voces* (1992) was followed by two dissertations later published in France, an Argentine dissertation, and my book in English. A consideration of their coincidences and variances begins this review of the critical literature. Ulla's 1992 collection of essays discusses both Ocampo's prose and poetic

2. Silvina Ocampo and Adolfo Bioy Casares in his study at 1650 Posadas,
Buenos Aires, March 1980.

creations, comparing them to those of her contemporaries, Borges, Bioy,
and Cortázar in prose and Neruda and Paz in poetry. She describes the use
of documents, especially letters, as structural elements of the stories, and
oxymoron and enumeration as rhetorical devices of both the prose and
poetry. Most importantly, Ulla proposes what she calls the extensive
redefinition of courtly love which underlies Ocampo's works in both genres.
In offering a close reading of the sonnet "Amor" with the story "Amada en
el amado," Ulla addresses issues of gender and desire which would initiate
a lengthy re-evaluation of Ocampo for the twenty-first century. This
pioneering work was the first of a string of book-length studies, including
another by Ulla herself.

Graciela Tomassini's *El espejo de Cornelia* (1995) was the first systematic study of Ocampo's complete list of published narratives. Using structuralist and reader response approaches, Tomassini analyzes all the stories written during the author's lifetime, excepting the ones intended specifically for children. She focuses her comments around a central idea, that Ocampo's fictional world is characterized, both structurally and linguistically, by paradox, "donde lo trivial suele expresar lo sobrenatural, la banalidad puede servir a un planteo metafísico y la belleza abre cauces en lo abyecto, lo cruel, lo insignificante o lo estereotipado" (24) [where the trivial may express the supernatural, banality serves to present the metaphysical, and beauty opens pathways to the abject, the cruel, the insignificant, and the stereotyped]. Starting from that premise Tomassini offers a thorough discussion of structural elements, such as point of view. She studies in detail certain linguistic patterns, such as irony, exaggeration, and enumeration; and the use of colloquialisms, popular sayings, and other "debased" language codes. These, she claims, often appear in combination with the most lyrical of prose poetry. In four chapters she discusses the stories in chronological order; her introduction offers a brief overview of scholarship to date and the bibliographies provide the most complete listing I have seen of short reviews and brief commentaries and interviews printed in Argentina in the years prior to its publication.

Annick Mangin's *Temps et écriture dans l'oeuvre narrative de Silvina Ocampo* of 1996 selects six stories in as many chapters for detailed analyses of the way literary time functions in Ocampo's narrative. Since this book is difficult to obtain and underappreciated within the critical canon, I believe a relatively lengthy commentary is worthwhile. It is immediately clear that this wonderful study is far more than a technical discussion of literary time: Mangin's analysis examines time as a coordinating structure of Ocampo's fiction, but also explores how narrative moments work with each other, with space, with characters, and with the enunciating moment. Within the stories, time is also a theme (a topic of narration); they are stories about time. As I did a few years later (see below), Mangin chose "El diario de Porfiria Bernal" for extended analysis, noticing that the time elements in the story are difficult to correlate. Since my interest, developed over several chapters, focused primarily on the feminist approach to its female characters I commented only generally on its structure vis-à-vis the time disjuncture, concentrating on the possibilities offered by its ending in an un-narrated future. I have to admit that I thought Ocampo herself had made an error involving the dates of Porfiria's diary. The story suggests that Miss Fielding's document begins before she has completed the reading of Porfiria's diary at the end of 1930; she then finishes the reading at the end of 1931. Are we to believe she had the diary in her possession for more than a year? It seems more likely that the diary was written as the events of the story take place;

Porfiria starts in the contemporary moment and then begins to get ahead of herself, anticipating events at a moment impossible to designate, but confirmed on October 5th when Miss Fielding has been in possession of the diary for a few weeks. Miss Fielding begins reading in September of 1930 and, logically, both her reading and the diary's conclusion should match on a fatal date in December 1930, not 1931. Mangin's analysis eschews this kind of literal quandary, preferring to see the disjuncture of the dates in the two documents as part of Ocampo's overall approach to the problem of time.

Mangin offers a far more philosophical argument about time than a mere structural argument would constitute. In the case of "El diario de Porfiria Bernal," the tension she ultimately traces is between reader and writer, between Miss Fielding who believes that reality precedes and is separate from her text, and Porfiria who believes her writing is not just recording reality, but controlling it. Nevertheless, Porfiria's power of divination depends on Miss Fielding's reading; depends on being incorporated within the signifiers of the journal and on being read. Memory, for Porfiria, resides on the same plane as creativity ("Inventar es más fácil que recordar" (53) [inventing is easier than remembering]) and therefore is no less fictional. For Mangin, the originality of this story is that Miss Fielding, the reader of the journal, gives up her power, capitulating to Porfiria's created future: "hablará por mí el diario" (54) [the diary will speak for me]. The tension between the two characters and between the two texts is a struggle for the future and is reflected in the difference between writing and reading, between the narrator and the narratee of both documents; it is a fight which the student eventually wins over her governess.

Porfiria succeeds in turning her governess into a cat and having her disappear in the streets of Buenos Aires. Instead of conforming to the image provided by the teacher, the student, through repetition, *inflicts* the violence of institutional education against the supposedly dominant force of the teacher. But it is also the case that Porfiria fights against the image of herself produced by her surroundings. In her part of the story Miss Fielding relays the severity of the restrictions imposed on Porfiria; we can see that outwardly Porfiria is submissive to the demands of the hierarchy of her household and conforms to the outward image of a Botticelli angel which is expected of her. She puts her literary talent and her powers of divination in the service of a vengeance that will allow her to move from dominated to dominant. We can see in retrospect that Miss Fielding's entire story is written as a defense of the image of her created in the diary. Filled with insecurity and doubt, her version is a plea for her innocence. She says that she had the best motives, acted as a mother, and was not herself responsible for the severity of Porfiria's education. But her account calls the reader's attention to its quality of apology, a reflection of an uneasy conscience that portends her final capitulation.

Miss Fielding, in effect, shows that she is incapable of conceiving another discourse from the one of confrontation that pits one against the other as either winner or loser. She loses sight of language's provisional quality: finally, words are just words; they make up a relative system of signs without reducing the represented world to what is said; there is always open space by way of the word of the other. Miss Fielding misunderstands the limit to language's power, but, as Annick Mangin has so carefully shown, Silvina Ocampo does not, and her story ends in a future beyond the frame of the narration, permitting an ambiguity that allows her readers to mark out the complexity of time and text.

I have lingered on just one chapter of Mangin's book in order to show that it deals with more than just the mechanics of narrative time. One unexpected aspect revealed by her analysis is how much Ocampo's narratives refer to the past, even as they may seem to be obsessed with predicting the future; Mangin also discusses at length the role of memory and forgetting in both the fear expressed by many characters regarding the passage of time and the construction of identity. This is the core of Ocampo's interest in childhood, the traces of memory on which identity is based. Mangin argues that for Silvina Ocampo, the child only seems to be lost to the adult, but the child is still present, active and eternally part of all life stages superimposed and contemporaneous to the adult. Childhood is the privileged space of both memory and imagination and, as in dreams, is the space free of the measure and sense of time. The fantastic appears in her works as a play of two dimensions of time, the irreversible and its various subversions. The existence of these two orders and their interplay give rise to a narrative universe where the real and the imaginary are no longer clear categories. The fantastic character of the stories depends, not on some external force, but on the narrative structures and the function of language. The two dimensions of time, the reversible and the irreversible, are at the same time reflections of the dynamic between reading and writing. In other chapters Mangin takes up what she calls the inversion of time (by focusing on "Autobiografía de Irene"), circular time ("La liebre dorada"), ubiquitous time ("El bosque de Tarcos"), the eternal present ("El impostor"), and in an epilogue she offers a lengthy conclusion by way of "Magush." This book deserves to be, even now, more widely read.

Belinda Corbacho's *Le monde féminine dans l'oeuvre narrative de Silvina Ocampo* of 1998 uses a restrained mixture of theoretical methods in order to examine the gendered inflections of Ocampo's stories. She starts by noting the feminine that is evoked in first names (Irene, Violeta, Porfiria, Malva, Amelia, Rosalía, Arminda, Piluca), through function (seamstress, domestic, upper class woman), but also by spatial modality (places, objects, clothing), and by certain motifs, ideas, symbols, or myths. The importance of female characters is the primary focus of the study, but the masculine is essential to Ocampo's stories, even if only evoked, mocked, or moved aside in stories where the feminine prevails. Corbacho's strategy selects specific stories for lengthy analysis, starting with "Las vestiduras peligrosas" [Dangerous dresses], which serves to illustrate her argument about Ocampo's use of the feminine as illusion or deception as well as creation. Other chapters take up the fantastic process of metamorphosis, killing as an act of vision, and the feminine construction of space.

Corbacho is particularly attentive to the mythical underpinning of many stories, which greatly enriches the reading. For instance, the conflict between the two characters of "Las vestiduras peligrosas," Piluca the seamstress and Artemia her employer, operates, according to Corbacho, as a complex inversion of the Artemis myth. Artemis, the goddess of the hunt, feels an aversion to men and tries to avoid their gaze; she preserves her power by remaining chaste and immortal. Ocampo's creative character, the artist Artemia, operates an inversion of the myth, actively seeking not only the male gaze, but bodily violation and death, the opposites of virginity and immortality. Furthermore, the antagonism between the two characters represents two different social groups, two spiritual states, and two attitudes toward femininity regarding men, work, and the world. Corbacho identifies Artemia's desire for "success" as a desire for recognition, further defined as a desire to be bodily raped and killed. Piluca, then, represents the forces of societal law. In creating an extravagant character like Artemia, the author puts in place an aestheticizing invention which constitutes the feminine as masquerade, as artifice. And the conclusion is a kind of double seduction, for as Corbacho points out, Piluca's is the gaze that centers the work; she is Artemia's chief witness, her voyeur. At the intersection of myth, folktale, and fantastic story, this narrative dissolves the borders of genre. Corbacho quotes Giulia Poggi, who calls this story an "antifiaba," an anti-fairy tale. The doubled female character poses the question of feminine representation by way of an exaggerated femininity on the part of Artemia and its denigration by Piluca. The two characters reflect unconscious forces which make the story difficult to decode in a rational way. Here Corbacho has no doubt identified its attraction to critics, who have made it one of Ocampo's most often analyzed stories.

The book's second long chapter on feminine transformation studies three stories, starting with "Isis." Corbacho argues that the fantasy of metamorphosis is about doing without the body, but in my view the terms of her argument suggest that what is really rejected is not the body, but human language and consciousness. Associating the child Isis with the myth of Echo, who is only able to repeat the end of other people's sentences, confirms the importance of language. Corbacho rightly points out that the story works to eliminate the possibility of chance in the final metamorphosis. The ending, which suggests that the zoo animal has assisted in Isis's metamorphosis, proves her premeditation. Isis does not act through knowing, through language, but by way of a mutual gaze with this creature. If Isis has foreseen her disappearance through the mysterious power of her eyes, the narrator does not see the transformation; she deliberately turns away at the key moment. As in her previous chapter on "Las vestiduras peligrosas," Corbacho sees two approaches to the world insinuated in this story: that of the look/observation (Isis) and of the word/discourse (the unnamed narrator). Corbacho acknowledges my analysis but thinks the two readings complement rather than contradict each other.[1] Her own conclusion states that "Isis" shows the superiority of the imagination over the real, but I would argue that it privileges the imaginary over the symbolic, the body over language.

Corbacho's discussion of "El automóvil" compares it to Dino Buzzati's "Suicidio al parco," which she cites only in French and dates to 1972. Elsewhere the story is listed as part of Buzzati's 1966 collection entitled *Il colombre*. The Italian writer is a contemporary of Ocampo, also an artist as well as a writer of fiction, so while Corbacho's argument makes no claim to a direct influence it is entirely possible that Ocampo's version is a deliberate inversion of Buzzati's story. Both have the same motif, the transformation of a woman into a car. The difference is that for Buzzati's character, the car is a rival of his wife, an object of luxurious consumption and seduction, whereas the car in Ocampo's story is a rival of the husband for his wife's erotic passion and a means of her bodily escape from his domination.

One of Corbacho's most original observations comes from a chapter devoted to feminine space where she utilizes Gaston Bachelard's *L'eau et les rêve* to trace Ocampo's use of water imagery. Ranging from Ocampo's first stories, such as "El mar," through "La red," "Azabache," "El chasco," and "Keif," Corbacho traces their participation in a poetics of space and the ways in which water inscribes itself in a fictional, dream/ideal, mythic, and original place. The writer's work is filled with water and the feminine in the form of nymphs, feminine deities, and mythical creatures such as mermaids. For Ocampo's human feminine characters, confined in interiors, for whom exterior space seems unknown or dangerous, who are deprived of identity or individuality, water becomes the only place of solace or liberation. Whether water is a mode of suicide ("Keif") or accomplishment of desire ("El mar"), the stories give water a restorative and revelatory vision of another life; it is a motif of deliverance, a kind of refuge for the feminine subject (Corbacho, *Le monde* 205).

In her conclusion Corbacho returns to Giulia Poggi's 1978 article to quote her in saying that Ocampo's approach to the fantastic is deliberately different from those of her Argentine contemporaries where her privileging of the feminine is willfully deformed and deforming (Poggi, "Las vestiduras" 145). Certain stories make evident through irony, the fantastic, or through the presence of an

---

1   Corbacho refers to an early article, "The Feminine 'I.'" An expanded version of this analysis is also available in *Fantasies of the Feminine*, especially 169–75.

all-powerful woman narrator the supremacy of masculine desire, which stimulates or obstructs the quest of the feminine character. The masculine announces its presence also through hearsay, rumor, or *le discours gnomique* [short, pithy maxims]. This is the law of the father that infiltrates the discourse of certain characters, like Piluca, that perpetuates the system. The fiction abolishes masculine supremacy in re-imagining myths of a sacred pagan feminine force (Artemis, Isis, Circe). Ocampo does not try to dismantle man's power, but to confront it with a diffuse and secret counterforce which reveals its limits, its alienation, or its dependence on the feminine (Corbacho, *Le monde* 211).

My book, *Fantasies of the Feminine* (1999), the first in English on this author, begins with a lengthy analysis of what was already recognized in Ocampo's stories, the fantastic and grotesque elements. These are seen as subversive of received notions of reality, with the analysis paying special attention to Ocampo's unique female characters, including the many children. Approaches to the fantastic and the grotesque do not explain completely the power of Ocampo's stories, however. The specifically feminist subversion of dominant modes of discourse is analyzed in subsequent chapters, including the ways in which Ocampo rewrites and re-imagines the gendered arrangements of plot, the definitions of good and evil, the meaning of violence, and the cultural blindness toward female desire. The book concludes with two chapters which address what is called "writing the feminine," strategies for creating outside the parameters of the established norm. These strategies include Ocampo's use of letters and other documents as an extension of a long tradition of epistolary fiction which she employs in order to play with the location of the narrative voice; the use of objects and extraneous details as a kind of coded feminine language (defined by the dominant culture as kitsch); the presence of mirrors as a particularly feminine approach to transcendence; and finally the creation of ambiguity and silence as specifically feminine means to undo the certainties of readerly expectations.

Noemí Ulla observes in her prolog to *Una escritora oculta* (1999) that Silvina Ocampo's works were not studied in the literature department of the Universidad de Buenos Aires until the 1980s. But in this volume of critical essays, Ulla is able to collect studies by scholars working in three different countries: France (Milagros Ezquerro, Belinda Corbacho, and Annick Mangin), Germany (Marily Martínez de Richter), and Argentina (Adriana Mancini). This chorus of international voices draws attention to the possibilities of psychoanalytic and feminist approaches to Ocampo's fiction. In her chapter Milagros Ezquerro discusses the story "La liebre dorada" and the odd blend of elements – typical of Ocampo's fiction – that it introduces: its strange narrator, an apparent first-person witness who nevertheless narrates as if omniscient; its textual references to Cervantes's "El coloquio de los perros" and Horacio Quiroga's "La insolación" (where the animals also talk); the inclusion of characters whose names are those of the author's friends (Jacinto and

Jorge Alberto Orellana); and the probable inspiration for the story in a personal experience combined with a visual image, possibly from a child's book. This and others of Ocampo's stories emphasize the unsettling nature of the author's fiction for a reader disoriented by their mixing of narrative levels.

Belinda Corbacho's chapter in the same volume expands on the observations about feminine space made in her book. Quoting Irigaray's suggestion that women perceive themselves bodily as interior, unknown space, Corbacho argues for attention to be paid to Ocampo's use of closed interiors, especially the house, or rather, rooms within a house. Taking "La escalera" [The stairway] and "El sótano" [The basement] as examples, Corbacho notes that the characters are completely defined by the locations noted in each title. Adriana Mancini's chapter also takes up this issue in a close reading of "La paciente y el médico" [The patient and the doctor]. The patient of this story occupies an enclosed private room, while the doctor walks through the streets of Buenos Aires, through the open public sphere where, nevertheless, he can "see" his patient by way of a photograph. The magical properties of photography are repeated elements in Ocampo's fiction as discussed in the chapter by Annick Mangin. Her close reading of one of Ocampo's most-discussed stories, "Las fotografías," concentrates on a double discourse in which the reader perceives a metaphoric level of profound and complex meaning revealed by way of the surface details, which seem trivial and ultimately cruel. By the end the death seems expected, and the reader has been made complicit in the tragedy. The narrator's indifference highlights and exaggerates the story's cruelty. As suggested by Esquerro's essay, Mangin also argues that the reader of this story is placed seemingly within the frame as one more character, equally guilty because unable to denounce the described behavior.

In the same volume Marily Martínez de Richter's "Triángulo de tigres" proposes a comparative study of the tiger motif in Ocampo, Borges, and Bioy Casares. As a first detailed look (following in Ulla's footsteps) at the differences that appear among the writers of this threesome, it is worth considering at some length. While her complete essay undertakes a persuasive comparison between Borges and Bioy, her conclusion stresses the ways in which Silvina Ocampo operated in opposition to both, a finding that in the future would be confirmed by others. A well-recognized recurring element of Borges's poetry and fiction, the tiger appears only once in Bioy's work, according to Martínez, in "El héroe de las mujeres," while tigers dot Ocampo's stories in more numerous ways.[2]

---

2   The tigers of Ocampo's fiction are more numerous than Martínez suggests: she lists an embroidered towel in "Y así sucesivamente," but doesn't list, for instance, the various embalmed tigers of "Esclava de las criadas." She suggests that Keif in the eponymous story is only half-tiger, half-dog. I would say that Keif is compared to a dog in various places but is fully identified as an Asian tiger.

The Ocampo narrative that she analyzes in depth is "El rival" [The rival] which seems to describe what Martínez calls a "tigre overo ... también llamado jaguar" [a tawny tiger, also called a jaguar] in direct contrast to Borges's insistence on the Asian tiger, "rayado, asiático, real" [striped, Asian, and regal] (quoted from *El hacedor* by Martínez 61). The three stories have in common the narration of a journey – defined as a heroic quest in the tales of Borges and Bioy but as a simple "encounter" in Ocampo – and a metamorphosis.

Ocampo's purpose is to deconstruct the language and conventions of romantic love, and parody the works of the other two. Martínez starts usefully with the author's interest in art, arguing for the influence of Cezanne, especially in terms of his affirmation of the geometric basis for all natural forms. The critic notes Ocampo's "cubist" description of the rival with his "pupilas cuadradas" [square pupils] and "boca triangular" [triangular mouth]. Martínez refreshingly admits that she simply did not understand the story on her first reading, completely perplexed by the ending, "no por fantástico sino por incomprensible" (75) [not because it is fantastic but because it was incomprehensible]. The narrative ends abruptly, with no attempt at explanation, but does imply a "perversity" of destiny and desire. Martínez suggests that Ocampo asks much, maybe too much, of her reader. The story's *ménage à trois* is narrated, as in Bioy's story, by one of its male characters who is puzzled by the girl's attraction to a man – the rival – whom he finds ugly; Ocampo's character discovers, however, that without the rival he is unable to act. It seems clear that all of the pairs in this story need a third term in order to function. In the story's perplexing ending the rival returns after a brief absence apparently transformed into a jaguar, recognizable by his distinctive "triangular" eyes, and enters the tent where the girl is sleeping. Martínez posits the ambivalence of Ocampo's ending as a direct response to Borges's serious epiphanic moments:

> Creo que Silvina se divierte imaginando el espanto del pudoroso Borges ante ese destino perverso ... a los "obscenos" tigres azules de Borges, puramente intelectuales, Silvina responde con una variante sodomita de la especie, a la solemnidad con que el Maestro trata al destino, opone una visión desacralizada, sexualizada, burlesca y paródica de su relación con los mortales. (84)

> [I think Silvina has fun imagining the horror of the reserved Borges faced with that perverse ending ... to Borges's purely intellectual "obscene" blue tigers, Silvina responds with a sodomitic version of the species: to the solemnity with which the Master expresses destiny, she opposes a desacralized, sexualized, burlesque, parodic vision of its relation to mortals.]

Ocampo's story is "insólito, transgresor, extravagante" [startling, transgressive, extravagant]. Martínez concludes by saying that the three authors, lifelong friends, maintained a discreet reticence about any disagreement they may have had between themselves: however, "los textos son mucho más elocuentes" (85) [the texts are much more eloquent].

Articles and Book Chapters 1996–2000

Important new studies began to appear in Argentina, for reasons that are not completely clear to me, around 1996. Perhaps the author's death in the last weeks of 1993 drew the attention of scholars in greater numbers. Many of these began to offer comparative readings of Ocampo with those of her immediate circle. As ever, Noemí Ulla was a pioneer in this effort. Her book *La insurrección literaria* (1996) devotes one chapter to a direct comparison of Ocampo with Cortázar where she focuses on parody and popular speech. Ocampo's use of the epistolary mode in many of her texts serves as a mask by which she is able to switch gender and "borrar todas las pistas de sí misma como autora" (Ulla, *La insurrección* 41) [erase all evidence of herself as author]. It is also a mode which permits the use of colloquial expressions; Ulla discusses the exactitude with which Ocampo imitates local dialect with the *voseo*, the diminutive, and the abundant use of nicknames. In the following year "Huellas de una poética" expanded on this argument to suggest that Ocampo's epistolary stories of *La furia* express a wide range of societal and intellectual elements within the speech patterns of Buenos Aires, ranging from the language appropriate to an aspiring author of "La continuación," to that of the little boy from the lower classes of "La casa de los relojes." In the use of colloquial speech Ocampo is much more adventurous than any of her immediate colleagues, including Cortázar, who wrote admiringly of Roberto Arlt but did not, in his own fiction, vary from the correct usage of Borges or Bioy. A decade later in *Variaciones rioplantenses* (2007) Ulla speculates that Ocampo's belated status within Argentine letters had to do with the preference among critics for politically engaged literature which devalued the imaginary works of an entire generation.

Guillermina Walas's "La mirada en la escritura" (1996) was the first article to compare Ocampo with a contemporary woman writer other than her sister Victoria by juxtaposing Norah Lange's *Personas en la sala* with Ocampo's "El diario de Porfiria Bernal." Both works raise the issues of feminine subjectivity and identity construction viewed by Walas as forming within a space of transgression from social norms. Ocampo's divided narrative provides a voice for two female speakers, both utilizing private, feminine, literary structures: the letter and the diary. Ocampo's two characters can be perceived as spying on each other in a complex game of competition and complicity. The unnamed narrator of Lange's novel stakes out her point of observation from within one closed space to view another, trying to understand the behavior of an intimate family group; in that way she is most like Ocampo's Miss Fielding whose version of events produces a study of the Bernal family. All three narrators reveal their fascination with minutely observed, intimate, feminine behavior. The most interesting of these voices is undoubtedly that of Porfiria whose diary becomes far more than a mirror held up to the writer, as in a traditional diary, but rather a form of revenge directed at Miss Fielding. The fact that Lange's spying character keeps her activities secret from her own family gives the act of watching and telling an air of transgression, particularly significant for Walas in the fact that both the observer and the observed are all female. Ultimately this air of secrecy is what the two texts have in common. Walas suggests that women writers of this era conceived of a feminine subjectivity by looking imaginatively at what was forbidden to those of previous generations or left out of the fictional works of men.

Andrea Ostrov utilizes international feminist theory in approaching Ocampo's texts. Her two articles published in 1996 and 1997 study the intersections between text and textile, gender and language in Ocampo's narratives, arguing that they often playfully subvert accepted norms of literary genre and human gender identity. The first describes Ocampo's subversion of the dichotomy active/passive as it relates to gender stereotypes. As others have noted, the female character who steps out of the passive role is labeled in some way as monstrous; Ocampo's works attempt to blur these definitions of "angel/monster" often through a parody of feminine masquerade. Both essays quote Enrique Pezzoni's suggestion that the subversive element of Ocampo's stories relies on an exaggerated compliance with gender norms. Ostrov gives several examples of female characters who take rules of comportment literally and play out "el fracaso estrepitoso de una puesta en escena de la femineidad" ("Género" 302) [the clamorous failure of a staging of the feminine], using "Las vestiduras peligrosas" as the primary example. The various dresses, wigs, makeup, and other artifices of femininity are viewed in the stories as inseparable from the body, thus negating a strictly essentialist concept of human subjectivity. The feminine in Ocampo's fiction is presented repeatedly as constructed and therefore disposable. Ostrov further argues that the many doubles of Ocampo's stories confirm an oscillating, rather than a fixed, identity. She concludes that every conceivable opposition – inside/outside, presence/absence, life/death, word/deed – is relentlessly overturned in story after story.

Adriana Mancini's long article "Amo y esclavo" [Master and slave] of 1998 is interesting in two ways: she recounts the events behind the publication of Jean Genet's *Las criadas* [The maids] in *Sur* and relates Genet's material to several stories by Ocampo. The translation of Genet's novel was a joint effort with José Bianco so that Ocampo's story dedicated to him, "Esclavas de las criadas" [Slaves of the maids], suggests the relationship between the two narratives. Mancini points out that, in contrast to Genet's novel in which the servants betray the master, Ocampo's story proposes the reverse. The servant cares for her sick mistress such that the latter ends up living for many years, while the wealthy ladies who try to steal the former away begin to die mysteriously. The treason, therefore, is between people of the same class, rather than across the class divide. The 1948 publication of the translation of Genet's novel marks a definitive moment within the *Sur* group, according to Mancini, after which a split developed, with the Ocampo sisters on opposing sides. Victoria's review of the translation describes the novel as "literatura sórdida" [sordid] and goes on to deride those who believe that "la mierda es más verdadera que la rosa" (quoted in Mancini, "Amo" 79) [shit is more real than a rose]. Mancini thinks, however, that the translation hardly copies the vulgarity of Genet's original, but rather smooths it out with "una escritura del decoro" [decorum].

Adriana Astutti begins her book on contemporary authors, *Andares clancos: Fábulas del menor* (2001), with a study of Borges which clarifies her use of the word "menor" to mean minor, as in minor author, though in the case of Silvina Ocampo, as we shall see, she expands it to play with the word's other meaning: "younger," as in the little sister. When she turns to Victoria and Silvina Ocampo, Astutti says her original intention was to compare Victoria and Virginia Woolf, especially where Victoria describes her desire (in the prolog to her first volume of *Testimonios*) to write like a woman and not use a masculine style or a man's voice. Astutti believes that Victoria managed to find that feminine voice in her own essays, but ultimately could not write fiction because she was unable to relinquish her identity as a particular person; she could not do what fiction writing requires, abandon herself to the other. Astutti suspects that Victoria discovered a genuine woman's voice in reading fiction, but it was written neither by Virginia Woolf, Emily Bronte, nor any of her other favorites: it was written by someone Astutti describes as closer, yet further away: her youngest sister, Silvina (154). Victoria is her only character, and she tells all in an "escritura indiscreta" [an indiscreet writing] while Silvina's writing is all fiction and stays firmly "del lado del secreto" (156) [in the realm of the secret]. Victoria writes essays and autobiography which aim to draw lines from one memory to another, to make a coherent account of cause and effect, using letters to fix dates, so that everything is realistic, organic, and truthful. Silvina loses herself in the unknown and the incoherent; her memories are isolated, devoid of a context she does not even try to provide. Victoria expresses herself as the big sister, "osada y combativa" [daring and combative] while Silvina is "un vago etcétera" [a vague etcetera] who nevertheless knows how to pierce the surface in a style which couches the disturbing within the commonplace (156). Silvina's world is at once uncanny and trivial; though often narrated from the vantage of childhood, the uncanny comes from misunderstandings or from a literal reading and is never *aniñada*, childish. Childhood characterized Silvina's self-image as well as her fiction (something that will be discussed by others below) in a gesture which crosses life and literature (157). The image of hunger in Victoria's works is a sign of lack, the desire to appropriate; in Silvina it is "el fluir del deseo, la sensualidad, una potencia inquietante" [the flow of desire, sensuality and a disquieting power]. Astutti exemplifies her arguments using Silvina's stories such as "Malva," "Los amantes," and "Mimoso," each of which uses grotesque bodily functions and clichés to produce the effect of comic horror, so antithetical to the cerebral high culture of *Sur*.

Graciela Speranza's chapter in *Homenaje a Adolfo Bioy Casares* (2002) makes a direct comparison between Silvina Ocampo and the works of her husband related to their voicing of characters identified as "other," usually by their social class. Speranza argues that Bioy maintains what she calls a prudent distance between the narrative voice and his characters (in her analysis of *El sueño de los héroes*, 288). His narrators speak with an elegance and correctness that distinguishes them absolutely from the lower-class characters who are parodied, whereas Ocampo's fiction shows "una voluntad verdadera de pasar al otro lado" (291) [a real willingness to cross to the other side], blending the narration of lower-class characters with the narrating voice. Speranza suggests that Ocampo's early interest in the serving class formed her acute ear for popular sayings, clichés, and gossip. For instance, Jovita Iglesias, her longtime head housekeeper, confirms that she frequently read in Ocampo's stories, especially "Las vestiduras peligrosas," "algo de lo que yo le decía, pero transformado" (286) [something like what I would say to her, but transformed]. In fact Speranza argues that Ocampo's stories work, not to stress the difference between social dialects, but to blur their lines: "la lengua oral popular se naturaliza en la lengua literaria sin subrayados ni excesos, sin incorrecciones ridiculizadas" (291) [popular oral language is naturalized within literary language without underlining it, without exaggeration or incorrect usage that is mocked]. In Ocampo's works, as in those of Manuel Puig, there is a fundamental lack of conviction in a single personal voice; rather, both authors show an interest in using literature to renovate the perception of authentic language, what Speranza calls "la primera persona del plural" [first-person plural]. This impulse to blur differences is what ultimately distinguishes Ocampo and Puig from the first-person singular of both Bioy and Borges.

In 2002 the Spanish literary review *Cuadernos Hispanoamericanos* dedicated a special issue to Silvina Ocampo, another critical milestone for scholarship on this author. The volume opened with translations into Spanish of two Ocampo prologs, one, originally written in English, for the Penguin translation of a compilation by Daniel Balderston entitled *Leopoldina's Dream* (1988); the other, originally written in French, for a 1964 translation of Borges's works published by Cahier de L'Herne. The English prolog is one of the few places where Ocampo speaks about her training as a painter. Of her two teachers she says that Léger spoke most favorably about her work and convinced her to value drawing; Chirico, on the other hand, was carried away by his love of color. Speaking about her turn from painting to fiction she goes on:

> That was how I began to grow disillusioned. I drew away from a passion that was also a torture for me. What was left for me? Writing? Writing? There was music, but that was as far beyond my reach as the moon. For a long time I had been writing and hiding what I had written. For so long that I suffered from the habit of hiding what I wrote.[3]

This is a rare non-fictional version of her personal experience with painting and writing. In another non-fiction moment, the prolog to Borges's stories, her purpose is to characterize his works for a French readership, but what we see is a set of seemingly random anecdotes, which is suggestive of her approach to memory in general. This translation from French allows a rare view of their friendship. She describes Borges's fear of masks, his love of pretty women, his art of conversation. Silvina laments that his sister Norah does not paint him, but says that his spirit is captured in a photograph taken of him by Bioy. In a rare reference to Argentine politics she speaks fondly of the group of writers who formed their circle when "aún no los habían separado ni la muerte ni las ideas políticas" [neither death nor politics had yet separated them]. She describes happy times over dinner, car trips, long walks, shared sadnesses, and "la angustia de una tiranía vergonzosa, a veces grotesca o trágica, cuya voz –terriblemente argentina, debo reconocerlo–, invadía nuestras calles y nuestros hogares" (12) [The anguish of a shameful tyranny, by turns grotesque or tragic, whose voice – terribly Argentine, I have to recognize – invaded our streets and our homes].[4] These translations are important contributions to a greater understanding of several aspects of Ocampo's life and work.

Reina Roffé's brief contribution to this volume, which she also coordinated, describes Ocampo's attitude when writing: "la niña mala que jugaba hasta las últimas consecuencias literarias (y antiliterarias)" (18) [the naughty little girl who plays out the literary (and antiliterary) consequences of her actions]. She rightly argues that Ocampo's feminism is to be found in her writing and not in her spoken pronouncements on the subject. With time, a wider readership is discovering the audacity and originality of her texts (20). Noemí Ulla's "En memoria de Silvina"

---

3   I am quoting the original English version, in *Leopoldina's Dream*, "Author's Introduction" x.
4   One of the extremely rare direct references to the first Perón government of 1945–55.

offers the perfect key to her poetic autobiography, revealing the references which may not be obvious in numerous of Ocampo's poems. We are pleased to translate it in the present volume for English-speaking readers.

Judith Podlubne's article for this special issue traces the genesis of Ocampo's narrative voices to the oral origins of the short story. It is the importance of the narrative voice itself, Podlubne argues, that Silvina Ocampo recuperates in *Viaje olvidado*. In this Ocampo goes against the schemes of theorists of the short story, such as Propp, who attend only to the actions of the plot and not to its narrative perspective. This is an original and detailed argument for Ocampo's deliberate strategy as a writer in opposition to the carelessness that Victoria saw in her 1937 review in *Sur*. Podlubne believes that Victoria was at least partially correct in her original review: Silvina's narratives are "recuerdos enmascarados de sueños" [memories masquerading as dreams] ("El recuerdo" 37). Neither "negligencia" nor "pereza" [laziness] flaw Silvina's first stories, nor anything like inexperience (Victoria's judgements), but a daring attempt to capture ancient forms embedded in childhood memory. Milagros Ezquerro's contribution also speaks to the traditional underpinnings of many of Ocampo's tales. Here the critic studies the ways in which a switch of gender changes other elements of the classic tale of Blue Beard in Ocampo's adaptation, "Jardín de infierno" (*Cornelia frente al espejo*). Ocampo's female Blue Beard transforms the story from one of many ancient tales of female curiosity, especially that of Eve in the biblical story of origins, to a consideration of female monstrosity. The character's methods are manipulation and indirection rather than brute force. And, characteristically, the story ends with an open possibility. As Ezquerro points out, it does not end with the aptly named Bárbara entering the room of the hanging corpses, but with her reading of what seems to be a suicide note. What if the note is a trap? The documents of Ocampo's stories, such as this note, serve the purpose of providing an open ending in which the reader must imagine the consequences of an act of reading.

Monographs and Articles since 2003

Marcia Espinoza-Vera's book-length monograph was the first to make extensive summative and comparative study of the different critical appraisals developed around Silvina Ocampo's work internationally up to this point in the early 2000s. Writing from Australia, this critic refers to a wide range of critical commentary on Ocampo in three languages, and offers detailed assessments of differing approaches to the specific stories she studies. Since her topic is ambiguity, Espinoza-Vera is able to contrast more than one reading of many of these works and guide her reader to an awareness of the rich variety of approaches and readerly reactions. Her separate chapters trace the details of narrative unreliability as functions of humor, as fantastic elements, and as gender issues. She utilizes critical theories developed in French, primarily structuralist, and in English, primarily feminist, and thus offers the most complete understanding to that date of the work done on Ocampo around the world.

Adriana Mancini's 2003 book, *Silvina Ocampo: Escalas de pasión*, provides a useful introduction which situates Ocampo within what she quotes Juan Rodolfo Wilcock as calling "la trinidad divina" [the divine trinity] with Borges and Bioy. Starting her review of critical reaction to Ocampo with the 1970s, Mancini cites various critics, especially Marcelo Pichon Rivière, as describing the contrast between the fame of the other two and the "abrumadora indiferencia" [stunning indifference] of the Argentine literary establishment to Ocampo. The book in general seeks to apply primarily French literary theory to Ocampo's texts and compare her works to authors from the twentieth century to whom she might usefully be compared (excepting any from Argentina beyond the two mentioned above). For instance, Chapter II uses Deleuze on the Baroque fold and Barthes on fading to compare Ocampo's narrative structures to those of Henry James, Marcel Proust, and Virginia Woolf, particularly in the ways all of these writers display what in the introduction was called "la promiscuidad deíctica" [deictic promiscuity], that is, the ability of the narrative perspective to evolve and float, breaking the established rules of point of view. In Chapter III Mancini arrives at her primary interest, Ocampo's rewriting of the language of love, for which Noemí Ulla is the uncredited precursor. Mancini continues with the vicissitudes of love in Chapter IV by discussing the love–hate dimension so frequently explored in Ocampo's texts. The reading of "La expiación" uses Barthes's *Fragments d'un discours amoureux* (1977) to argue that a fascination with the rival amounts to a love–hate relationship with its own rich resonance in Ocampo's stories. Mancini quotes Sylvia Molloy's reflections on what she has called "lo dicho no dicho" [the unspoken spoken] in which the exaggerated insults of certain narrators amount to a proclamation of love. Saying the opposite of what is intended is one way to suggest taboo themes such as the homoerotic. Genette argues that figurative language is the only way to express erotic passion and for that reason it is easily associated with magic.

Chapter V is dedicated to magic and the erotic, and here Mancini associates several of the stories with autobiographical material she believes links directly to the fiction. She thinks, for instance, that the change of title of "La muñeca" [The doll] from its original, "Yo" [I], calls attention to the self-reference of the story about a little girl who can predict the future.[5] The story "La sibila" [The sibyl] was originally intended by Ocampo to name the volume, ultimately entitled

---

5   The story was published as "Yo" in *Sur* 272 (1961): 47–57. Later it was included in *Los días de la noche* with the title changed.

La furia. Jovita Iglesias, according to Mancini, attributed to Borges the thought that the similarity of the two words sibila/Silvina would not be good for the book's cover. The change, though, is notable in that it occludes the attention the author clearly wanted to draw to the story of a little girl, like the author, with the gift of clairvoyance. The final chapter utilizes Julia Kristeva's theory of the abject to discover the erotic elements in certain perverse stories. "Mimoso" is read as a tale of revenge in which the act of preparing a poisonous dish produces an "erotismo grosero" [disgusting eroticism] which then leads to the hilarious dinner scene filled with clichés and double meanings. Mancini reads "La calle Sarandí," one of several rape stories in Ocampo's works, as one example of the abject as a language of poetry and silence. Finally, "El retrato mal hecho" views the murdering servant and the mistress/mother as doubles, the abject a willingness to convey what repels. Mancini leaves silent any gendered reflections on these stories, a silence which resonates oddly in the context of her chosen theoretical frame for this section, the work of the leading French feminist.

Andrea Ostrov's *El género al bies* (2004) is a comparative study of five Latin American women writers whose works are viewed through the lens of French feminist theory and its complication or revision by English-language theorists such as de Lauretis, Butler, and Hutcheon. Ostrov also acknowledges work by her Hispanic counterparts such as theorist Nelly Richard and Ocampo scholars from around the world, making her bibliography and critical comparisons the most useful to this point. The five chapters situate Silvina Ocampo in the company of María Luisa Bombal, Ana Lydia Vega, Tununa Mercado, and Diamela Eltit. Each of the authors is discussed according to their representation of the female body, especially as an image of the text itself. The chapter on Ocampo discusses the female body as mask or performance; her texts work not only to transgress, but to reveal the mechanisms of coercion in a rigidly gendered world. While Ostrov claims to concentrate on the works of *La furia*, her analysis ranges widely over the entire corpus of Ocampo's fiction. Ostrov makes no claim to influence among these writers, but by grouping them together she allows readers to appreciate Silvina Ocampo's prescient modernity from within this gathering of her esteemed younger, in some cases much younger, peers.

Included in a book about Argentine film director María Luisa Bemberg (2000) is Fiona Mackintosh's study of the film adaptation of Silvina Ocampo's story "El impostor." Bemberg's script was completed shortly before her untimely death in May of 1995. John King's introduction to the volume gives a fine sense of Argentina in the relevant time periods and the difficulties a woman would have encountered being taken seriously in the artistic realm. The photos of Bemberg as a debutante will be of interest to Ocampo readers, since the two women were distant relatives and their social circles overlapped. For the screen adaptation, Bemberg consulted with both Ricardo Piglia and Alejandro Maci (who would eventually direct the film), and the film itself was completed after her death. The story, as Mackintosh notes, comes from Ocampo's least typical volume (*Autobiografía de Irene*), the one most influenced by Borges, and is much longer than any of her others (nearly 80 pages). In Mackintosh's comparison of the two genres, she argues that Bemberg emphasizes the class conflicts inherent in the plot and downplays Ocampo's philosophical and metaphysical musings in order to ground the film in a social and emotional reality: "So whereas Ocampo's text obsessively questions memory, dreams and reality, Bemberg focuses on more direct visual questioning of seeing and perception" ("El impostor" 205). If Bemberg thereby "domesticates" Ocampo's text, she still offers a film script which employs a complex mix of literary ingredients: the detective novel, the gothic, the fantastic, and social critique. Both film and narrative versions imply that perceptions of reality can be undermined on many levels, challenging the boundary between dream and reality and between madness and sanity. The title is left unclarified: who is the impostor here? Bemberg understood from Ocampo that what we see is never the whole story.

In 2003 Mackintosh published *Childhood in the Works of Silvina Ocampo and Alejandra Pizarnik*. Her comparative study convincingly argues for a literary link between the two, a poetic and personal connection which since then has been more widely recognized. Mackintosh usefully includes Ocampo's poetry and stories in the analysis, as only a few other critics, notably Noemí Ulla, had yet done. In her discussion of Ocampo's biography she names Norah Lange as a literary "sister" (8) and briefly compares the ways that both Ocampo and Lange were described by members of their intellectual circle as playful and childlike in their bearing as women, not just in their literary interests. Nevertheless, she says, Ocampo differs from Lange by offering a doubled and contradictory image: "Silvina Ocampo shifts seductively between adult and child worlds in her presentation of self and her construction of narrative personae" (9). In her primary argument Mackintosh shows how Ocampo's use of childhood memory blurs concepts of age and wisdom; her playful language questions established expectations of adult and child. Pizarnik, on the other hand, finds herself both personally and literarily drawn to a kind of aporia which leads her to depression and death in her fiction and suicide in her life. Mackintosh's excellent analysis of childhood in Ocampo not only considers her poetry but also those stories written directly for children. In all genres the children are as capable of suffering as any adult; secrets, games, and issues of identity and power are accorded an emotional weight unique to literary experience. Mackintosh devotes separate sections to birth, sexuality, death, and transgression where Ocampo's children cannot be easily separated from adults in their insight or agency. The concluding remarks argue that though Pizarnik seems at first glance to be a more subversive writer, Ocampo's works still shock in their juxtaposition of the ordinary and familiar with the cruel.

Fiona Mackintosh's further work on Ocampo takes several original tacks: in one set of articles she continues her study of visual images as they relate to Ocampo's poetry and narratives and in another set she delves into Ocampo's little-studied poetry by way of her translations from English. Two articles offer direct comparisons of Ocampo's short stories and illustrations by Norah Borges. In these, Mackintosh clarifies that the two women became friends in their late twenties and collaborated on various occasions. Norah, of course, was Jorge Luis Borges's younger sister who, like Silvina, studied art in Paris. On their return they joined with Xul Solar and others in an exhibit which was reviewed in the pages of *Sur* (by Julio E. Payró). In addition, both young women illustrated works by many of the writers of their day, including Bioy Casares and Borges. Norah drew the illustration for the original book cover of Silvina Ocampo's *Las invitadas* (1961). Mackintosh (2009) contrasts the artistic point of view of the two women by way of this cover illustration, which is actually an image of one of the stories, "Tales eran sus rostros." The story's plot involves a group of deaf children who turn into angels. The thematics of the narrative speak of one of Norah's favorite artistic subjects, angels as children, but as Mackintosh argues, Norah chooses to avoid the easy solution of painting children with wings. Rather, she selects a moment earlier in Ocampo's story when the deaf children are communicating in sign language. Norah is thereby able to express her own view of children as "innocent, angelic and other-worldly," and avoid Silvina's insinuation of "the messy details of life" or the hint of monstrosity in their metamorphosis. An earlier article (2004) discusses a book the two had planned together as a joint project, *Breve santoral* (1984). Mackintosh's essay describes it as a kind of collection of *estampas*, images in drawing and poetry, for twelve religious and/or historic figures. Norah provided an image for each and Silvina a poem. The points of similarity between the two women are clear from their interest in childhood, in a simplicity of line, in a neo-primitive approach to representation, and in their mutual respect as artists. Nevertheless, Ocampo's more subversive version can always be deduced in these poems.

"'My Dreams are a Field Afar'" (2007) is Mackintosh's study of Ocampo's translations from English verse. Using a critical structure articulated by Richard Gavril, she argues that Ocampo felt a "literary consanguinity" with certain poets, that these formed a set of "linguistic ghosts" which she was worried about inadvertently plagiarizing. In detailing this relationship with English poetry, the critic focuses on the 1948 volume for which Ocampo wrote the prolog and carried out several of the translations, *Poetas líricos ingleses*. It is no surprise to learn that Ocampo's prolog is not a literary overview, but a personal account of her own reaction to the poetry, especially of her passionate reaction to Shakespeare's sonnets. Mackintosh also studies other translation projects: Ocampo's own poetry volumes include her translations from both

French and English where they reside with her original poems, suggesting, as Mackintosh notes, that Ocampo considered the process of translation as another kind of creative writing; there are also works published in *Sur*, among them the lengthy translation with Patricio Canto of De Quincey's "The Affliction of Childhood" (1944). Mackintosh quotes Ocampo (from Ulla, *Encuentros* 128) in saying that in reading generally she hopes to find inspiration for her own work, something that "I could have written" (10), hence the intersection between "her overlapping roles as reader, writer and literary translator" (11). Ocampo chose to translate Pope's "Eloisa to Abelard," a suggestion of her interest in the epistolary form as well as what Mackintosh notes as her important theme of despair; Marvell's "To his Coy Mistress" demonstrates her willingness to produce gender ambiguity; De Quincey's poem reflects her interest in the childhood fascination with closed and locked doors. In these and in her five translations of poetry by John Donne, Ocampo is careful to reproduce a sense of the rhyme and meter of the originals while adapting the meaning at times to her own voice. Mackintosh points to ways in which the structure of the originals influences Ocampo's own, especially her preference for the sonnet and for rhyming couplets; the themes of the translated poetry appear not only in Ocampo's verse, but in her short stories as well.

Emily Dickinson is a special case for Ocampo. She published an entire volume of translations in 1985, *Poemas de Emily Dickinson*, apparently based on work done over many years. Mackintosh's exquisite readings (2005) demonstrate her knowledge of both poets. The elements of the nineteenth-century poet which appeal to the twentieth-century Argentine writer are characteristics the two have in common: the themes of homesickness, memory, and oblivion, insects, plants, and other natural images, an aphoristic syntax and an interest in gender ambiguity. Nevertheless, Ocampo's translations reveal distortions that may be the result of faulty understanding of the original language, or reflect a difference in worldview impossible to surmount. No doubt Dickinson's quirky punctuation and capitalization would give any translator difficulties, but Mackintosh finds that Ocampo shows no interest in reflecting the originals in these elements. In general, Mackintosh shows that the poems which suggest religious belief or hope are those for which Ocampo shows least respect, translating them almost always in terms darker, more painful, and at times more shocking; to use Mackintosh's terms, they are "rougher and less trusting."

Fernanda Zullo-Ruiz's close reading of "El pecado mortal" [The mortal sin] is the most extensive analysis of this story in recent years, in which she argues that the power, class, and gender issues that often mark Ocampo's stories of childhood are here mapped in the spatial arrangements of the family mansion where the action takes place. The narrative carefully divides the functions of the various floors between the lower main levels where the rituals of life and death play out (parties and funerals) and the upper level, designated as "superior" by the narrator with an ironic double meaning, devoted to "la pureza y la esclavitud" [purity and slavery], that is, to the children's playroom and various servant workrooms. The isolation of this top floor and the proximity of the various spaces establish what Zullo-Ruiz argues is the precondition for the events which unfold. The Catholic doctrines that oppose body and soul govern the language and its multiple layers of misunderstanding. The mythical references contribute to this story's development of betrayals, by the Church, by parents, by friends, and finally by way of the transgression against the young character's own body. Zullo-Ruiz defines the ritual of Communion as a second transgression, one that Muñeca must enact for her own survival. The adult narrator defines this second coercion as the mortal sin of the story's title, thus transforming herself in her own mind from victim to perpetrator.

My article, "'Literatura como pintura:' Image, Narrative and Autobiography" (2006), addresses the plastic arts as they appear within Ocampo's narratives. This study concentrates on the last two compilations of stories prepared during the author's life, *Y así sucesivamente* (1987) and *Cornelia frente al espejo* (1988), in which she uses artistic images in combination with overt references to herself as the writer of the text. A brief overview of Ocampo's previous work argues that the striking images that appear in her fictions reveal the ways Ocampo associates the creative process involved in painting and photography with that of writing. Certain repeated images establish a kind of personal code of associations. Several of the analyses entail ekphrastic readings of well-known paintings which form important components of the story: Dürer's engraving *The Knight, Death and the Devil* functions as the organizing structure of "El bosque de Tarcos"; Sir Joshua Reynolds's *The Age of Innocence* is an important detail in "Los retratos apócrifos"; and Michaelangelo's image from the Sistine Chapel of the Sibyl of Erythraea is a key to "Lección de dibujo." The essay's conclusion suggests that Ocampo's writing technique may borrow more literally from painting than has been imagined: her break from the well-ordered plot in both theme and structure entail a more spatial development of narrative order.

Julieta Yelin approaches Ocampo's work via the writers of *Sur* and more specifically their response to the works of Franz Kafka. Yelin begins by dividing Borges's strictly textual approach to Kafka from that of Eduardo Mallea. Predictably, Mallea reduces (Yelin's word) Kafka to his biography and reads his stories as allegory. The second half of the article takes up Kafka's animal stories, many of them published together under the title *Bestiario*. Yelin finds that Kafka himself objected to the title, arguing that his stories were not parables, as the anthology's title suggests. Bringing Deleuze and Guattari to bear, Yelin clarifies that metamorphosis for Kafka is a disintegration of all forms, the opposite of metaphor. The conclusion to this section presents Kafka's approach to metamorphosis as a way to question the opposition of animal and human nature. With these issues in mind Yelin proceeds to analyze the animal stories of three authors of the 1950s, Mario Di Benedetto, Julio Cortázar, and Silvina Ocampo, as members of this new tradition, all of whom take a Borgesian view of Kafka in order to remake the tradition of the bestiary in fiction. In the case of Silvina Ocampo, Yelin refers to "Isis" and "Fuera de las jaulas" to show how Ocampo's fiction questions the unique wholeness of human identity and how it constantly blurs difference between human and animal nature.

Judith Podlubne's excellent book, *Escritores de Sur* (2011), is the most extensive examination to date of Ocampo's eccentric place within the generation of writers contemporaneous to her. From Podlubne's detailed examination of the debates about literature from inside the *Sur* group we gain a comprehensive idea of Ocampo's originality and a basis for viewing the various misunderstandings involving this writer, from those arising from her relationship to Borges to that with her sister, Victoria. The ongoing challenge within the *Sur* group of writers was the growing gap between "dos morales literarios antagónicos" [two opposite ideas of literary morality]: one is described as humanist or moralistic (Victoria Ocampo, Eduardo Mallea, Guillermo de Torre); the other as formalist (Borges, Bioy). Later Podlubne clarifies that of the two, Bioy is the formalist while Borges arrives at a new framework for the whole debate: "un modo radicalmente nuevo de pensar este asunto, un modo afectado por la experiencia de la desaparición del hombre en el lenguaje" (22) [a radical new way of thinking through this issue, a way affected by the experience of man's disappearance in language]. As Borges is defending himself through the 1940s against attacks on his writing as "deshumanizada" [dehumanized] (à la Ortega) and "antiargentina" [anti-Argentine], José Bianco and Silvina Ocampo enter the equation to triangulate the dichotomy in two different ways.

Podlubne views Bianco as a kind of bridge between the two camps, having begun his career as a writer closer to the Mallea side of the divide, characterized by the belief that art and literature were means by which culture could defend itself against the debasement of the masses. This group believed that one mode of creative achievement was the total identification of the artist with his art: an exceptionally beautiful work often implies an exceptionally beautiful life. So, when Victoria says, "Soy simplemente un ser humano en busca de expresión" [I am simply a human being in search of expression], what sounds like modesty is actually the description of the highest value of artistic creativity (Podlubne, *Escritores* 50). José Bianco seemed to ally himself with this group in the sense that he wrote at an early stage in his career in favor of a literature of moral responsibility. However, Borges's introduction to his novel *Las ratas* (1943) (re)casts Bianco as a formalist, and this seems to have been his preferred identity. Podlubne situates him as the mediator between the two camps: while exemplifying the careful attention to formal craft, he preferred to pay attention to the reality of the reader (193), thus making him a voice for the several creative forces which converged in *Sur*. Silvina Ocampo, on the other hand, upended both edges of this debate, breaking with known forms and already understood ways of narrating.

Silvina Ocampo made her literary debut in the pages of *Sur* in 1936 with the publication of one story from her soon-to-be released volume, *Viaje olvidado* (1937). Podlubne addresses Victoria's infamous review by referencing Enrique Pezzoni's suggestion that everything that Victoria found to criticize in Silvina's first published work – and her review is the most insightful of the early reactions – would later be considered "los hallazgos" [the achievements] of Silvina's original voice (258). Victoria expresses exasperation that Silvina transforms memories which then do not match her own; she feels threatened by the confusion of dream and reality, of the known with the unknown. She uses words like "deformación" [deformity] and "disfrazada de sí misma" [disguised as herself], a wonderful, apt phrase which Podlubne (and Pezzoni) recommend we simply read favorably rather than negatively. The irritation with style is the most famous objection Victoria elaborates; she believes it was not a deliberate creative strategy on Silvina's part, but a function of her lack of control of the language. What Podlubne calls "la voz rarísima" [her strange voice] is, for her, Silvina's most original creation, an originality permitted precisely by the oddness of the style. The most interesting question in all of Silvina's fictions is the undecidability of the narrative voice. From where does it arise? On the level of pronouns (first-person disguised as third-person and vice versa), on the level of plot, on the level of tone and vocabulary everything is slippery, nothing is clarified. Podlubne identifies the ambiguity of the stories as their essential feature: "lo que se cuenta está siendo contado por una figura inaprensible, como si la lengua hablara sola y sin dirigirse a otros" (290) [what is told is being narrated by an inaccessible figure, as if language were speaking itself without addressing others]. Not only does *Viaje olvidado* fall completely outside the ideal of "escribir bien" [good writing], but is indifferent to the demand to construct perfect plots. Which is to say that it veers from the criteria for good writing from both sides of *Sur*'s divide.

This overview reveals the important new threads in the approach to Ocampo's literary production: on one front there is now an attempt to view a wider set of her undertakings, including the large body of published translations; on another there are new paradigms emerging for understanding her place in Argentine literary history. After having been nearly written out of such histories for a number of years, particularly in the 1970s, she is now being reconsidered as a unique force of her own. More recently, various critics have read individual stories in light of literary theory and have begun to write comparative studies which situate Silvina Ocampo more clearly within and beyond her immediate intellectual and personal circle.

2

Re-reading *Autobiografía de Irene:* Writing and Its Double in the Narrative of Silvina Ocampo[*]

ANDREA OSTROV

In recent decades, Silvina Ocampo's narrative has attracted readings from several critical approaches which have contributed to the illumination of different zones and stress diverse aspects of her textual production; dominant among them are gender studies, the fantastic as a literary genre, her treatment of cliché and of childhood, her relationship and place among the primary members of the *Sur* literary group (Borges, Bioy, Bianco, Victoria Ocampo), and her work's autobiographical character. In the present essay I would like to inscribe the following considerations within the last of these currents in order to interrogate the place that writing acquires in the author's poetics, not just as a signifying structure but also as an object of reflection, as itself a theme or pretext for fiction. In other words, my intention is to present a meta-literary reading on the basis of key stories which markedly problematize the writing act.

The presence of doubles, metamorphosis, and transformations, so common in these stories, has long been pointed out as a manifestation of the fantastic through which the notion of a unified identity can best be questioned in order to provide a more complete and more unsettling concept of both subjectivity and reality. In many of the narratives by this author it is possible to propose a specific connection between the presence or appearance of duplicity and some form of reflection or textualization of writing. If the focus here is in no way exclusive, the stories that make up *Autobiografía de Irene*, the second of Silvina Ocampo's story collections published in 1948 ("Epitafio romano" [Roman epitaph], "La red" [The net], "El impostor" [The imposter], "Fragmentos del

---

[*] The translations of quotations from Derrida are taken from published essays listed in the Works Cited, indicated alongside the original versions consulted by Ostrov. All quotations from the works of Silvina Ocampo are included in the original Spanish with translations appearing immediately following. These and other quoted material from Spanish were translated by Patricia N. Klingenberg.

libro invisible" [Fragments of the invisible book] and "Autobiografía de Irene" [Irene's autobiography]), become paradigmatic in this sense; in Cecilia Graña's words, "a reflection on writing and narrative mechanics is evident" since "the very condition of writing seems to expose itself completely" (71).

"Epitafio romano," the story that opens the volume, in its very title refers to a particular type of writing: the inscribed epitaph, which is explicitly related to the preservation of identity in the sense that its function is to identify the buried remains and preserve the memory of a proper name. The plot of this story explodes the link that one expects between the epitaph and the burial: in Flavia's tomb there is no body, no referent to sustain the expectation of truth that defines the genre. However, everyone believes that Flavia is dead because the epitaph – like all writing – shows itself to be a signifier that does not represent, but rather produces, truth effects. Not by happenstance does the story's structure turn around two axes of meaning that constantly interlace and cross each other: writing and infidelity. Beyond the anecdotal – Flavia's infidelity, Claudio Emilio's jealousy, and the symbolic assassination of the former – the story's textual complexity stages the act and function of writing and reading. Both the anonymous, extradiegetic, first-person narrative voice and the voices of the characters insert explicit and implicit literary references. At the mention of two classical authors – Virgil and Plautus ("Con frecuencia [Claudio Emilio] *citaba a Plauto, dice la voz narradora*" [8, my emphasis] ["Frequently Claudio Emilio *would cite* Plautus," says the narrator]) – the text then juxtaposes these with obvious Borgesian allusions: "Como los senderos de un jardín que se alejan o se acercan arbitrariamente, formando modestos laberintos…" (10) [As the paths of a garden which recede and approach arbitrarily, forming modest labyrinths…]. On the other hand, the story establishes a textual relationship with the body of epitaphic inscriptions that reaches us from ancient Rome, recorded in the *Corpus Inscriptionum Latinarum*. In this way the plot reveals itself as a meeting place (*lugar de citas*) where divergent voices merge.

The intertextual dimension, often specifically stressed in Silvina Ocampo's stories, constitutes a privileged tool for dramatizing the function and processes of writing. The clarification of literary "debts" makes visible the need for reading as a condition of writing and, by extension, the latter's textual origin. Since every quote implies a clipping, an extrication from its original context, it also supposes inevitable differences, gaps, and distortions of both meaning and original purpose:

> by virtue of its essential iterability, one can always lift a written sintagma from the interlocking chain in which it is caught or given without making it lose every possibility of functioning … Eventually, one may recognize other such possibilities in it by inscribing or *grafting* it onto other chains. No context can enclose it. (Derrida, "Signature" 93, original emphasis)

At the same time, it is precisely the successive quotes from Flavia about love that unleash the conflict of the plot, which engages the two protagonists under the guise of a debate surrounding the theme of the original and the copy. This dichotomy is introduced in the text by way of a description of a religious rite, for whose enactment mannequins are used as replacements for female human bodies meant for sacrifice:

> Todos los años [Claudio Emilio] veía a los fieles arrojar sobre las aguas del Tíber (para aplacarlas) treinta maniquíes vestidos. Protestaba: "Para aplacar la violencia de las aguas ¿no sería más eficaz y económico arrojar treinta mujeres verdaderas?" (8)

> [Every year Claudio Emilio would see the faithful throw thirty dressed mannequins upon the waters of the Tiber (to placate them). He would protest, "In order to placate the violence of the waters wouldn't it be more effective and economical to throw thirty real women?"]

The dialog between the two spouses is structured according to the idea of plagiarism, a legal term which refers to illicit appropriation of an artistic or intellectual creation – in this case the poems by Claudio Emilio – but their conversation opens up a wide field of theoretical reflection on the discursive production and function of language. Perhaps one of Ocampo's most important stories in this sense is "La pluma mágica" [The magic pen] (*Las invitadas*). There, the narrative voice refers to the impossibility of escaping plagiarism: "Sabes que todo lo que yo escribía, todo lo que se me ocurría ya estaba escrito por alguien en alguna parte del mundo y que por ese motivo llegó un momento en que no pude publicar nada, pues los lectores menos sagaces me hubieran acusado de plagio" (153) [You know that everything I would write, everything that occurred to me was already written in some part of the world and for that reason there came a moment when I couldn't publish anything because the least knowledgeable readers would have accused me of plagiarism]. This story exposes the basic alienation of the signifiers, the words' lack of ownership. Although as signifiers or markers words are structurally repeatable, pronounceable, they constitute the original theft of language:

> The letter, inscribed or propounded speech, is always stolen ... It never belongs to its author or to its addressee ... which amounts to acknowledging the autonomy of the signifier as the letter's historicity; before me, the signifier on its own says more than I believe that I mean to say, and in relation to it, my meaning-to-say is submissive rather than active. (Derrida, *Writing and Difference* 178)

In fact, in this story it is the pen that confers on its possessor the talent to write. The speaking subject is clothed in an irreducible secondary quality in relation to the organized field of language, that cultural field from where lexicon and syntax are extracted, from where one reads before one writes (Derrida, *Writing and Difference* 178).

In "Epitafio romano," Flavia argues in favor of difference, originality, and uniqueness in order to hide her infidelity, paradoxically in terms of the similarity between original and copy:

> ¡Oh, Claudio Emilio! Tus amigos plagian tus versos pero yo los reconozco. Dime, ¿te agradaría que los confundiera? Porque soy hermosa, y también para que las ames, mis amigas plagian mis túnicas, el color de mi cabello, tan difícil de lograr, las ocho trenzas de mi peinado ... Reconoces sobre mi pecho, desde lejos, la rosa artificial y la rosa verdadera; sin equivocarte puedes distinguir el buen poema del malo, ¡pero puedes confundirme en pleno día con mis amigas! (9)

> [Oh, Claudio Emilio! Your friends copy your poems but I recognize them. Tell me, would you be more pleased if I confused them? Because I am beautiful, and so that you will love them, my friends plagiarize my tunics, the color of my hair, so difficult to achieve, the eight locks of my hairstyle ... You distinguish, from afar, the artificial rose on my breast from the real; without fail you can tell a good poem from a bad one, but even in broad daylight you can confuse me with my friends!]

On the other hand, her husband, in a reverse but also paradoxical move, argues for the sameness and repetition in order to finally identify – among the friends who copy her – the true Flavia:

> Las cosas se repiten demasiado: un solo día es igual al resto de la existencia. Una sola amiga es igual a todas tus amigas. El vuelo de aquel pájaro ... lo volveré a ver en este mismo jardín que honra a Diana. Estas palabras que estamos diciendo ¿no las dijimos ya otro día? (10)

> [Things repeat themselves too much: one day is the equivalent of the rest of existence. One friend is equal to all of your girlfriends. The flight of that bird ... I will see again in this same garden that honors Diana. These words that we are uttering now, didn't we already say them another day?]

The evident contradiction between what they say and what they do demonstrates that the debate strategy which both characters display unfolds in a series of statements that constitute, definitively, a deceptive plot which has no fidelity to the true thoughts of either. In fact, there is no representation of ideas, no correspondence between word and deed: words fail to reveal the profound truth of the subject but instead produce effects that alternate between obfuscation and disclosure. In this sense the supposed plagiarism of which Flavia is victim by way of her friends – and by which she hides her adventures – enacts the etymological link with *plaga* (net, trap). In other words, *plagiarism, betrayal, trap, net* make up a network of meanings that are disseminated and that mirror each other at different textual levels.[1]

Now, if at first Flavia resorts to plagiarism to enable her betrayals ("¿En dónde encontraba Flavia amigas tan parecidas? La misma estatura, el mismo talle, los mismos senos" [10] [Where did Flavia find friends so similar to her? The same height, the same size, the same breasts]), Claudio Emilio responds with an identical strategy, since it is precisely a *crimen plagii* or *plagium* (that is, a kidnapping) that is the punishment he inflicts on his wife when he discovers her in "other arms" (12). Flavia, in effect, is whisked from the world of the living and locked up by her husband on his estate on the Tiber. Her supposed death occurs in a fire caused by Claudio Emilio himself who fakes the scene such that the verisimilitude – just as in Borges's "Emma Zunz" – hides the truth of the events:

> Incendió su casa de Roma ... Salvó a sus hijos y retiró algunos objetos de valor, algunos retratos. Anunció la muerte de Flavia. Se recogieron en una urna las pretendidas cenizas, y los retazos de una de sus túnicas (Claudio Emilio los había colocado cuidadosamente entre los escombros) fueron enterrados con pompa. (12)

> [He burned their house in Rome ... He saved the children, and a few valuable objects, several portraits. He announced Flavia's death. Her supposed ashes were gathered in an urn together with pieces of one of her tunics (Claudio Emilio had placed them carefully among the rubble) and buried with ceremony.]

Obviously, the writing of an epitaph is necessary to identify Flavia's tomb and transform her disappearance into an "accidental death." The referential pact of the genre will definitively sanction her death:

> Tus hijos, tus padres, tus hermanos, tus amigas, el mundo entero cree que has muerto. Si te acercas a ellos, si les hablas, creerán que eres una aparición, tendrán miedo de ti y te darán alimentos; pero no lograrás reincorporarte a

---

[1]   On this point, critics have pointed out Silvina's fascination with polysemy, multiple meanings of words, and the way she takes advantage of semantic ambiguity as part of her narrative (Tomassini, "La paradoja" 378).

la vida. El día en que mueras realmente, nadie asistirá a tu muerte, nadie te
enterrará. (15)

[Your children, your parents, your siblings, your friends, the entire world
believes that you have died. If you approach them they will think you are a
ghost, they will be afraid and they will give you food; but you will not be
able to reincorporate into life. The day that you really die no one will attend
your death, no one will bury you.]

However, in Flavia's tomb there is no body – either alive or dead – where the
referent is embodied. The epitaph – the writing – is organized literally based
on absence, image without original, appearance of presence, negation of all
exteriority: "Ninguna precisión, ningún busto de mármol me guían para describir
ese rostro joven y resuelto" (7) [No specifications, no marble bust, guide me in
describing that young and resolute face], announces the narrative voice at the
story's beginning.

   The imposture is completed by the lines that compose the long epitaph,
poems attributed to the voices of the dead woman's intimate friends and
family, though they were actually written by the single voice – or the hand
– of Claudio Emilio. The first-person narrative voice (unidentified by gender)
makes his/her intervention explicit in the process of translation of the Latin
verses when a footnote clarifies: "He puesto rimas a la traducción de los versos
latinos" (13) [I have made rhymes out of the Latin lines]. This explicit reference
to translation invites a special attention to the construction of the words carved
"sobre una lápida decorada con instrumentos musicales, figuras de adolescentes
y guirnaldas" (13) [on a stone decorated with musical instruments, adolescents
and garlands], since the writing of the epitaph's verses is sustained and based
on the exercise of translation – by its author – of the scene of infidelity. Indeed,
the words chosen by Claudio Emilio for his composition seem to allude to his
wife's betrayal by way of sintagmas and signifiers that refer to a different
scene. Thus, for example, in the four lines attributed to Flavia's parents, the
mention of "racimos" [bunches] can be linked to her dress, "color de las uvas"
(9) [the color of grapes]; but more explicitly, where it says "venerando tus
favores" (13) [honoring your favors], it is easy to read this as a kind of anagram
for *favores venéreos* [sexual favors]. For her part, the younger sister mentions
"incendio" [fire] and "arrepentidas llamas" (13) [regretted flames] which, in
addition to introducing the dimension of guilt, establish a counterpoint to "las
penumbras ardientes" (8) [burning shadows] where earlier Claudio Emilio
had imagined his wife. In the lines of the older sister – "tus labios tendrán
sed como las ramas" (13) [your lips will be thirsty like the branches] – the
erotic meaning of thirst is clear; but in addition, if we take into account that

houses of prostitution in the past were designated by a branch with leaves and/or flowers hung over the door – from which the Spanish term "ramera," meaning "prostitute" comes – the comparison with *ramas* introduces an allusion to the prostitution that Claudio attributes to his wife: "Flavia y su insistente perfil, su cabellera con ocho trenzas ... ¿se prostituía?" (9) [Flavia and her insistent profile, her hair with eight curls ... was she prostituting herself?]. Her children, in turn, make reference to "la paloma" [the dove], a bird consecrated to Venus by the Romans since they considered salaciousness or lust its salient characteristic. Her cousin insinuates irrepressible erotic passion with the phrase "sin gobierno" (14) [without restraint]; her brother, the "mystery" of her adventures; and her husband, finally, alludes to "brazos" and "lazos" (14) [arms and ties]. In other words, the long text of the epitaph is structured around allusion, semantic ambiguity, the multiplicity of meaning, the instability and undecidability of the referent, at the same time that it dramatizes the apocryphal nature of writing, the adulteration of the origin, the imposture and the imitation of other's voices.

Consequently, the reality effects produced by the writing are unpredictable. The three different endings that the narrator proposes introduce their own interpretative possibilities; each one presumes a questioning of the ultimate property of meaning. The different endings are offered immediately following a scene of reading: two years after Flavia's death, Claudio Emilio directs his wife to her tomb and "sin apartar de ella los ojos, aguardó a que leyera el epitafio" (13) [without taking his eyes off of her he waited while she read the epitaph]. The three different alternative endings narrate the possible readings – the possible meanings – that the deceased enacts on reading her obituary. The first suggests a perfect agreement between the couple, since Flavia accepts her destiny and thanks her husband for "haberla ennoblecido prematuramente con los privilegios que solo puede otorgar la muerte" (14) [having ennobled her prematurely with the privileges that only death can bestow]. The effect sought by Claudio Emilio through his detailed writerly construction of his wife's "death" is here imposed unequivocally.

The second ending implies a turn of the screw regarding the first as it presents a line of escape which shakes the edifice constructed and planned by Claudio Emilio. Faced with his implacable words – as quoted above – and the sinister reality that he describes to her, Flavia makes use of the multiplicity of meaning in order to dispute the last word: "Es cierto, todos creen que he muerto, salvo tú: tú eres el único equivocado" (15) [It's true that everyone thinks I am dead, except you: you are the only one who is wrong]. However, it is in the third ending where a total inversion is produced by virtue of which the fabricator of revenge falls prey to his own net, and the victim becomes the more intelligent executioner.

Claudio Emilio pide clemencia a los dioses y amor a Flavia. La lleva a su casa. Nadie la reconoce y ella asegura ser una mendiga que un demente ha violado, después de vestirla con la túnicas que robó de una urna sagrada. La locura de Claudio Emilio es tal vez inevitable; nadie entiende sus explicaciones claras e ingeniosas. (15)

[Claudio Emilio asks forgiveness from the gods and love from Flavia. He takes her home. No one recognizes her and she claims to be a beggar who has been raped by a crazy man, after dressing her in the tunics that he robbed from a sacred urn. The insanity of Claudio Emilio is possibly inevitable; no one understands his clear and ingenious explanations.]

The great paradox consists of the fact that this ending maintains the impossibility of reversing the meaning effects established by the writing. Flavia's death is – although false – irreversible, as witnessed by her epitaph, and her planned exile from life is suddenly transformed into the unexpected insanity – or exile of reason – of her jailor, trapped between the lines of his own discursive snare.

The progression of the three possible conclusions dramatizes the scene of empowerment and the different power relations generated by writing. The act of writing necessarily implies a position of power that, nevertheless, finds its limit in the reading. In effect, only in the first instance does Claudio Emilio control the reach of what is written. On the other hand, in both the second and the third, Flavia as a reader signs the text by putting an unexpected twist on it that, in addition, has pragmatic effects. It is there, then, in the *post-scriptum* that takes place in any reading moment, that the meaning is sanctioned – or constituted – always *a posteriori*.

"La red" [The net], the second of the stories included in *Autobiografía de Irene*, also proposes a reflection on writing and its link to a certain duplicity. The title puts into play several meanings of the Spanish word "red:" plot or weaving, that is writing, but also (as in the previous story), trap, subterfuge, ambush. The body of the story's butterfly – like language, like the signifier – makes these two sets of meanings cohere.

Duplicity becomes evident at the level of the story's structure (enunciation), since the entire first-person narrative by Kêng-Su is framed by another narrator who at the beginning of the story simply introduces the voice of her friend and underlines her speech with brief stage directions; later this voice begins to take form, first by establishing short dialogs with Kêng-Su and then by definitively taking charge of the narrative. Certain details allow one to propose a mirror relationship between the two narrators. Toward the end, the primary narrator faints from exhaustion on managing to reach the shore, just like Kêng-Su in her part of the narration. After Kêng-Su's disappearance in the sea, the friend finds in her beach tent "la tira de papel, con el ídolo pintado" (28) [the strip of paper with the painted image] which had supposedly protected her from harm. And finally she concludes, "Cuando pienso en Kêng-Su, me parece que la conocí en un sueño" (28) [When I think of Kêng-Su, it feels like I met her in a dream]. This doubt introduced in the last sentence about the real or dreamed existence of the young woman allows the possibility of considering the two characters as a splitting of a single subject, as doubles of each other. But it is also possible to establish subtle links between Kêng-Su, the character and second narrator, and the butterfly whose body is speared by a pin in order to fix it in place: Kêng-Su describes the butterfly as "amarilla con nervaduras anaranjadas y negras" (17) [yellow with black and orange veins], the identical colors with which she describes herself since she has black hair that she holds with a "tira de papel amarillo" (24) [a strip of yellow paper], mentioned above. At the same time she recognizes that, once trapped, the butterfly "abría y cerraba las alas como siguiendo el ritmo de mi respiración" (18) [opened and closed its wings as if following the rhythm of my breath]. The doubling of Kêng-Su and the butterfly culminates in an identification of gazes, as the character confesses: "A veces, al mirarme en el espejo, veía sus ojos sobrepuestos a los míos" (26) [Sometimes, on looking at myself in the mirror, I would see its eyes superimposed on mine].

The story presents a power struggle related to writing. Beyond the intrinsic cruelty, Kêng-Su's initial act – piercing the body of the butterfly with a gold pin – transforms the insect into a figure of difference – a signifier – recognizable and identifiable. Simultaneously, the arbitrary attempt to pin and detain it pretends to definitive inscription, a final fixing of the direction (*sentido*) of its flight:

> Entre mis peinetas y mis horquillas, había un alfiler de oro con una turquesa. Lo tomé y atravesé con dificultad el cuerpo resistente de la mariposa ... Luego clavé el alfiler con su presa en la tapa de una caja de jabones ... La dejé en mi habitación, ensayando su inmóvil vuelo de agonía. (18)

> [Among my combs and hairpins there was a gold pin with a turquoise. I took it and punctured with some difficulty the resistant body of the butterfly ... Later I tacked the pin with its prisoner on the cover of a soap box ... I left it in my room, rehearsing its immobile flight of agony.]

However, the unexpected disappearance of the butterfly reveals the impossibility of fixing meaning, it delineates precisely the point of escape in the plot. At the same time its liberation inverts the power relation implicit in the perforation of the body, since from here on it will be Kêng-Su's body that is punctured by the consequences of her act. On the one hand she is systematically assaulted by "los párrafos marcados con pequeños puntitos que parecían hechos con un alfiler" (19) [the paragraphs marked with little pricks that seemed to be made with a pin] in her copy of *El libro de las recompensas y las penas* [The book of recompense and punishment], whose pages are mysteriously left open for her. On the other, the embroidery of a tapestry she is working on takes on a life of its own: "A veces tenía que deshacer una rama entera de mi labor: insensiblemente había bordado con lanas amarillas, en lugar de hojas o de pequeños dragones, formas de alas" (22) [Sometimes I had to take out an entire branch of my stitching: unconsciously I had embroidered with yellow wool, instead of leaves or small dragons, forms of wings]. Not only do the tips of her fingers show "marcas de [sus] labores ... [que] ... parecían pinchazos de mariposa" (21) [marks made by her needlework that looked like pricks of a butterfly], but *all* of her reality is discovered to be pierced with these inscriptions: "En aquel momento pensé que mi visión del mundo se estaba transformando y que muy pronto mi piel, el agua, el aire, la tierra y hasta el cielo, se cubrirían de esos mismos puntitos" (23) [In that moment I thought my vision of the world was being transformed and soon my skin, the water, the air, the earth and even the sky would be covered with the same little points]. That is to say, the signifying mark that the character inscribes on the body of the insect is repeated, infinitely and autonomously, in different contexts in which it acquires different meanings and opens new ones never foreseen by her. Certainly, the mounting siege by the butterfly begins to concentrate on Kêng-Su's eyes: "Buscaba mis ojos, el centro de mis ojos, para clavar en ellos su alfiler" (25) [It sought my eyes, the center of my eyes, in order to stick the pin in them]. The final duel, the revenge of the butterfly, consists of the closure of vision, the interruption of reading, the subtraction of meaning from the one who pretended to detain its circulation, to fix its movement.

In "El impostor" [The imposter], the long story or novella that follows "La red" and that occupies the very center of the volume, Rómulo Sagasta – the second narrator, author of "Consideraciones finales" [Final considerations] – takes up the story after he has read the preceding document which the extra-textual reader has just read as well: that is, the manuscript signed by Luis Maidana in which he tells of his traveling to and staying at Armando Heredia's cattle ranch, having been charged with the mission to watch over him, a request from the latter's father. Sagasta also travels to the ranch at the request of Armando's father – a personal friend – supposedly with the same mission as Luis Maidana. But on his arrival he discovers that his friend's son has just committed suicide. His inquiries about Armando's life, his friends, his visitors, accompanied by a reading of the manuscript attributed to Maidana, lead him to the conclusion that the latter never existed, that the one who wrote the notebook was Armando himself, victim of a doubling of his personality, a result of schizophrenia. Apparently, the illness also explains the suicide: Armando had killed himself in a desperate attempt to free himself from Maidana, that persistent and menacing double.

The sudden irruption of Sagasta as narrator seeks to validate the impressions that Luis Maidana's manuscript has left with him and his deductions about it. Thus, the story makes its textual origins explicit: Sagasta writes about a reading. In this way reading and writing converge in the story's structure without distinction. What is more, Maidana wrote and signed his tale in the blue notebook that had belonged to Armando Heredia, with penmanship identical to the latter; even the story's title seems to propose a link between imposture and the act of writing: as in "Epitafio romano," the writing subject is definitely an imposter, inasmuch as nothing guarantees the truth of the matter nor the certainty of the referent. Toward the end, Sagasta himself affirms: "A veces pienso que en un sueño he leído y he meditado este cuaderno, y que la locura de Heredia no me es ajena" (111) [Sometimes I think that I read and meditated on this notebook in a dream and that Heredia's insanity is not alien to me]. And immediately following, a paragraph differentiated from the previous text by a different typeface and whose narrator remains unidentified adds: "No hay distinción en la faz de nuestras experiencias; algunas son vívidas, otras opacas; algunas agradables, otras son una agonía para el recuerdo; pero no hay cómo saber cuáles fueron sueños y cuáles reales" (111) [There is no difference in the surface impression of our experiences; some are vivid, others opaque; some pleasing, others an agony of memory; but there is no way to know which were dreams and which reality]. Not only does this suggest that the narrator-character Luis Maidana has no real existence except as a double of Armando Heredia, but it also opens the possibility that both are only the mental constructions of Rómulo Sagasta. If the act of writing implies a decentering of the subject, a splitting – pathological in this case – of Armando Heredia into the fictional narrator called Luis Maidana (and eventually of Rómulo Sagasta into the two previous characters), it does no more than dramatize the scene and condition of writing itself (Mangin, *Temps* 171).

The enormous complexity of this novella, like that of the story which gives its title to the entire volume, deserves a more exhaustive analysis than is possible to produce here. Let it suffice to point out that the same relation between duplicity and writing also organizes the structure of "Autobiografía de Irene." At the beginning of the narration the character lays claim – as is to be expected in an autobiography – to the writing of the tale: "La improbable persona que lea estas páginas se preguntará para quién narro esta historia ... Tal vez sea para mí que la escribo: para volver a leerla, si por alguna maldición siguiera viviendo" (128) [The improbable person who may read these pages will ask for whom I write this story ... Perhaps it is for myself that I write it: in order to read it again, if by some bad luck I continue living]. However, at the end, we discover that the *other* – the anonymous, unknown, mirrored double of the protagonist – is the one who is writing it.[2] The dialog between the narrator and the stranger she meets in a plaza concludes precisely with the project of the future writing that Irene, with her gift of clairvoyance, has been able to predict:

> –Irene Andrade, yo quisiera escribir su vida.
> –¡Ah! Si usted me ayudase a defraudar el destino no escribiendo mi vida, qué favor me haría. Pero la escribirá. Ya veo las páginas, la letra clara, y mi triste destino. Comenzará así: *Ni a las iluminaciones del veinticinco de Mayo* ... (149)

> [Irene Andrade, I would like to write your life.
> Ah, if only you would help me to cheat destiny by not writing my life, what a favor you would be granting me! But you will write it. I already see the pages, the clear hand, and my sad destiny. It will start like this: *Not even to the fireworks of the 25th of May* ...]

That is to say, Irene reads the story of her autobiography – not yet written – that the reader has in his hands. The perfect circularity of the text – since the final paragraph duplicates the first – multiplies its specularity such that the reading and the writing form an eternal continuum.

The stories analyzed thus far suggest that an imposture – whose flip side is the loss of identity by the subject, the dissolving of the clear lines between the *I* and the *other* – is constitutive of writing: the signature as a mark of identity fails to guarantee the authorship of the text (both the epitaph written by Claudio Emilio and Luis Maidana's version are definitively apocryphal), never mind the authority or stability of meaning. In this sense it is important to note that the five stories which comprise *Autobiografía de Irene* propose a relationship between writing and death. In different ways, death is present in each of them. The title of the first, "Epitafio romano," is emblematic since it refers to a genre whose very conditioning premise is death; "La red" ends with the disappearance of the protagonist in the sea; in "El impostor," Armando Heredia has committed suicide. In "Fragmentos del libro invisible" [Fragments of the invisible book] the prophet includes in his book the text of his autobiography – that is, the story that we read – when he finds himself near death. In "Autobiografía de Irene," finally, the narrator clarifies that the moment of her death is approaching.

---

2   Annick Mangin identifies "the splitting inherent in any writing act, between an author and a character who says 'I,' even in an autobiography" (*Temps* 83). However, what is explicit in this text for the genre of autobiography – as we have already noted – becomes constitutive of all writing: whoever writes is always the *other*, in that what is written always exceeds the limits of the I.

Therefore, the writing confirms its link, not only with duplicity – as a manifestation of the decentering of the speaking subject – but with death, the ultimate absence. As a condition of writing, death in these stories comes to radicalize the absence of the speaking subject, the non-presence of the meaning-to-say or the intention of meaning – in Derridean terms – as structurally constitutive of the textual economy: "The text is not conceivable in an originary or modified form of presence ... The 'subject' of writing does not exist if we mean by that some sovereign solitude of the author" (*Writing and Difference* 211, 226).

In "Fragmentos del libro invisible" a certain mobile and dynamic concept of writing is made explicit, contrary to the values of preservation that are traditionally attributed to it and that would imply the establishment of secure meaning. The prophet-narrator claims to have written:

> dos libros invisibles cuyas frases imprimí únicamente en mi memoria, sin recurrir a la tinta, al papel y a la pluma ... esos groseros instrumentos que fijan, que desfiguran el pensamiento: esos enemigos de la metamorfosis y de la colaboración. El que se atreva a imprimir mis palabras las destruirá ... Mi libro, en caracteres impresos, se tornaría menos importante que un puñado de polvo. (115)

> [two invisible books whose phrases are imprinted solely in my memory, without recourse to ink, paper and pen ... those blunt instruments that fix and disfigure thought; those enemies of metamorphosis and of collaboration. He who dares to print my words will destroy them. My book, in printed characters, will become less important than a handful of dust.]

Indeed, this narrator appreciates the errors that his disciples make when repeating the phrases of his books, and with full consciousness he rescues the productivity they bring: "Estas equivocaciones todavía me deleitan: suelo modificar mi texto de acuerdo con ellas" (116) [These errors delight me: I usually modify my text in accordance with them]. Thus the *Invisible Book* is presented as the ideal of a writing that resists closure, the univocal, the ownership of meaning, the ending of circulation, and the certainty of the origin. Consequently, hermeneutics as a reading strategy is invalidated in favor of interpretative freedom and textual unfaithfulness. In relation to this, Graciela Tomassini stresses that "the mode of existence of the invisible book is, therefore, the mode of existence of any text, whose polyphony is multiplied in the reading (Tomassini, "Menos" 181). Metamorphosis may not be just a distinctive characteristic but the very condition of writing. Not by accident, the butterfly of "La red" embodies – at least according to the reading above – a signifier that is *already* the result and effect of metamorphosis. At the same time it is right to consider under this term the sum of the perlocutionary effects of language, that is, the material consequences of a speech act. In "Fragmentos del libro invisible" the material objects originate in dreams and the imagination of the characters:

> A veces en medio de nuestros diálogos instaba a mis discípulos a cerrar los ojos y a estudiar la oscuridad ... Mis discípulos tenían que describir estos mundos, uno por uno, detalladamente ...
>   Uno de mis discípulos descubrió en mi mano, al abrir los ojos, una hierba amarilla que nació en los dominios de la oscuridad. Él solo la había visto y la encontró en mi mano. (118)

> [At times amidst our dialogs I ordered my disciples to close their eyes and study the darkness ... My disciples had to describe those worlds, one by one, in detail.
>   One of my disciples discovered in my hand, on opening his eyes, a yellow herb that was born in the darkness. He alone had seen it and found it in my hand.]

If in fact the materialization of dreamed or imagined objects is a recurrent theme in Silvina Ocampo's narrative, such as in "El cuaderno" [The album], "Los sueños de Leopoldina" [Leopoldina's dream], or "El goce y la penitencia" [Pleasure and punishment] (just to mention examples that appear in *La furia*), in the case of "Fragmentos del libro invisible" it is not just *any* object. The narrator continues:

> Esta planta se llama "Planta Dorada." El viento llevará sus semillas al Monte del Líbano y a las sendas que conducen a Damasco. Florecerá en mayo y será invisible durante el día. La buscarán los alquimistas porque puede transmutar los metales. (118–19)

> [This plant is called, the "Golden Plant." The wind will carry its seeds to Mount Lebanon and to the roads which lead to Damascus. It will flower in May and be invisible during the day. Alchemists will look for it because it can transmute metals.]

In the first place, this is about a plant, a living being, that does not remain identical to itself through time but rather reproduces, flowers, and in addition becomes alternately visible and invisible. Beyond that, by way of its power to "transmute metals," it in turn generates transformations, metamorphoses. Hence the chain of perlocutionary effects initiated here by the invisible books forms an unlimited succession. It is therefore as if what still does not exist, the future, is subordinated – according to the narrator – to the idea that "los siglos renueven las palabras de mis libros y originen un nuevo caudal de objetos que perfeccionarán la felicidad o el dolor" (126) [The centuries will renew the words of my books and originate a new bounty of objects that will perfect happiness or pain].

The narrator of this story defines himself as a prophet (113), a word that in meaning and etymology condenses the two fundamental and constitutive aspects that the notion of writing acquires in the texts of Silvina Ocampo. On the one hand, a prophet is the one who claims the ability to announce what will later become reality, in such a way that his words are defined by their perlocutionary effects. On the other, the prophet is not the origin of his discourse, since it is an *other* subject (for example God in the religious context) who speaks through his voice. Thus duplicity and ubiquity of origin are also essential markers of the act of prophecy. Taking this into account, it is possible to propose that in these texts, writing acquires the status of prophecy understood not so much as an inevitability or fate but more as an affirmation of the discursive – and therefore multiple – dimension of the real.

The perlocutionary effects of discourse are dramatized in exemplary fashion in "El diario de Porfiria Bernal," a long story included in *Las invitadas* (1961). Here, the English governess reads the diary of her pupil and confirms that everything that was written a year previously is coming true, down to the exact date, even the moment of her transformation into a cat. In this tale, the metamorphosis is literal: Miss Fielding – *Mish* Fielding, after her change – flees through the room's window and is lost in the streets of Buenos Aires. Both the pact of truthfulness and the self-reference that the writing of a diary supposes are here altered, in the sense that Porfiria does not write of her own lived experiences but of the future metamorphosis of her governess. On the other hand, the demand for truth that the latter prescribes for her pupil on suggesting that she write a diary like English girls do does not consist, in this case, of a referential faithfulness but paradoxically of the performativity of her statement. The writing of the diary confers a performative power whose effects are produced in the moment of reading. Miss Fielding rigorously "obeys" the content of the diary as she reads it. If she stopped reading, the transformation would not happen, but it is written that she will not stop reading and will arrive at the ending. Here again the problem of the written text's origin is considered. Porfiria herself recognizes a certain degree of alienation from her own writing: "Es como si una voz me dictara las palabras de este diario; la oigo en la noche, en la oscuridad desesperada de mi cuarto ... Temo el desenlace como lo temerá Miss Fielding" (171) [It is as though a voice dictates the words of this diary; I hear it in the night, in the desperate darkness of my room ... I fear the conclusion as Miss Fielding will fear it].

However, in other stories the modification of the real by way of writing acquires different variables that do not imply such an extreme metamorphosis as the governess's but rather present a continuum between writing and reality. In "Epitafio romano," for example, we read the following words of Claudio Emilio:

La vida nos encierra continuamente en invisibles prisiones, de las cuales solo nuestra inteligencia o nuestro espíritu creador pueden liberarnos. En alguna prisión de mi vida he creído ser feliz; en otras he creído ser desdichado; en otras humillado. La vida, como el amor, como el poema, se corrige fácilmente y es buena para los estudiosos. (8)

[Life encloses us constantly in prisons from which only our intelligence or our creative spirit can free us. In some prison of my life I have believed myself to be happy; in others I have believed myself to be unhappy; in others, humiliated. Life, like love, like a poem, is easy to correct and is good for scholars.]

Beyond the irony of that last thought is the clear equivalence between life and writing. The possibility of correcting the plot of a life as if it were a text implies an obvious conception of the real as a discursive construct, overdetermined by the laws of language. But in addition the paragraph exhibits the functioning of this same idea in the sense that the three "prisons" that Claudio Emilio mentions retain a relationship, respectively, with the three endings that the story proposes. Following that logic, it is possible to think that these "invisible prisons" are no more than the successive meaning effects that the reading of the epitaphic poems unravels. If in the first ending Flavia appears to be understanding and grateful to her husband for saving her honor and that of her children, it is reasonable to expect that the character feels happy, just as he would be unhappy with the possibility of being the "only one who is wrong" (15) in accordance with the subsequent reading by his wife. Congruently, the third option – in which Flavia frees herself from her prison and he is consigned to insanity – confers the ultimate humiliation. So, not only is the "death" of the woman the consequence of a writing, but also the very course of Claudio Emilio's life will depend on Flavia's reading. In essence it is about the prison of words or – in Fredric Jameson's terms – the prison house of language.

A similar example of the relation between the real and writing, in which a life is "corrected" like a text, is "La continuación" [The continuation] – and the title is essential – a story included in *La furia* (1959). Here the narrative voice expresses the effects that the task of writing produces in her life: "Al abandonar mi relato, hace algunos meses, no volví al mundo que había dejado, sino a otro, que era la continuación de mi argumento (un argumento, lleno de vacilaciones, que sigo corrigiendo dentro de mi vida" (18) [On abandoning my story a few months ago, I did not return to the world I had left behind, but to a different one, which was the continuation of my plot (a plot filled with vacillations that I continue to correct within my life)]. That is to say, the narrator's life is organized as a plot – as a text – whose corrections are felt not just on the linguistic plane. It is not the movement of a pen which corrects the tale but the crossing-outs, the reorderings and the new beginnings that the writer imposes on her existence. Similarly, in "El diario de Porfiria Bernal," when Miss Fielding interrupts the narration to cede the word to the diary of her student, she says: "Hablará por mí el Diario de Porfiria Bernal. Me falta *vivir sus últimas palabras"* (171, emphasis added) [Porfiria Bernal's diary will speak for me. I can only *live out her last words*].

In "Fragmentos del libro invisible" an identical proposal is enacted:

> Dios me verá como yo vi las imágenes en la oscuridad. No me distinguirá de las otras imágenes. *Soy la continuación desesperada de mi libro, donde encerré a mis discípulos, a mi madre y a mí mismo.* (126, emphasis added)

> [God will see me as I have seen the images in the dark. He will not tell me apart from the other images. *I am the desperate continuation of my book, where I enclosed my disciples, my mother and myself.*]

What is more, the two first phrases of the fragment cited suggest the impossibility of establishing certainty about the dimension of the real. As in a structure of Russian dolls, the same subject of the writing and the other elements of his context become mere images observed by a god on another level of reality. Something similar had been announced in a previous paragraph in the same story:

> En los senderos de los jardines hay piedritas en cuyo fondo se encuentran diminutos jardines, millones de diferentes jardines; penetrar en ellos no es imposible. En cada gota de rocío hay otra noche en miniatura, con sus estrellas. (123)

> [In the pathways of the gardens there are little stones in whose depth one can discover tiny gardens, millions of different gardens; entering there is not impossible. In each drop of dew there is another miniature night with its stars.]

Also in "Epitafio romano:

> las formas se repiten en ellas mismas: en la hoja del árbol está dibujada la forma del árbol en miniatura; en el caracol, la terminación del mar con sus ondas sobre la playa; en una sola ala, imperceptibles alas infinitas; en el interior de la flor, diminutas flores perfectas. (11)

> [forms repeat in themselves: in a leaf of a tree is sketched the form of the tree in miniature; in the shell, the end of the sea with its waves on the beach; in a single wing, imperceptible, infinite wings; inside the flower, tiny, perfect flowers.]

The explicit underlining of the material world's fractal structure mirrors and duplicates the unfathomable structure of a writing which folds and refolds over itself in order to re-flect (on) its own condition. The origin of the text consequently dissolves itself within those same folds in which the levels of reality are multiplied in a play of mirrors. The prophet of "Fragmentos…" introduces the question:

> Oh, trama suspendida en el espacio, tejido luminoso y abyecto, que unirá el presente al pasado y el pasado al futuro. ¿Dónde nació tu primer hilo? Somos el mero sueño de algún dios? ¿Somos una escala prismática? (125)

> [Oh, plot suspended in space, luminous, abject weaving that will unite the present to the past and the past to the future. Where did your first thread originate? Are we the mere dream of some god? Are we a prismatic scale?]

"Del color de los vidrios" [The color of glass] (*Cornelia frente al espejo*, 1988) is, in my opinion, a story where the reflections about writing we have been discussing up to now converge in a special way. Here the metaphor of glass represents meta-literarily the difference between writing and reading in terms of refraction.

The character-narrator, in charge of a building, constructs over a long period of years a house – a text – made out of glass, using pieces or fragments of bottles that mysteriously arrive, accumulate, and multiply, and that can be heard to tinkle in the basement of his living quarters.[3] The emphasis placed on the sound of the glass bottles added to the process of fragmentation and recombination of them in order to construct an*other* structure facilitates the proposal of a homologous relationship between these objects and the linguistic signifier. The bottles *sound* – like words – and allow successive decontextualizations and recontextualizations which permit the generation of new meanings and new functions. Thus the process of constructing the house imitates the act of writing and specularizes the referential structure of a text. At the same time, the house once constructed can fly: it can change its location, its context, be approached from different perspectives, by different observers. Its potential to insert itself in other spaces reinforces the *graft* as a principle of construction and a founding procedure of textuality: "a written sign carries with it a force of breaking with its context, that is, the set of presences which organize the moment of its inscription. This force of breaking is not an accidental predicate, but the very structure of the written" (Derrida, "Signature" 92).

---

[3]   According to Graciela Tomassini, this text "proposes a kind of parable of the process of textual production … The metaphor of the house-*bricolage*, developed narratively, can be read as a complete aesthetic of a textual production" (118). Dámaso Martínez also reads the glass house as a metaphor of a conception of literature opposed to realism (158).

The choice of glass as a prime material for the edification of a house makes it visible and transparent, a privileged object of the gaze of observers and curious onlookers:

> Toda la casa es de vidrio por dentro y por fuera; por dentro los muebles, los pisos y los cielos rasos, ventanas y puertas; por fuera todo el frente. A todas horas el público nos verá haciendo todo lo que se hace en la intimidad: arrodillarnos, lavarnos, peinarnos, bañarnos … barrer, cocinar, remendar, lavar, planchar. (72)

> [The whole house is made of glass inside and out; inside the furniture, the floors and the skylights, windows and doors; outside the complete façade. At all hours the public sees us doing everything that one does in private: kneeling, washing up, combing our hair, bathing … sweeping up, cooking, mending, washing, ironing.]

However, the image of the house's interior that one obtains from outside does not guarantee a direct correspondence with what is really occurring there:

> Las imágenes que veían eran raras. Las rajaduras de los vidrios deformaban los cuerpos, las posturas, los movimientos. Si besaba la boca de mi novia, para los observadores de afuera, besaba su zapato; si acariciaba su frente, acariciaba una botella … Las rajaduras del vidrio inventaban posturas, las multiplicaban, pero *nunca reflejaban la verdad*. (72, emphasis added)

> [The images that they would see were strange. The cracks in the glass deformed our bodies, postures and movements. If I kissed my girlfriend's mouth, for the observers outside, I was kissing her shoe; if I caressed her brow, I was caressing a bottle … The cracks in the glass invented poses and multiplied them, but they *never reflected the truth*.]

Like a lens, the mediation of the glass intervenes in decisive ways on the perception of the object. The vision – or the reading – then implies an inevitable distortion: the original and true meaning is inaccessible – or nonexistent – and the act of seeing – or reading – here reveals its dimension as construct. The materiality of the house – the glass – or that of the text – the writing – do not *reflect*, do not reproduce a mirror image of the real, but a *refraction* – they deviate, modify and transform.[4]

The narrator specifically clarifies, "mi cuento se titula *El cuento de vidrio* y no de cristal," and then reiterates: "mi cuento se refiere al vidrio de las botellas

---

4   Something very similar occurs in "Cielo de claraboyas" (*Viaje olvidado*, 1939), where a little girl who looks through the glass of a skylight tells of a supposed crime which takes place in the apartment on the floor above.

y no del cristalino" (66) [my story is entitled *The story of glass* and not of crystal ... my story refers to the glass of bottles and not to that of crystalline]. What is more, the crystalline lens of the eye as the organ of vision is ironically discarded: "Los americanos han inventado un millón de cosas descartables: los platos, las jeringas, los senos, los ojos (o parte de los ojos: el cristalino, por ejemplo)" (66) [The Americans have invented a million disposable things: plates, syringes, breasts, eyes (or at least part of the eye: the crystalline lens, for example)]. The obvious and insistent choice of glass in opposition to crystal is not, in my view, a mere plot detail. On the contrary, I think that it contributes in a decisive way to the presentation of a specific conception of writing and reading. If the crystalline lens as a "natural" organ of vision generates precisely a naturalized perception of what we consider reality, glass makes possible new combinations, new expressions. It is hardly accidental that none other than the author of "The Metamorphosis" is mentioned as the ideal writer in this story: "Los [cuentos] de Kafka nunca dejan de ser los mejores del mundo" (65) [Kafka's stories never cease being the best in the world]. Just as was announced in "Fragmentos del libro invisible," no text remains static, identical to itself; no meaning can be fully localizable. The lens made of glass – and not crystalline – will generate multiple meanings, indecipherable, contradictory, whose effects will be always – as Silvina's stories suggest – unpredictable.

Translated by Patricia N. Klingenberg

3

Sur in the 1960s: Toward a New Critical Sensibility[*]

JUDITH PODLUBNE

The Remains of *Sur*

In the entry for July 18, 1963, the diary *Borges*, that masterpiece of malicious gossip and resentment with which Adolfo Bioy Casares redeems himself from the silliness and detachment of his fiction, records an appropriate and, in many ways, telling episode:

> Después del almuerzo voy a Sur, donde hay una reunión que se repite cada dos o tres años. Están Murena, Girri, Pezzoni, María Luisa Bastos, Borges, Mallea, González Lanuza y Victoria. VICTORIA: "Los he llamado para ver qué se puede hacer para dar vida a Sur." (Yo pienso que se podría prender una estufa eléctrica.). ALGUIEN: "Hay gente que ya no colabora." OTRO: "¿Quién?" ALGUIEN: "Algunos por causas obvias, como Martínez Estrada. Otros como Soto ..." GONZALEZ LANUZA: "Porque es perezoso. Si se le pide colaborará. ("Estamos salvados," me dirá después Borges). Se podría llamar a Martínez Estrada a un debate." BORGES: "Yo no quiero hablar con Martínez Estrada." GONZALEZ LANUZA: "Bueno, eso es lo que no hay que hacer. El diálogo ..." BORGES: "Para discutir hay que estar de acuerdo sobre algo. Si yo quiero jugar al truco y vos al tute no podemos jugar un partido ... Además, no sé por qué Sur se va a convertir en una tribuna para comunistas." ALGUIEN: "Los debates de antes ..." UN SEGUNDO: "Eran otros tiempos. Estaban Pedro [Henríquez Ureña], Amado [Alonso] ..." (925)

> [After lunch I go to *Sur*, where there is a meeting that is repeated every two or three years. Present are Murena, Girri, Pezzoni, María Luisa Bastos,

   [*]   Originally published in *Badebec* 2 (March 2012), a publication of the Centro de Estudios de Teoría y Crítica Literaria de la Facultad de Humanidades y Artes de la Universidad Nacional de Rosario.

Borges, Mallea, González Lanuza and Victoria. VICTORIA: "I have called you to see what can be done to give life to *Sur*." (I think that one could turn on a space heater.) SOMEONE: "There are those who don't participate." ANOTHER: "Who?" SOMEONE: "Some for obvious reasons, like Martínez Estrada. Others like Soto ..." GONZALEZ LANUZA: "Because he is lazy. If you ask him he will cooperate ("We're saved," Borges will later tell me.) One could invite Martínez Estrada to a debate." BORGES: "I don't want to talk to Martínez Estrada." GONZALEZ LANUZA: "Well, that is what should not be done. Dialog ..." BORGES: "In order to argue one must be in agreement about something. If I want to play *truco* and you *tute* we cannot play a game ... Besides, I don't know why *Sur* should become a forum for communists." SOMEONE: "The debates in the past ..." A SECOND: "They were different times. Pedro [Henríquez Ureña] and Amado [Alonso] ..."]

The meeting dies away in repetition and nostalgia. Overall flies the ghost of José Bianco, who had resigned shortly before. The reserve and the lack of ideas from those who supported Victoria's intentions, and the alienation, the asides, and the sarcastic jokes of those who continued to attend in spite of their differences, produced a recognizable dynamic, by then clearly crystallized,

3. Silvina Ocampo, Enrique Pezzoni, Alejandra Pizarnik, Edgardo Cozarinsky, and Manuel Mujica Láinez, on the Casares estate; photo taken by Adolfo Bioy Casares on October 3, 1965.

which nevertheless did not impede the continuation of the journal for several more years. Present also were the newest contributors, though Bioy does not record their participation. One could attempt a quick reading of the careful toponymic exercise that the fragment recreates: with the exception of Victoria, whose first name suffices, and of María Luisa Bastos, who requires a complete name, the others are mentioned by their surname only. When the conversation begins just a few are retained. Bioy replaces proper names with indefinite pronouns, as if the same ones were speaking in order to say the same things – all with the effect of diminishing the prominence given by the group to individual voices. The scene presents with biting humor the slow death that Victoria's gathering diagnoses.

A few months after this meeting, in December of the same year, Alejandra Pizarnik wrote two letters to Ivonne Bordelois from Paris in which she proposed different projects for *Sur*. The image of the journal reflected through her youthful enthusiasm contrasts painfully with the fatigued vision transmitted by her elders. For Pizarnik, who the year before had published her first contribution to the journal (an article on Yves Bonnefoy, written with Bordelois) and whose fourth book, *Árbol de Diana*, had been published by *Sur*'s book publishing branch, the journal is the space for risky ventures: an opportunity to translate and write about what she was reading in Europe and could recommend with assurance:

> No sé si sabés quién es Bruno Schultz. Una suerte de segundo Kafka, célebre ahora en París. Murió en campo de concentración y dejó cuentos extrañísimos, originalísimos y fascinantes. Nadeau lo publicó en su colección. Te propongo esto: traducir un cuento suyo y publicarlo en *Sur*. Ya le dirás a María Luisa Bastos ... Naturalmente, Schultz escribió en polaco pero nosotros lo traduciremos del francés ... Entre nuestro bello traducir y mi apellido, todo se arreglará. Además haré un artículo (o "haremos," si preferís), rico en detalles o interpretaciones. Por supuesto que el asunto vale la pena, es literatura de primera calidad y de paso *Sur* publicará por primera vez–en Argentina–a un escritor que, según va la cosa, será pronto tan conocido como K. (*Correspondencia* 238)

> [I don't know if you know who Bruno Schultz is. A kind of second Kafka, famous these days in Paris. He died in a concentration camp and left very strange, very original and fascinating short stories. Nadeau published him in his collection. I propose the following: translate one of his stories and publish it in *Sur*. You can tell María Luisa Bastos ... Naturally, Schultz wrote in Polish but we will translate from the French ... Between our beautiful translation and my surname everything will work out. Then, I will write an article (or "we will," if you prefer), rich in details or interpretations. Of course it is worth it; it is literature of the first caliber and in the process

Sur will publish for the first time – in Argentina – a writer that, according to some, will soon be as well known as K.]

The second project involved the translation of Karen Blixen, the real name of Isak Dinesen, "una autora de cuentos perfectos, dirá, que no deslucen cerca de los de Chéjov" (*Correspondencia* 241) [an author of perfect stories that do not lose their luster in comparison with Chekhov]. Although neither of these suggestions prospered, the letters show, indirectly, a perception of the journal that transcends one individual perspective: they demonstrate a shared impression among several of the younger contributors of the time. It has been suggested that one of the principal causes of the decline of *Sur*, beyond the natural aging of its historic members and collaborators, was the aging of its intellectual mission. *Sur* failed to navigate the profound transformations rising up in the second half of the twentieth century and, as tends to happen with cultural enterprises of long life, clung to the values and style of contribution that had characterized its first decade (Gramuglio 202). The reasons for its loss of influence have been traced with rigor and exhaustive detail by the intellectual histories of the journal and of the period. Maintaining a focus on continuity, these histories inevitably characterized the publication as having a homogeneity and systematic quality, and therefore tended to downplay the contingencies, the rifts, and the disruptions that stressed the journal at this time.

The series of testimonies, oral and written, the anecdotes, stories, and gossip – so much gossip, ever more passionate and moving! – was disseminated for some time during the last decade, discreetly and fragmentarily, by some of the most important protagonists and by those close to them; I would venture to say that this regained for the last stage of *Sur* a porosity that complicates the stony, flat perspective provided by the histories. If this tale interests me – one that waited to declare itself until the elders had absented themselves, and new dialogs could be established – it is because it transmits the agitation and power that the remains of this intellectual project radiated over many of the most distinguished critics, poets, and writers of the following decades. I am not referring to the sanctioned commonplace that suggests that the generation of the 1950s, congealed in the journal *Contorno*, nourished themselves intellectually and emotionally with readings from *Sur* and discussions with Murena.[1] Rather than these

---

[1]   John King describes the dynamics of *Sur*'s administration during the late 1950s with a quote attributed to Patricio Canto: "*Sur* es una monarquía constitucional. Victoria Ocampo es la reina ... que no gobierna. Pepe Bianco es el primer ministro, Murena es el favorito del primer ministro, quien es él que realmente gobierna" (*Sur: A Study* 153) [Victoria Ocampo is the queen who does not govern. Pepe Bianco is the prime minister, Murena, the court favorite who is the one actually in charge]. King characterizes *Contorno*, founded in 1953, as one of the "little magazines" which rose up to criticize *Sur*. The list of contributors – the Viñas brothers, Adolfo

intellectuals, already much studied (although it doesn't hurt, it seems to me, to reconsider the so-called modernizing reach of their contributions to Argentine literary criticism), who made confrontation and denunciation their practice, I am interested in that group of young people of diverse origins who coincided during the 1960s in the offices of *Sur*. This subgroup, in the majority, were friends and lovers of each other and of the elders, who, without forming a school of thought (all of them *rara avis*, as Jorge Panesi once said of Sylvia Molloy), connected at *Sur* and in other nearby places, as was inevitable in the Buenos Aires culture of the time, like the artistic gatherings of artists in the El Taller gallery and the literary salons of Esmeralda Almonacid. María Luisa Bastos characterized this group as "varios ... intelectuales jóvenes –futuros profesores, críticos, periodistas– [que] hicieron en las páginas de *Sur* sus primeras experiencias como escritores, generalmente redactando notas o reseñas" ("Dos líneas" 15) [various young intellectuals – future professors, critics, journalists – who in the pages of *Sur* had their first experiences as writers, generally providing notes and reviews]. I wonder not just about what motivated them, but also about what effects these first critical experiences had on the plains of Argentine literature.

There is no doubt that their personal relationships and sexual liaisons played a significant role in the gathering of this subgroup, which coexisted among the original members with attitudes that ranged from recognition and exasperation to the expectation of renewal. It seems, according to the vague tale that wove the legend of the last decades, that after the resignation of Bianco in 1961, Victoria toyed with the possibility of retaking the reins of the journal in order to avoid the repetition of any similar incident.[2] Enrique Pezzoni, the oldest of the younger group (he had joined *Sur* at the end of the 1940s), was lying in wait as the natural candidate for the vacant post, although he was not interested in accepting it, it is said, so as not to have to deal with Victoria. Anticipating the proposal, Pezzoni agreed with Murena, at the head of the editorial staff in those years, to introduce María Luisa Bastos, their mutual friend, to Victoria. The agreement resulted in the appointment of Bastos to a position which in fact restricted her function: she would not be the editor in chief, but rather the director's secretary. I think that the results of this arrangement – the modernizing reach of their directives, their translations, and essays – failed for different reasons to be appreciated in the following decades because of changes and

Prieto, Portantiero, Noé Jitrik, León Rozitchner – "the most important literary critics of the time ... would write in opposition to, rather than within, *Sur*" (157). (translator's note)

2   Bianco's exit from *Sur* after twenty-three years at the helm resulted from a dispute with Victoria Ocampo – which she made public – over his decision to take part in cultural activities organized by the Cuban publisher, Casa de las Américas (King, *Sur* 172). (translator's note)

displacements in the world of literature and ways of reading that began to operate in the inner workings of the journal in order to extend its reach beyond itself. In the early 1990s Oscar Terán still insisted on a reductive opinion, blind to the movement that shook the publication: "mientras [la crítica literaria] se torna más profesional –y sobre la cual pronto han de influir las propuestas estructuralistas–, *Sur* permanece atenida básicamente a un estilo tradicional de abordaje del hecho literario" (87) [While literary criticism is becoming more professional – and is soon to be influenced by the notions of structuralism – *Sur* remains basically tied to a traditional style of literary approach]. To mention for the moment just one of the displacements that occurred at the journal, whose influence is enough to warrant a reconsideration of the importance that the younger critics joining *Sur* were to have in the later development of Argentine criticism, I need to recall the interpretation of the work of Borges that the 1952 essay by Pezzoni proposed on the appearance of *Otras inquisiciones*. This essay was published two years earlier than the implacable book by Adolfo Prieto, *Borges y la nueva generación*, and delineated a line of readings that extends to *Las letras de Borges* by Sylvia Molloy in 1979, and I would say even includes *Borges y el cine* by Edgardo Cozarinsky and *Borges ante la crítica argentina* by María Luisa Bastos, both in 1974.

Already interested in these questions, in 2011 I asked Sylvia Molloy to tell me about what *Sur* was like in that era. I had just read *Desarticulaciones* and I found or imagined that the writing of those fragments had permitted her to relive those years with the rare intensity that literary narratives afford: "No quedan testigos de una parte de mi vida, la que su memoria se ha llevado consigo. Esa pérdida que podía angustiarme, curiosamente me libera: no hay nadie que me corrija si me decido a inventar" (Molloy, *Desarticulaciones* 22) [No witnesses to that part of my life remain, to the part that their memory has carried off with them. That loss which might cause distress, curiously liberates me: there is no one to correct me if I decide to invent.] I don't know, and it doesn't matter, how much Molloy invented that afternoon; I know that scarcely had she begun to recount her story than I abandoned my notes so as not to interfere with the effervescence that she transmitted as she went along. I noted things down immediately after we had parted. The beginning of these notes is the literal transcription, I think, of an account that, according to what I heard (according to what I wanted to hear, probably), worked as a kind of guide for her memory of those days: "En esos años, *Sur* era un lugar en el que se podía disentir, incluso con *Sur*" [In those years, *Sur* was a place in which one could disagree, even with *Sur*]. The affirmation ventured an entry to the matter I was traversing and exceeded the personal relations that formed the special emphasis of her version. In a period during which, as pointed out by Terán, totalizing responses, violent certainties, and doctrinaire Manichaeism invaded the style of theoretical contributions and blocked possibilities for a plural and open debate, a period during which politics, in Sartrean code, became the ultimate cause of diverse cultural practices, *Sur* (like the Di Tella Institute, although following other forms and aesthetic convictions, of course) made space for dissent, for a sexual and critical dissidence. The analogy between the Di Tella Institute and *Sur* does not imply, in principle, more than an idea extracted from a series of testimonies in which one notes contradictions, similarities, and mutual antagonisms, among the participants of both spaces. Edgardo Cozarinsky records his attendance at the opening nights of the Di Tella, while Raúl Escari,[3] the former avant-gardist, has fun identifying himself with his admired Silvina and Victoria Ocampo. The memory of both Cozarinsky and Escari coincides on one point still little studied: the rejection of what Escari designates as *the prejudices of the reigning intellectual left* of those years – the left and even some of the members of *Sur*, I would add, if one remembers the ferocious homophobia that wafts from *Borges* by Bioy. As on so many other occasions, political morals of different stripes affirm aberrant agreements on this point.

I have no desire to fall into the naive and no less prejudicial awkwardness of attributing critical dissent to sexual dissidence; nevertheless, one comment by Cozarinsky does make a convincing connection. Cozarinsky said: "La disidencia sexual, en cuanto marginalidad (aun tácita, postergada, olvidada, pero siempre palpitante), ayuda a no ilusionarse con las volubles mayúsculas de la Historia" (*Blues* 112) [Sexual dissidence, as marginal (still tacit, forgotten, but always latent), helps us to avoid illusions about the erratic, changeable capital letters of History]. I wonder if it might not be this kind of radical, active skepticism – more Nietzschean than nihilist, taking up a distinction that Cozarinsky applies to Murena – a discreet yet somehow jubilant skepticism, that permitted this subgroup to maintain links to their artistic and literary interests without feeling pressurized to respond directly to the ideological imperatives of the moment. Their skepticism made it possible for the younger group of *Sur* to dissent, tangentially but surely, both from the journal's intellectual program, by then completely outdated, and from the virulent attacks on this program by different sectors of the left. As Jacques Rancière points out, dissent is not to be confused with the conflict of ideas, but rather it supposes

> una organización de lo sensible en la que no hay realidad oculta bajo las apariencias, ni régimen único de presentación y de interpretación de lo dado que imponga a todos su evidencia. Por eso toda situación [puede ser]

3   The Di Tella Institute provided a cultural space for experimental and modernist art and theater; Raúl Escari was a leader of avant-garde efforts to reconsider artistic expression and its relation to mass media. For more, see Inés Katzenstein, listed in the Works Cited. (translator's note)

hendida en su interior, reconfigurada bajo otro régimen de percepción y de significación. (51)

[an organization of sensibility in which there is no reality hidden under appearances, no single regime of presentation or interpretation that convinces everyone with its evidence. For that reason every situation can be split in its interior, reconfigured under another regime of perception and signification.]

Dissent operates on this point as the condition (the assurance) of the unstable character of an age, a work, an interpretation – of whatever identity that pretends to affirm itself as such. From this point of view, I would speculate that the re-reading of Silvina Ocampo's narrative that those young critics undertook in the second half of the 1960s constitutes one of the most luminous and fertile *scenes of dissent* to be promoted by the journal.

The Silvina Ocampo Event

In 1966 José Bianco compiled, for the publisher Eudeba, the first anthology of stories by Silvina Ocampo, *El pecado mortal*. The selection included stories from three of the four books that Silvina had published up to that point: *Autobiografía de Irene* (Sur, 1948), *La furia y otros cuentos* (Sur, 1959) and *Las invitadas* (Losada, 1961) – a total of twenty stories, most of them very brief, that in the years since have been listed among the best known of her works. At the urging of Pezzoni, who by this time was the editor in chief of *Sur*, Alejandra Pizarnik published her well-known essay "Dominios ilícitos," a reading of the anthology that displaced, in a brand new and unexpected direction, the different interpretations that had accompanied these narratives. It was a change of direction in the wake of conclusions announced by George Bataille in *Eroticism*, an author Pizarnik read in those years with a fervid identification ("Cada vez me asombra más nuestro aire de familia" [I am ever more astonished by our family spirit], she would write in her *Diary*). Bataille's book, translated by María Luisa Bastos, was published in 1964 by *Sur*'s book publishing wing (I am guessing at Pizarnik's recommendation). This was a new direction, devoted to an appreciation of Silvina's stories based on the dreadful and delicious ambiguity that defines them: "La conjunción entre la fiesta, la muerte, el erotismo y la infancia, procede de una misma perspectiva fulgurante, posible de discernir, distintamente, en todos los relatos" (Pizarnik, "Dominios" 94) [The combination of celebration, death, eroticism, and childhood proceeds from the same stunning perspective, differently discernible in all of her narratives]. With an impulse that expands on the decision by Bianco to baptize the anthology with the name of one of the most voluptuous stories in the collection, Pizarnik's reading displaces the heart of these works from a habitual ambivalence between the real and the unreal, about which all the reviewers of *Sur* and *La Nación* were in agreement, to situate it in the incohesive convergence of ancient paradoxical forces:

> La ambigüedad de Silvina Ocampo se acuerda con su facultad de trasponer un hecho apacible y común en otro que, sigue siendo el mismo, sólo que inquietante. Es decir: se traslada al plano de la realidad sin haberlo dejado nunca. Asimismo se traslada al plano de la irrealidad sin haberlo dejado nunca. Claro es que términos como realidad e irrealidad resultan perfectamente inadecuados. (91)

> [Silvina Ocampo's ambiguity accords with her ability to transport a pleasant and common event into something which continues to be the same thing, only disturbing. That is to say: it is carried to the plane of reality without ever having left it. Similarly it is carried to the plane of unreality without ever having left it. Naturally terms like *reality* and *unreality* become completely inadequate.]

Ever since the controversial review written by Victoria Ocampo on *Viaje olvidado*, in which a graceless older sister found unforgivable the literary circulation of her family memories, and especially since the publication of *La furia y otros cuentos* in 1959, the disquiet and dismay that Silvina's stories provoked had found an effective limit by the dispatching of them to the bounded refuge of fantastic fiction. The recognition that Bianco's book afforded the author (in addition to numerous reviews in and beyond *Sur*, she received the Municipal Prize for Literature) failed to hide the anxiety and discomfiture that her tales evoked among the very critics who praised them. The warmly favorable commentary by Tomás Eloy Martínez published in *La Nación* is an eloquent example of this tension: "Una primera lectura de *La furia* puede suscitar malestares, cambios de ánimo, deslumbramientos. Ciertas frases, alguna sola palabra violenta desencadenan entonces el estupor y la inquietud física" (25) [A first reading of *La furia* may evoke unease, mood swings, bewilderment. Certain phrases, a single violent word, then unleash astonishment and physical agitation.] The warnings are mitigated a few paragraphs afterward when the writer finds that the majority of the cruel anecdotes that he has just listed "corroboran que, (aunque es pasmosamente creíble), el mundo de Silvina Ocampo es irreal" (25) [confirm that (although it is astonishingly believable) the world of Silvina Ocampo is unreal]. On that same note Eugenio Guasta published his review in number 264 of *Sur*. Immediately after evoking the article by Eloy Martínez, Guasta declares, "El mundo de *La furia* existe en sí mismo y es un ámbito clausurado. Silvina Ocampo crea, más allá de este mundo real, otro mundo, que ella imagina, con aire extraño, en el que sin embargo nos encontramos con reconocibles elementos de la realidad" (62) [The world of *La furia* exists in itself and is a cloistered space. Silvina Ocampo creates, beyond this real world, another world, that she imagines, a strange atmosphere, in which nevertheless we meet with recognizable elements of reality.] This statement is the threshold of an imprecise and unsubtle conclusion, destined to domesticate the inconveniences of these narratives. Like Eloy Martínez and Mario Lancelotti, the other reviewer of *Sur*, Guasta underlines the poetic value and the metaphysical tension in the stories. There is no need to point out that these are the completely anachronistic and stereotyped general qualities with which it was still common at this time to cleanse the excesses of feminine sensibility.

Contrary to the recognition that Ocampo's work was gaining within *Sur*, and without noticing the spirit of correction that surrounded it, and above all without renouncing the transcendental pretensions that supported this impulse, Abelardo Castillo published, in *El grillo de papel*, a devastating review in which he repeated various of the imputations that the intellectuals on the left had been directing at the major writers of *Sur* through the previous decade. Castillo wrote:

> El círculo mágico, la inventada realidad donde un narrador introduce al que lee, obligándolo a creer en resucitadas, horlas o pescadores sin sombra, esa que angustia en Kafka y escuece en Chéjov: la atmósfera del relato, no aparece aquí. Hay, es verdad, una constante tenebrosa, malvadísima, una suerte de frívolo draculismo que se repite en todas las historias, pero la frivolidad no es intensa ... *La furia* no alcanza a producir horror: ... acaso, como escribió Edgar Poe, porque el horror legítimo viene del alma y sólo arrancándoselo de allí puede llevárselo a sus legítimas consecuencias (Prólogo a *Cuentos de lo Grotesco y lo Arabesco*, 1840). (Castillo 17)

> [The magic circle does not appear here, that invented reality where a narrator, obliging the reader to believe, introduces him to the dead brought back to life, to horlas, to fishermen without shadows, things that produce anxiety in Kafka and friction in Chekhov. There is, it is true, a shadowy, evil constant, a kind of frivolous Draculism that is repeated in all the stories, but the frivolity is not intense ... *La furia* fails to produce horror ... perhaps, as Edgar Poe wrote, because legitimate horror comes from the soul and only grabbing it from within is one able to carry it to its legitimate consequences.]

The stories of *La furia* for Castillo lack the seriousness and profundity – a vital commitment, he all but said – that distinguishes "great fantastic literature." This lack, which conditions the frivolity and superficiality of its effects, is intensified by the inexperience of Ocampo's narrative. The problem is not just with the themes but also and more importantly in the treatment the author gives them. From this point of view Silvina is fundamentally a defective narrator, a bad storyteller, incapable of "articulating with exactitude the rigorous mechanics of the short story" and ready to sacrifice its darker content to a lighthearted and distracted spirit:

> El cuento es ante todo una elaboración artística; por lo tanto, indeclinablemente debe guardar armonía entre concepto y forma: equivocar los términos, exagerar uno de ellos, equivale al fracaso. Si, como en *La furia*, el concepto está dado por una constante tenebrosa y la artimaña es coquetamente divertida, se produce un tropiezo, no sólo literario sino de sospechoso donaire. (17)

> [The short story is above all an artistic elaboration; thus it should, without leaning either way, maintain harmony between concept and form: to mistake the terms, to exaggerate one or the other, is to fail. If, as in *La furia*, the concept is presented by an unwavering darkness and the artifice is coquettishly humorous, it produces a fumble, not just a literary one, but one of inappropriate wit.]

Having declared his platonic affiliation, it is no surprise that his commentary perceives as error the same quality that later critics recognized as one of the principal accomplishments of the stories: I refer to the contrast that is established between the lighthearted, innocent tone of the narrators and the atrocious nature of the events narrated.

Indifferent both to the cautious recognition that Ocampo received within *Sur* as well as to Castillo's condemnation of her narrative, the path of reading that Pizarnik inaugurated in her article invents, Rancière would say, a new order of perception and meaning for these works, an order attentive to the multiple layers of meaning: "Aquí es todo más claro, y a la vez, más peligroso. El peligro consiste en que los textos dicen incesantemente algo más, algo que no dicen" ("Dominios" 91) [Here everything is clearer and at the same time more dangerous. The danger consists in that the texts incessantly say something more, something that is unsaid]). The "centro magnético" [magnetic center] of these stories is located in "el modo de hacer visibles las pasiones infantiles" (91) [the way to make childhood passions visible]. Pizarnik, in a few paragraphs, outlines a brilliant reading of "El pecado mortal," the story that narrates in a superegoistic and impersonal voice, inflamed by the very thing it seeks to censure, the irrepressible and guilty desire that a child at the age of First Communion feels for Chango, the main servant of the house. For Pizarnik the principal characteristic of Ocampo's work consists of "ciertas uniones o alianzas o enlaces: la risa no se opone al sufrimiento; ni el amor al odio; ni la fiesta a la muerte" (94) [certain unions or alliances or ties: laughter is not opposed to suffering; nor love to hate;

nor celebration to death]. Following the findings established by Pizarnik's critical discourse, the challenge assumed by the young generation at *Sur* in subsequent interpretations was to sustain this primordial ambiguity, to defend it from palliatives of meaning with which one might try to untangle it, in order to preserve its indeterminacy within the state of childish neutrality transmitted by the narratives.

The forms of excess that Molloy read in her essential (and by now canonical) essay published the year after "Dominios ilícitos," in number 320 of *Sur*, "Silvina Ocampo: la exageración como lenguaje," rediscover this foundation of primordial ambiguity not just in the voices and the conduct of the characters but also in the modes of narration. The reckless will to verbalize that Molloy's essay illumines and describes in detail invokes for Ocampo's stories an anomalous form of decentered melodrama, a kind of eccentric drama in which the unresolved disputes between good and evil revive, exacerbated by the manifestation of archaic and childish impulses that expropriate from narrators and characters their subjective armor:

> No hay para estos relatos una salida –una asimilación a la "realidad"– decorosa. Una vez sometidos a las acrobacias éticas y lingüísticas que les impone [Silvina] pierden la posibilidad de volver, como las tragedias, al orden tranquilizador del que se han alejado. La exageración logra una distancia definitiva. No hay cabida para las declaraciones deliberadamente normalizadoras … Condenados a la exageración que les señala la autora, relato y protagonista quedan fijados en ese exceso que los arroja fuera de ellos ("La exageración" 22–23)

> [For these narratives there is no decorous exit, no assimilation to "reality." Once submitted to the ethical and linguistic acrobatics that Silvina imposes they lose all possibility of return, as in tragedy, to a calming order from which they have been removed. The exaggeration establishes a definitive distance. There is no room for deliberately normalizing declarations … Condemned to the exaggeration to which the author sentences them, story and protagonist remain fixed in that excess.]

From this fixation, from this bewilderment, which Cozarinsky calls "la tara secreta" [the secret weight] of Ocampo's narrators, proceeds, as the critic rightly points out, the ability of her works to name as if for the first time a sovereign innocence disposed to affirm contradictory passions whose coexistence makes them unique. The introduction to the anthology *Informe del cielo y del infierno*, which Cozarinsky published in 1970 some months after Molloy's essay, and from whose conclusion I have just quoted, is invoked by Pezzoni in the entry about Silvina Ocampo that he wrote for the *Enciclopedia de la Literatura*

Argentina, directed by Pedro Orgambide and Roberto Yahni that same year. In his entry Pezzoni insists that, even when an incessant battle between enemy forces agitates her works, Ocampo absents herself from ethical judgments. I leave for another time the analysis of these specifications, their personal nuances, and the consequences that this kind of conversation about Ocampo's narrative had in the critical and literary production of these writers. If I wanted to recompose it, even in a hasty and summative way, it is because it seems to me that not only did they dramatize the divisive moments of this always deferred encounter between a literary work and its readers, but also because I deduce that in this conversation a new form of Argentine critical sensibility unfolded: a reluctant form regarding cultural emblems and ideological fetishes of the era, disposed to allow itself to be affected by an incomparable rarity of the literary experience; a form of sensibility that, permeable to the unrepeatable character of her narrative, made a place for the "ambiguous," "extreme," "exaggerated," and "excessive," the Silvina Ocampo event.

Translated by Patricia N. Klingenberg

4

Reading Cruelty in Silvina Ocampo's Short Fiction:
Theme, Style, and Narrative Resistance

ASHLEY HOPE PÉREZ

Silvina Ocampo's stories often evoke a distressing fictional world: children frequently witness, commit, or suffer acts of violence; death and murder occur with startling regularity; self-mutilation and rivalry abound; vengeance outstrips offense; and a sinister atmosphere hovers over even those stories that avoid direct engagement with cruelty. Beginning with Mario A. Lancelotti's 1962 review of Ocampo's fourth short story collection, *Las invitadas*, references to the stories' cruelty have become *de rigueur* in Ocampo criticism, yet they are often accompanied by a certain uneasiness or bent toward justification. Jorge Luis Borges declared his perplexity before Ocampo's "strange taste for a certain kind of innocent and oblique cruelty," which he explained as "the astonished interest that evil inspires in a noble soul" (Ocampo, *Leopoldina's Dream* 2).[1] This pronouncement possesses the ring of authority we expect from Borges, but the reference to "innocence" and a "noble soul" also betrays a certain patronizing and dismissive stance rather than serious consideration of the role of cruelty in Ocampo's fiction.[2] Even Ocampo herself displayed a certain ambivalence regarding cruelty in her fiction. At times she seemed to take pride in the sharp edges of her tales, and she expressed her delight in "El vestido de terciopelo" [The velvet dress] which she describes as "un cuento muy cruel" (Ulla, *Encuentros* 72) [a very cruel story]. But she also responded negatively

---

[1]   These remarks were reprinted in English as the preface to *Leopoldina's Dream*, Daniel Balderston's translation of selected fiction by Ocampo. Borges's text appeared originally in French as the foreword for a French-language collection of Ocampo's fiction with the title *Faits divers de la terre et du ciel* (Gallimard, 1974).

[2]   Regarding this assessment of cruelty in Ocampo's fiction, Fiona Mackintosh notes that Borges "recuperates and domesticates" Ocampo's treatment of cruelty (*Childhood* 114), and Gisle Selnes argues that Borges mistakenly assumes that a woman's engagement with cruelty must be a mere "flirtation" with "foreign obscenities" (520).

to critics' tendency to fixate on cruelty: "me parece que es un poco exagerado decir que [los cuentos] son crueles" (48) [I think it is a bit exaggerated to say that the stories are cruel].[3] At one point she argued that cruelty was only relevant to a handful of stories and distanced herself from these "cuentos de crueldad" which she claimed were "totalmente distintos del resto" (72, 91) [the stories of cruelty are completely different from the rest].[4] Ocampo retracted this remark a moment later, and the shift in the conversation suggests that what bothered her was less the presence of cruelty in her fiction than the degree to which it hampered positive critical attention. In part, this frustration stemmed from Ocampo's belief that negative reactions to the cruelty of her stories had prevented her from receiving Argentina's Premio Nacional for fiction (92). While her poetry received a number of prizes, including the Premio Nacional de Poesía for both *Los nombres* (1953) and *Lo amargo por dulce* (1962), her fiction was never recognized with a major award.[5]

The label "cruel" may be particularly damning in part because of the unique contours of the concept of cruelty. Understood most broadly as indifference to (or pleasure in) the pain of others, cruelty resides not in an act itself but in an individual's relation to suffering. Whereas a focus on violence primes us to emphasize effects (e.g., the body count), cruelty implies a judgment that (a) one has acted (or has refrained from acting) for the purpose of deriving pleasure from another's suffering or (b) one has failed to react in response to another's suffering. Kicking a dog is violent regardless of circumstance, for in any case physical harm is done to the dog, whether by accident or intentional abuse. By contrast, this act would only be described as cruel if it were accomplished without care for the pain caused or out of pleasure in that pain. Even in daily experience, the attribution of cruelty to others is bound to subjective judgment. In the case of literature, to describe a body of work as "cruel" places the stress on the author's deviance: she must delight in imagining or causing suffering. But such a judgment lets the reader off too easily, as I will argue, and it misses the surprising ethical dimension of some literary engagements with cruelty. In *La ética de la crueldad*, José Ovejero describes three incarnations of cruelty in literature and art: spectacular cruelty, conformist cruelty, and ethical cruelty. Spectacular cruelty might be thought of as the displays of violence without compassion that produce frissons or cheap thrills that are quickly reabsorbed into the narrative, as in the clearly codified cruelty and violence of horror or

---

3   Translations from Spanish for this essay were made by Patricia N. Klingenberg. (editor's note)
4   "El vástago," "El vestido de terciopelo," "La casa de los relojes," "La furia," and "El sótano" are among the stories that she briefly repudiated (Ulla, *Encuentros* 72, 91).
5   The ratio of critical attention paid to Ocampo's short fiction as compared to her poetry, however, suggests that Ocampo's stories may have the most enduring appeal.

detective genres (38–40). Ovejero's second type of cruelty, conformist cruelty, is most notable for presenting us with cruelty that conforms to our expectations; what we read affirms values we already hold, which usually align with the writer's or narrator's (16–20, 43–45). By contrast, ethical cruelty resides primarily in the terms by which the reader is asked to engage with the text. Rather than fulfilling the readers' expectations, ethical cruelty in literature forces readers to re-evaluate the values that guide their reading and to consider their less complimentary implications (61).

Notwithstanding Ocampo's passing suggestion that cruelty be quarantined to a particular subset of her stories, the pervasiveness and subtlety of her engagement with cruelty suggest its centrality to the broader workings of her fiction. My focus encompasses thematic elements in Ocampo's fiction, and I build on existing approaches to Ocampo by examining the impact of her resistant aesthetic on readers' textual encounters with narrated cruelty. Embracing Ovejero's view that particular engagements with cruelty may possess a distinctive ethical character, I argue that the challenge of cruelty in Ocampo's fiction resides as much in how it becomes present to readers as it does in the stories' thematic content. In particular, I focus on the role of stylistic and narrative elements in frustrating readers' attempts at emotional connection with characters and narrated circumstances. I will also explore how Ocampo's resistant aesthetic creates peculiar dilemmas for readers that may intensify feelings of uncomfortable responsibility.

Reading Cruelty in Ocampo: Fantasy, Solidarity, and Femininity

During past decades, cruelty in Ocampo's fiction has often been discussed as a mark of her engagement with the fantastic tradition. Ocampo's early collaboration on the *Antología de la literatura fantástica* (first edition, 1940) with Borges and her husband, Adolfo Bioy Casares, may have encouraged critics to emphasize the fantastic elements in her fiction.[6] In a 1968 review of a new compilation of Ocampo's stories, Alejandra Pizarnik criticized José Bianco, author of the collection's introduction, for repeating the already clichéd recurrence to the fantastic ("Dominios" 95). Sylvia Molloy assesses this tendency as a "prophylactic" measure by which stories are resituated in "una zona inocua 'donde esas cosas en realidad no pasan'" ("Silvina Ocampo" 23) [a harmless zone where these

---

6   Ocampo's story "La expiación" was included along with works by Bioy Casares and Borges in the considerably revised second edition of the anthology, which has been credited as a major influence on the shift in Latin American literature away from the regional realist novel. Interestingly, despite the anthology's title, many of the stories included in this eclectic collection are well outside the frame of what most of Ocampo's critics mean when they describe her work as fantasy; the anthology includes, for example, works by James Joyce, Tolstoy, and the anthropologist James Frazer.

things don't really happen]. The interpretive pressure that accumulates around cruel events ("esas cosas") dissipates when they are reframed as features of fantasy, marks of a breach in reality.

It is worth noting, however, that twenty of the thirty-four stories in Ocampo's 1959 collection, *La furia, y otros cuentos*, do not include any explicit element of fantasy. While often disturbing, they are nevertheless within the realm of the possible, if not the probable, as is the case in "El vástago" [The heir] in which a child is given a loaded gun to play with in hopes – perfectly fulfilled – that he will "accidentally" shoot the grandfather who tyrannizes the family. "La voz en el teléfono" [The voice on the telephone] offers a retrospective and unrepentant narration of the deadly entertainments pursued by a four-year-old boy and his friends during a birthday party: the speaker instigates and successfully executes a plan to set fire to his home with the mothers locked inside. Of the remaining fourteen stories, most are not definitively fantastic but rather hold open multiple explanations in irresolvable tension.[7] "El vestido de terciopelo," which we will examine at greater length, can be read as a story of a velvet dress that mysteriously suffocates the woman trying it on, but it also holds open the possibility of human cruelty as the cause of the woman's death. The attribution of supernatural properties to objects is also tempting in the frequently discussed story, "La casa de azúcar" [The house made of sugar], in which a newly married woman receives a package with a dress that seems to initiate her transformation into the woman who previously occupied her house. Because the woman's jealous husband narrates the story, we can also read the fantastic as a product of his obsessive delusions or as an elaborate cover story for his own neglect and potential misdeeds. While readings focused on fantasy offer significant insights, an overemphasis on fantasy sometimes diminishes the crucial ambiguity of Ocampo's stories.[8]

Another frequent approach to interpreting cruelty in Ocampo's fiction is to frame it as an expression of the frustration and rage experienced by those relegated to the margins of society. Ocampo's stories often center on children, servants, housewives, the disabled, the elderly, and those oppressed by their

---

[7]   See Sylvia Molloy's "Simplicidad inquietante" for a discussion of this characteristic of Ocampo's fiction (245).

[8]   Commenting on the tendency to recur to fantasy when speaking of Ocampo, Valentín Díaz notes that the fantastic should be understood as one possible interpretative frame rather than as "una explicación suficiente" for the particularity of Ocampo's work (92). For readings that present ambiguous events as if they were clearly fantastic, see Erika Martínez Cabrera's "Fantástica criminal" (132–33), the chapter on women writers and fantasy in Cynthia Duncan's *Unraveling the Real* (179–201), the description of "La casa de azúcar" and "Las fotografías" in "Aspectos esotéricos en *La furia*" by Ricardo Romera Rozas (312 and 315), and Hedy Habra's "Escisión y liberación."

domestic ties; among her narrators, we can count busybodies, hairdressers, tutors, thieves, and small animals. Erika Martínez Cabrera argues that cruelty in Ocampo's stories serves as a universal strategy for the relatively powerless to react against subjugation (132).[9] Viviana Bermúdez-Arceo, Mónica Zapata, and Marta López-Luaces focus more narrowly on children, each arguing (with slight variations) that cruelty functions in Ocampo's stories to show the hypocrisy of adults who make children into pawns of malicious schemes and to explore the retaliatory vengeance of children against an oppressive adult order (Bermúdez-Arceo 283–86; Zapata, "Entre" 359; López-Luaces 62–65).[10] The notion of thematic cruelty as an expression of solidarity with the marginalized holds strong appeal, yet in general Ocampo blocks the forms of identification that would seem necessary to bring the plight of the "other" home to the reader.

Several critics incorporate a focus on fantasy into their examinations of Ocampo's stance toward marginal figures, often arguing that cruelty in Ocampo's fiction stands for a playful, subversive distortion of reality that is particularly associated with women writers.[11] In particular, Cynthia Duncan focuses almost exclusively on what she describes as the "distinctly feminine point of view" offered in Ocampo's fiction (*Unraveling* 181).[12] We should note, however, that male first-person narrators slightly outnumber female narrators in *La furia*, and

9   See also Patricia Klingenberg's path-breaking discussion of the victimization and revenge of women, children, and "deviants" as a crucial dimension of Ocampo's critique of marginalization and hegemony ("Mad Double" 38).
10   Bermúdez-Arceo, Zapata, and López-Luaces adopt some of the critical gestures first introduced by Blas Matamoro's early study of Ocampo in *Oligarquía y literatura* ("La nena terrible," 1975), which focuses on the figure of the transgressive child. For Matamoro, the child's cruelty is a mode of response to the repressiveness of parents and educators, whose crimes necessarily precede the child's (197). In contrast to those who have followed him and celebrate Ocampo as an advocate of the marginalized, however, Matamoro's Marxist reading of Ocampo sees her fiction as an unrealized social critique without revolutionary significance. For him, Ocampo's apparent allegiance to the marginalized is just a new form of appropriation, and her stories are less acts of solidarity than acts of accumulation of "others" into marginal menageries. My discussion of the anti-cute in Ocampo (see below) responds indirectly to Matamoro's critique; for another thorough response to Matamoro's analysis, see Klingenberg's *Fantasies of the Feminine* (93–96).
11   See "Women Writers of the Fantastic" in Duncan's *Unraveling the Real*, Klingenberg's *Fantasies of the Feminine* (especially chapters 1 and 3), Marcia Espinoza-Vera's "Unsubordinated Women," and Habra's "Escisión y liberación." Duncan, Klingenberg, and Espinoza-Vera employ the framework proposed in Rosemary Jackson's *Fantasy, the Literature of Subversion*. Selnes argues that scenes of cruelty mark a feminine difference in fantastic literature, but she takes a more critical stance toward Jackson's model (523–24).
12   Despite this insistence, in earlier writings, Duncan engages more fully with the role of male narrators. Her perceptive essay, "Double or Nothing? The Fantastic Element in Silvina Ocampo's 'La casa de azúcar,'" discusses the mysterious Violeta as a double, not of the principal female character, but of the male narrator. Selnes also discusses the prevalence of male narrators in Ocampo's work, arguing that the distinctive profile of the "Ocampo narrator" is shared by men and women alike (522, 526).

many stories focus almost exclusively on relationships between men (e.g., "El mal," "El vástago," "Magush," "Nosotros," "La última tarde," "Los amigos"). This dimension of Ocampo's fiction is often occluded by the emphasis on women's experience or a "feminine" perspective.[13] As we will see in the next section, Ocampo's resistant aesthetic both activates and frustrates the horizon of expectations associated with women writers in the Latin American context.

Whether critics focus on fantasy, the plight of the marginalized, or feminine concerns, the most common tendency is to examine cruelty primarily as a theme or as a dimension of plot. But it is not just the *what* but also the *how* that unsettles readers of Ocampo, not just the content of the stories but also how that content is styled and framed.[14] In a number of Ocampo's stories, cruelty is narrated as if it were an obvious or natural dimension of the experiences being related. After describing a prank that angered his father and brothers, the thief who narrates "La sibila" [The sibyl] observes,

> Me acostaron en el piso, y mientras unos me sujetaban, otro me clavó la astilla adentro de la oreja. Después, naturalmente, para que yo no hablara, me metieron en una bolsa que tiraron al río. Los vecinos me salvaron. Me pareció raro. (*La furia* 78)[15]

> [They threw me to the floor, and while others held me down, another stuck a splinter of wood in my ear. Then, naturally, so that I wouldn't talk, they put me in a bag which they threw in the river. The neighbors saved me. I thought it was strange.]

Cruelty emerges "naturalmente" in this account; only his rescue strikes the speaker as strange. Similarly, in "El sótano" [The basement], a prostitute expresses no surprise that she has been locked in the basement of a building that is about to be demolished, and cruelty goes unremarked by characters or narrators in many other stories. This approach contrasts starkly with stories

---

[13]   Additional examples of a stress on "feminine" concerns include María Noemí Balbi's "Silvina Ocampo y sus niñas inquietantes," Helena Araújo's "Ejemplos de la 'niña impura,'" Marjorie Agosín's "Mujer, espacio, e imaginación," and Eva Santos-Phillips's "La representación femenina en la narrativa de Silvina Ocampo."

[14]   A handful of critics connect cruelty to narrative and stylistic elements. For example, Annick Mangin notes that the cruelty of a given scene in Ocampo's fiction is made more unbearable because it is never denounced ("Fotos" 59), and Martínez Cabrera suggests that the humorous, indifferent tone in Ocampo's stories is deliberately inadequate to the narration of brutality, triggering our sensitivity to cruelty in the plot (130). Rosalba Campra sees the cruelty of characters' actions as instances of parodic excess intensified by the ostentatious neutrality with which they are recounted (196).

[15]   Page numbers for stories from *La furia, y otros cuentos* (1959) refer to the Alianza Tres 1993 edition. Other quotations from Ocampo's fiction are drawn from *Cuentos completos*.

that dramatize a joy in cruelty that the reader can feel *against*. In Juan Rodolfo Wilcock's "La fiesta de los enanos" [The feast of the dwarves], for example, the narrator describes one of the dwarves as "excitado extrañamente por el color de la sangre" (62) [strangely aroused by the color of the blood]. By registering the strangeness or abnormality of this excitement, the narrator opens the way to readers' judgment. Similarly, the dwarves' acts of mutilation are described as being motivated "por un resabio de consideración humana" [a bad habit of human consideration]; this ironic reversal of values allows readers to intuit – and share – the narrator's disapproval (62).[16] By contrast, Ocampo's narrators rarely mark cruelty as abnormal, depriving us of the satisfaction of uniting with them against it. This is one of many ways that Ocampo's fiction resists the strategies by which we often manage thematic cruelty in literature.

Silvina Ocampo's Resistant Aesthetic

The reception of a given writer's work depends in part on its compatibility with reigning interpretative practices,[17] and critical objections to Ocampo's stylistic nonconformity can be seen as early as Victoria Ocampo's tepid review of *Viaje olvidado* (1937). Victoria's essay on Silvina's first collection of stories mixes muted praise with unflattering remarks, as when she compares the stories' portrayal of things and people to what one finds in cartoons (119). Toward the end of the essay, Victoria's assessment of her sister's narrative style turns especially harsh:

> Todo eso está escrito en un lenguaje hablado, lleno de hallazgos que encantan y de desaciertos que molestan, lleno de imágenes felices –que parecen entonces naturales– y lleno de imágenes no logradas–que parecen entonces atacadas de tortícolis. ¿No serán posibles las unas sino gracias a las otras? ¿Es necesaria esa desigualdad? Corrigiéndose de unas, ¿se corregiría Silvina Ocampo de las otras? Es ése un riesgo que a mi juicio debe afrontar. Antes de renunciar a la destreza, es preciso que se haya tomado el trabajo de investigar qué porcentaje de negligencia entra en la composición de sus

---

16 In "Los cuentos crueles de Silvina Ocampo y Juan Rodolfo Wilcock," Daniel Balderston presents Ocampo and Wilcock's treatment of cruelty as comparable, an assessment that seems to be based in part on their collaboration on *Los traidores*, a drama in verse.

17 See Peter Rabinowitz's *Before Reading* on the impact of critical practices on the possibility that a work will gain canonical status (11–14, 212–21). See also Juan Carlos González Espitia's *On the Dark Side of the Archive*, which examines the literary characteristics that influence whether a work can be received as part of the "open archive" (as opposed to the "dark side of the archive") (178–79). A related discussion in José Ovejero's *La ética de la crueldad* examines thematic cruelty as one of the elements that may mark a work as scandalous at first but that often loses its transgressive character over time (108–9).

defectos y qué pereza la lleva a no ser más exigente consigo misma cuando todo nos demuestra que puede serlo. (120)

[Everything is written in a spoken style, filled with discoveries that enchant and awkward phrases that annoy, filled with pleasing images – that seem natural – and with those so badly done they seem to be suffering from a stiff neck. Are the ones only possible thanks to the others? Is this unevenness necessary? Would correcting the latter mean Silvina Ocampo would be correcting the former? That is the risk that I believe she must take. Before rejecting skill it is necessary to take the trouble to find out what percentage of negligence enters into the creation of her defects and what carelessness makes her demand so little of herself when everything shows us that she is capable of more.]

In Silvina's resistance to the formal perfection of the "well-made" story, Victoria sees only evidence of laziness, negligence, and limited artistic aspiration. The severity of Victoria's critique may reflect her (perceived) authority over Silvina, both as the writer's eldest sister and as her publisher.[18] Given her powerful position at *Sur*, Victoria likely voiced her objections during the editorial process but was unable to persuade Silvina to "correct" her style and bring it in line with prevailing canons of taste.[19] The rhetorical questions in Victoria's review – "¿No serán posibles las unas sino gracias a las otras? ¿Es necesaria esa desigualdad?" – seem to challenge what might well have been Silvina's justifications for her stylistic choices. One can imagine Silvina insisting that the strength of her images resides in the interplay between stylistic grace and deliberate awkwardness; one can also imagine Victoria's incredulity and concern with distancing herself from an aesthetic that did not match her own. Perhaps Victoria wished to find in her sister a figure more like their contemporary, María Luisa Bombal, whose impressionistic fiction was published in *Sur* and celebrated for its "feminine" lyricism, deep interiority, formal elegance, and ability to eloquently evoke the social strictures endured by Latin American women. Nevertheless, the "flaws" Victoria identified in *Viaje olvidado* – Silvina's use of vernacular language, "stiff-necked" images, obsessive focus on objects, and distortion – emerge as crucial elements of the resistant aesthetic Silvina Ocampo developed over the course of her career as a fiction writer.

[18] In addition to her work as editor and patron of the literary magazine *Sur* where many of Silvina Ocampo's stories appeared initially, Victoria Ocampo also directed the *Sur* editorial house that published the first editions of a number of Silvina Ocampo's collections of fiction and poetry.

[19] In José Amícola's estimation, Ocampo assiduously resists the structural perfection that became an article of faith in the growing cult of Borges (136). For Hiram Aldarondo, Ocampo's thematic preoccupation with cruelty is part of her strategic renunciation of "una belleza recatada, clásica, tranquilizadora" (*El humor* 13–14) [a demure, classic, calm beauty].

This resistant aesthetic may have been partly motivated by a kind of oppositional response to the expectations for "feminine" literary comportment. On the one hand, Ocampo seems to have been frustrated by the set of expectations brought to bear on writing by women; on the other, she gravitated toward the settings, scenes, and characters that tend to trigger those very expectations.[20] In addition to featuring women, children, servants, and laborers, Ocampo's stories often present domestic scenarios that unfold in a Buenos Aires petit-bourgeois milieu.[21] Detailed descriptions of interior decorating, sewing, cooking, and fashion are common, and household objects crowd the stories. Titles like "El cuaderno" [The scrapbook], "Los objetos," "La propiedad" [Property], "Carta perdida en un cajón" [Letter lost in a drawer], and "El vestido de terciopelo" [The velvet dress] suggest the innocuous simplicity of items in the inventory for an estate sale. Some stories center on family and community celebrations such as dinners, birthday parties, baptisms, and weddings,[22] and the premonition of disaster that hovers over these events in *La furia* illustrates Ocampo's deliberate narrative impropriety. A baptism catalyzes cruelty in "La casa de los relojes," and in addition to the deadly outcomes of birthday parties, "Las fotografías" centers on a party held for a paralyzed teenage girl to celebrate her release from hospital. Apparently overwhelmed by being photographed repeatedly to memorialize this "festive" day, the girl collapses and dies. While the narrator provides lavish descriptions of the decorations and refreshments, she never comments on the partygoers' cruel failure to recognize or respond to the girl's distress.[23] In "La boda" [The wedding], a bride dies suddenly after a young girl plants a deadly spider in her headpiece, ostensibly in hopes of winning the approval of the bride's rival.

Beyond the actions of particular characters, many Ocampo stories seem to suggest that cruelty resides within the domestic sphere itself. Despite the absence of fatalities, a dark mood hangs over "El cuaderno" [The scrapbook], which centers on Ermelina, a young woman at the end of her pregnancy. Left alone

20   Klingenberg reads Ocampo's fiction as "a prolonged assault on every aspect of literary representation of the feminine" (*Fantasies* 11).

21   While Ocampo does employ other settings, Buenos Aires is featured in so many of her stories that it becomes a kind of default expectation for any story that does not clearly indicate a particular setting. In "Los objetos," which describes a woman's uneasy recovery of objects she lost over the course of her life, the narrator appears to reprimand the reader for making assumptions about the story's setting: "¡para qué imaginar Buenos Aires! Hay otras ciudades con plazas" (*La furia* 106) [why imagine Buenos Aires? There are other cities with plazas].

22   For a fuller exploration of this topic, see Aldona Pobutsky (79–97).

23   From the Brazilian tradition, Clarice Lispector's "Feliz Aniversário" (*Laços de família*, 1960) offers an interesting intertext for "Las fotografías." Taking the perspective of an elderly woman during a family celebration of her birthday, the story reflects her disgust with the command performance expected of her as well as her refusal to comply with her family's behavioral expectations.

by her husband who is out watching a holiday parade, she receives a visit from a neighbor who brings along her two sons and a scrapbook. As Ermelina thumbs through the notebook, she declares that an image she sees is the face she would like her child to have. She leaves a note for her husband that says, "la figura que está en la hoja abierta de este cuaderno es igual a nuestro hijo" [the figure on the open page of this notebook is just like our child], and then leaves for the hospital (*La furia* 74). According to her view of her child in the story's last lines, this expectation is perfectly fulfilled in his "cara rosada" [rosy face], which she recognizes from the notebook (76). Even with these seemingly fantastic explorations of maternal impression, the framing of Ermelina's "recognition" leaves open the possibility that her perception is altered by sedatives used during the delivery – or perhaps by maternity itself. What makes this story particularly interesting is that the possible intrusion of the fantastic cannot be seen as a source of cruelty. Instead, a gloomy atmosphere emanates from the domestic space of Ermelina's apartment, which remains "en tinieblas" [in twilight] even when she opens the curtains (71). An elaborate description of the bed Ermelina received as a wedding gift from her employer comes with the claim that "esa cama era el testimonio de su felicidad" (71) [that bed was the testimony of her happiness], and yet the eerie stillness of the apartment and the husband's absence seem to cast this claim to happiness in doubt. "El cuaderno" might be read as offering a subtle feminist intervention; the deadpan narration serves in part as an ironic indication of the degree to which the "disaster" signaled by the story's menacing mood is not an outside event but rather resides in Ermelina's own passivity and domestic complacency.[24]

The focus on feminine confinement and isolation in marriage in "El cuaderno" suggests a possible thematic connection with María Luisa Bombal's first novella, *La última niebla* (1935), in which a nameless narrator struggles against her circumscribed and isolated existence on a remote hacienda with an indifferent husband. Despite thematic similarities between the stories, however, the authors' narrative framing and stylistic choices lead to dramatically different reading experiences. Bombal vividly dramatizes her unnamed speaker's refusal to be stifled, at one point figuring her frantic cries, "¡Yo existo, yo existo!" (38), as she bathes nude in a pond, and imagination emerges as a defense catalyzed by social constraint. Ocampo's Ermelina placidly observes the decline of her creativity, which her supervisor in the hat shop declares a consequence of

---

[24] This reading does not, however, exhaust the possibilities of the story. Evelyn Fishburn points out that even the most persuasive feminist interpretations of Ocampo "serve only to open up certain possibilities of meaning ... but can never be offered as more than a tentative and partial reading" of the particularity that always exceeds the "attempted 'explanation'" (108). She is responding in part to readings of Ocampo's fiction that, as Carlos Gamerro also discusses, sometimes seem to know their "conclusions" before engaging with the text (152).

marriage (72), but neither Ermelina nor the narrator registers the absence of her husband as a nameable source of frustration. In *La última niebla*, the world yields to the speaker's imaginative advances; whether staring into a fire, walking in the woods, or sitting alone in a parlor, the intensity of her feeling spills over and into objects and characters around her. In contrast to Bombal's many invitations for identification with the speaker, whose isolation and desperation prime us to be flooded with sympathy, readers gain little purchase for feeling with Ermelina. Even as contractions render her movements painful, a touch of the grotesque distances us from her: "caminaba con rapidez, y, por el esfuerzo que hacía para no separar demasiado las piernas, con una extraña cadencia de baile" (75) [she walked rapidly, and because of her effort to avoid separating her legs too much, with a strange dance-like gait]. Far from a small, soft bundle, Ermelina's newborn child is all hard surface; his face has "el mismo color chillón que tienen los juguetes nuevos" (76) [the same loud color that new toys have].

Emphasizing the contrasts between Bombal's and Ocampo's approaches might seem to position Bombal as a foil for Ocampo, but what I most want to stress is how these differences relate to the horizon of expectations readers bring to each writer's fiction. An early review of *La última niebla* by Amado Alonso celebrated Bombal's lyricism, her "typically female" evocation of the character's emotional life (25), and her attention to the speaker's "temperamento íntegramente femenino" (27) [entirely feminine temperament].[25] To Alonso and many of his contemporaries, the virtues of Bombal's writing – especially her emphasis on the interior world of her characters – were intimately linked to her status as a woman writer.[26] Much as the individual with inferior social standing may be expected to lubricate an awkward interaction (the nervous laugh to ease tension, the sad story to elicit sympathy), the implication appears to be that a woman writer ought to enable a comfortable economy of emotional exchange between reader and text, often by facilitating identification as Bombal does.

One can imagine how expectations primed by such assumptions would be disappointed by Ocampo's less compliant fiction, particularly in terms of her refusal of depth.[27] In the case of "El cuaderno," an emphatic flatness is evident when Ermelina observes her neighbor's children:

25   This essay, "Aparición de una novelista," was first published in 1936 in *Nosotros* and was later used as a preface to the second edition of *La última niebla*.

26   My article, "Translating María Luisa Bombal's *La última niebla*," briefly touches on how these assumptions about Bombal's fiction hamper attention to other aspects of her narrative that are not so strongly identified with femininity.

27   Despite being traditionally associated with underdevelopment or literary weakness, flatness is beginning to draw critical attention as a valuable narrative feature. For example, see Herlinghaus on poverty as a "narratological attitude" (47–49).

De repente Ermelina vio que el menor de los hijos de la vecina se parecía extrañamente a la sota de espadas; era una suerte de hombrecito pequeño aplastado contra el suelo, vestido de verde y rojo. El otro parecía un rey muy cabezón con una copa en la mano, donde bebía una cantidad incalculable de agua. (74)

[Suddenly Ermelina saw that the younger of the neighbor's sons strangely resembled the jack of spades; he was a kind of little man flattened against the floor, dressed in green and red. The other looked like a king with a big head and a goblet in his hand, from which he was drinking an immeasurable amount of water.]

Despite formal marks of the diminutive – "el menor" and "hombrecito pequeño" – the stress on deformity in this passage blocks any possibility of finding the children endearing. Terms like "extrañamente," "aplastado," and "incalculable" highlight Ermelina's sense that the children are strange, unknowable creatures,[28] and the choice of playing cards as metaphor in the description frames the children as two-dimensional, stylized figures.

The impenetrable surfaces and hard edges of Ocampo's characters might be understood as a deliberate effort at protection from what has been somewhat awkwardly termed the "aesthetic of cuteness." Daniel Harris argues that cuteness – whether in stuffed animals, small children, or literature – is not an inherent characteristic, but rather an aesthetic that is *inflicted* on persons or objects. In his formulation, cuteness prioritizes the affective needs of beholders and creates "a class of outcasts and mutations, a ready-made race of loveable inferiors whom both children and adults collect, patronize, and enslave in the protective concubinage of their vast harems of homely dolls and snugglesome misfits" (179). Intensified by ugliness, helplessness, unhappiness, and injury, cuteness almost always has a sadistic dimension (Harris 179). As Sianne Ngai notes, cuteness requires that its object have "some sort of imposed-upon aspect … the look of an object not only formed but all too easily de-formed under the pressure of the subject's feeling or attitude towards it" (816). The imposition of cuteness is intimately linked to the fantasy of penetrability also visible in expectations of affective access in narrative. Even in the world of children's toys, the vulnerability and violence associated with the imposition of cuteness comes through in descriptions of "tempting exteriors" and "tactile immediacy"; for

---

[28] This feature of Ocampo's fiction draws frequent comment. For example, Richard Browning notes the distancing effect of seeing "grotesque, violent or sexual acts" performed by figures we expected to be innocent (103), and Graciela Tomassini describes the cruelty of children as one dimension of Ocampo's "demitificación de la infancia" (*El espejo* 38). Thomas Meehan mentions the "creciente abismo entre niños y adultos" in Ocampo's stories (35), and Mackintosh highlights Ocampo's stress on the inaccessibility of childhood from the perspective of adulthood (*Childhood* 98).

example, FAO Schwarz advertises a teddy bear as "just asking to be hauled and mauled" (Harris 180). We might draw a parallel between the sympathetic character whose implied depth invites identification and a huggable toy that "asks for" deforming embraces.

By contrast, Ocampo flouts the expectation of psychological depth associated both with nineteenth-century realism and the impressionistic fiction of the early twentieth-century vanguard. Like the black dresses, notebooks, photographs, portraits, toys, and other objects that make repeat appearances in her stories, her characters often read more like props than people.[29] This is the case even when characters serve as narrators; as dramatic monologues, the narratives are persuasive in their commonplaces and contradictions, but they deny access to an interior beneath the verbal construction, as we will explore more fully in "El vestido de terciopelo." For Ocampo, flatness is both a hallmark of textuality and a trait worth defending, and it functions in part to prevent the groping entry and unrestrained projections associated with the imposition of cuteness. Ocampo arrays her characters in what Harris calls the "anti-cute," two instances of which can be found in criminality and monstrosity (185). Unflattering portraits of monstrous mothers, child criminals, and animal accomplices – what Valentín Díaz describes as "una galería de pequeños *freaks*" (92) [a gallery of little freaks] – emerge in this light as an act of protection that deliberately limits opportunities for readers to forge emotional connections with the characters. Speaking of her own story, the narrator of "Los objetos" insists, "si no les parece patética, lectores, por lo menos es breve" (*La furia* 107) [if it doesn't seem moving, readers, at least it is brief]; this apparent show of concern with the readers' emotional connection in fact highlights Ocampo's refusal to grant it. Ocampo's fiction challenges the notion that her stories ought to serve as conduits for feeling, and her narrative and stylistic choices resist readers' efforts to feel their way into her fiction or to use emotion to guide interpretations that would release them from the stories' disconcerting hold. In the readings that follow, my aim is to attend as fully as possible to the narrative particularity of Ocampo's fiction and to explore how her resistant aesthetic shapes readers' encounters with cruelty in her fiction.

---

29   Claims to the contrary also appear with some frequency. For example, Adriana Castillo de Berchenko describes Ocampo as an "hábil creadora de personajes" [a deft creator of characters] who makes light work of representing children "con auténtica carnadura física y emocional" [with physical and emotional body] (181–82). In my view, such an assertion reflects the stringency of our interpretative habit to preserve the mimetic dimension of a narrative even when its synthetic components are insistently foregrounded. See James Phelan's discussion of this tendency in the introduction of *Living to Tell About It* (1–30).

Frustrated Feeling in Ocampo's Early Fiction

Ocampo deliberately deforms the domestic sphere she portrays, estranges us from
the characters who populate it, and renders emotional response dubious at best.
To reinforce the notion that the stylistic and narrative characteristics that define
Ocampo's resistant aesthetic were already apparent in her earliest fiction, I want
to look first at two of Ocampo's stories from *Viaje olvidado*.[30] "Los funámbulos"
and "El retrato mal hecho" center on the death of children and the unexpected
responses of their mothers, and they present readers with particular barriers to
narrative or affective resolution. In "Los funámbulos" [The flying trapeze artists]
a mother is introduced as "la planchadora sorda" [the deaf ironing woman] and
only later identified by name as Clodomira (*Cuentos completos* I 41). Despite the
narrator's stress on her disability, deafness is not the source of the "puerta cerrada"
[closed door] that she imagines separates her from her sons as they perform
acrobatics on the third-story balcony. Instead, Clodomira is troubled by her sense
that the boys are plotting "algún extraño proyecto" [some strange project], a project
she cannot discern no matter how hard she tries to read their lips (42). Their plans
may remain impenetrable to Clodomira, but the reader guesses what lies ahead as
soon as the narrator offers an account of the circus experience that inspired this
"fervor acrobático" (43). During the intermission, one of the brothers jumps into
the ring. At first, he merely emulates the performers, but soon "era el caballo blanco
de la bailarina, el pruebista *de saltos mortales*" (42, my emphasis) [he was the
ballerina's white horse, the acrobat of *death-defying jumps*], transformed, if only
in his imaginings, into part of the circus. Although Clodomira screams her son's
name from the sidelines during his performance, her "terror furioso" turns into
admiration when she sees the audience's reaction (42). These events ominously
foreshadow the story's outcome to the reader, but Clodomira shows no sign of
concern at her sons' various acrobatic engagements, from balancing on broken
chairs to posing on the narrow window ledges of the apartment, and the story ends
with the following fulfillment of the boys' "designios obscuros" [dark designs]:

> Un día no sentían ya el frío de la tarde sobre los brazos desnudos. Parados en
> el borde de una ventana del tercer piso, dieron un salto glorioso y envueltos
> en un saludo cayeron aplastados contra las baldosas del patio. Clodomira,
> que estaba planchando en el cuarto de al lado, vio el gesto maravilloso y
> sintió, con una sonrisa, que de todas las ventanas se asomaban millones de
> gritos y de brazos aplaudiendo, pero siguió planchando. Se acordó de su
> primera angustia en el circo. Ahora estaba acostumbrada a esas cosas. (42)

---

[30] See Ocampo's discussion with Ulla on the kinship between this early collection and *La
furia* (*Encuentros* 133–37).

[One day they no longer felt the afternoon cold on their naked arms. Standing on the edge of a third-floor window, they made a glorious leap and wrapped in a gesture of greeting fell flattened against the tiles of the patio. Clodomira, who was ironing in the room next door, saw the marvellous gesture and felt, with a smile, that from all the windows millions of shouts and applauding arms leaned out, but she continued ironing. She remembered her first anxiety at the circus. Now she was accustomed to those things.]

Descriptions saturated with triumph ("salto glorioso," "gesto maravilloso") carry over into Clodomira's mute fantasy of a building full of admirers applauding the boys from their windows like spectators at the circus. It is as if she has become so absorbed in their transformation that she imagines that, like the circus acrobats they pretend to be, they will be cushioned by a "red elástica sobre un colchón enorme" (42) [an elastic net over an enormous mattress].

Any celebration is sharply undercut for readers by the jarring image of the boys' bodies "aplastados contra las baldosas del patio," but there is no break in the mother's placid appreciation. Clodomira's imaginative extension of the circus fantasy – and the fact that she does not stop ironing when she sees her boys jump – signal a failure of understanding that intensifies the story's distressing dimensions. The uneasy anticipation felt by readers from the first mention of the boys' acrobatics on the balcony seems to demand that the mother at least recognize the danger involved in their games. Yet the boys' deathly leap appears to her more as a moment of triumph than a loss, and the vague commonplace that closes the story – "Ahora estaba acostumbrada a esas cosas" – reflects her resistance to registering the unfolding disaster, leaving readers alone with the knowledge of its outcome. Rather than dramatizing the cruelty of a given character, as would be the case if Clodomira had wished for the death of her sons or if they had deliberately killed themselves to cause her suffering, the cruelty of this tale resides in the tension between Clodomira's innocuous, festive vision and the image of the boys' bodies smashed against the hard patio tiles. Ocampo activates a certain horizon of expectations associated with fantasy as Clodomira's son "becomes" a trapeze artist when he breaks into the circus ring, but the promise of fantasy – wherein the buoyancy of the boys' imaginings should toss them back up like a trampoline – shatters against the narrative insistence on illustrating the actual outcome of this performance.

In "El retrato mal hecho" [The badly made portrait], another mother's reaction to the death of her own child lacks the affective content that we expect, providing an interesting comparison to Clodomira's reaction in "Los funámbulos." The absence of maternal feeling is figured in this mother's indifference to her children's advances; even as they seek out her embrace, Eponina remains "encerrada en las aguas negras de su vestido" [locked in the black waters of her dress] (*Cuentos completos* I 32). Her desultory detachment is further figured in the ostensibly permanent direction of her gaze away from the children, which creates the impression that "una mitad del rostro se le había borrado" (32) [half of her face had been erased]. As the mistress of a wealthy family, Eponina is condemned to live "en postura de retrato mal hecho" [in the pose of a badly made portrait], a figure that indicates the imposed stasis of her "privileged" position. For Eponina, "la vida era un larguísimo cansancio de descansar demasiado" [life was an infinite fatigue of resting too much], and the exhaustion inspired by too much leisure is only intensified by contrast with the activity of Ana, the servant whose labor sustains the household. Ana also carries the maternal burden rejected by the mistress of the house; whereas Eponina "había detestado a sus hijos uno por uno a medida que iban naciendo" [had detested her children one by one as they were born], Ana's arms "eran como cunas para sus hijos traviesos" [were like cradles for her mischievous children] (32).

After establishing this background, the narrative focuses in on "el 5 de abril de 1890, a la hora de almuerzo" (32). This specificity seems to suggest that an event of some import is about to unfold, but instead we read over Eponina's shoulder as she thumbs through a European fashion magazine while she waits for lunch to be served. Half a dozen elaborate descriptions cited from her reading appear to stall the narrative further until finally a revelation is paratactically appended to the end of the growing series:

> "Las hojas se hacen con seda color de aceituna", o bien: "los enrejados son de color de rosa y azules", o bien: "la flor grande es de color encarnado", o bien: "las venas y los tallos color albaricoque." Ana no llegaba para servir la mesa. (32–33)

> ["The leaves are made with olive-colored silk" or "the trellises are pink and blue" or "the large flower is blood red" or "the veins and stems are apricot." Ana still had not arrived to serve the table.]

Tacked on somewhat awkwardly and without transition, the revelation of Ana's absence interrupts Eponina's leisure, which, as already noted, is itself a kind of labor. During the search that follows, Eponina is the one who finds the disheveled servant in the attic. Even this climactic moment is tinged by the language of fashion; not only does she notice that Ana's apron is stained with blood, she also observes her "cintura suelta de náufraga" (33) [loose waist of the shipwrecked]. "Lo he matado," Ana says, pointing to the trunk she is sitting on, and next:

Eponina abrió el baúl y vio a su hijo muerto, al que más había ambicionado subir sobre sus faldas: ahora estaba dormido sobre el pecho de uno de sus vestidos más viejos, en busca de su corazón.

La familia enmudecida de horror en el umbral de la puerta, se desgarraba con gritos intermitentes clamando por la policía. Habían oído todo, habían visto todo; los que no se desmayaban, estaban arrebatados de odio y de horror.

Eponina se abrazó largamente a Ana con un gesto inusitado de ternura. Los labios de Eponina se movían en una lenta ebullición ... (33)

[Eponina opened the trunk and saw her dead son, the one who had most tried to climb her skirts: now he was asleep on the breast of one of her oldest dresses, in search of her heart. The family, mute with horror on the threshold, broke into intermittent shouts, clamoring for the police. They had heard everything, they had seen everything; those who did not faint were seized with hate and horror. Eponina wrapped Ana in a long embrace with an unusual gesture of tenderness. Her lips moved in a slow effusion ...]

Whereas the family reacts to Ana's apparent confession, the reader may find another detail troubling: no one had noticed that the child was missing. Only his death sets him apart from the indefinite groups of "chicos" and "hijos" mentioned elsewhere in the story, always at the margins of adult affairs. Still unnamed, we learn only that he is the child who made the greatest effort to break down Eponina's indifference and "subir sus faldas"; the futility of this effort is reinforced by the depiction of the boy "dormido sobre el pecho de uno de sus vestidos más viejos, en busca de su corazón" [asleep on the breast of one of her oldest dresses, in search of her heart]. The age of the dress recalls Eponina's sense that her children are "ladrones de su adolescencia" [thieves of her adolescence] (32), and the empty garment serves as a metonym for the absent mother. This figure finds further extension in the mother's first instance of speech in the story, which are also its last lines:

"Niño de cuatro años vestido de raso de algodón color encarnado. Esclavina cubierta de un plegado que figura como olas ribeteadas con un encaje blanco. Las venas y los tallos son de color marrón dorado, verde mirto o carmín." (33)

[Four-year-old child dressed in blood-red satin. Cape covered by a ruffle shaped like waves trimmed with white lace. Veins and stems of gilded purple, myrtle green or crimson.]

Despite Ana's blood-spattered apron, this description suggests clothing as pristine as if it were in a magazine illustration. Following the unnoticed absence of the child, Eponina's speech accomplishes a second disappearance by cloaking the boy in the anonymity of fashion. Her words would be equally apt descriptions of an outfit laid out on a bed or worn by a mannequin, and she incorporates language lifted straight from her reading (e.g., "color encarnado" and "las venas y los tallos"). Crossing the axes of gothic horror and the banal register of women's fashion magazines, Ocampo emphatically evades any engagement with the sort of pathos-laden depictions of maternal love that her contemporaries might have considered more fitting for a woman writer. Against the artistic tradition founded on sympathetic portraits of grieving mothers, from the Virgin Mary cradling Christ's lifeless body to the mothers of soldiers, Ocampo fashions a mother who elects to embrace the apparent murderer of her child rather than the child himself.[31]

While the forced proximity between the grisly tropes of the gothic and the mundanity of fashion is vexing enough, the description "marrón dorado, verde mirto o carmín" (my emphasis) suggests that rather than seeing the child before her, Eponina has projected a fashion illustration onto him. Were she describing the three colors that actually appear on her child's clothing, "y" [and] would have been the logical conjunction; instead, the use of "o" [or] suggests a kind of parasitic intrusion of the language used in catalogs and magazines to describe color choices for garments. The story seems to suggest that Eponina has been colonized by the discourse of women's magazines so thoroughly that it now speaks through her. Even in this early story, we find in Eponina's closing words clear evidence of a hallmark of Ocampo's narrative intransigence: verbal mimicry trumps mimetic detail.

Whereas in "Los funámbulos" no one but the reader registers the horror of the children's death, in "El retrato mal hecho," the family explodes in outrage, complete with screaming, fainting, and calling for the police. The horrified family members might seem to serve as readers' textual avatars, performing dismay or disgust before the characters whose misdeeds constitute the cruelty at hand. If this were the case, we would find in the story a fine illustration of what José Ovejero describes in *La ética de la crueldad* as the perverse cleansing function cruelty can sometimes serve in literature by enabling easy judgment or affirming a set of values we already hold (43–45). But in "El retrato mal hecho," this possibility is undercut by the melodrama of their response and by the fact that the social order represented by the family is implicated in Eponina's paralysis of feeling and in the boy's death.

---

[31] For an excellent discussion of this scene, see Amícola's reading of the story in "Silvina Ocampo y la *malseánce*" (133–34).

Even beyond the enigmatic pronouncement of the last lines, where readers most crave clear access to descriptive details that would lend coherence to a scene, they encounter instead the smooth artifice of language. The uncertain particulars of the child's death block the satisfactions of judgment; the ambiguity of Eponina's gesture and speech at the story's end blocks the satisfaction of identification. Eponina's embrace of the servant appears to suggest a momentary affective thaw on her part, a show of tenderness never enjoyed by her children. But the gesture is opaque. Does Eponina intend to relieve Ana of her self-declared status as murderess, suggesting that she would never believe the servant capable of intentionally injuring the child? In other words, does Eponina take "lo he matado" [I have killed him] as a hyperbolic description of some kind of accident? Or might her embrace mark approval of the child's murder, recognition of a need that such an act might satisfy? Is Eponina relieved to find in Ana evidence that she is not alone in her anti-maternal deformity, not the only "retrato mal hecho"? Does she signal her gratitude that Ana has fulfilled the wish that she – straitjacketed in the codes of propriety represented by her magazines – cannot act upon? The discourse of the story is most often colored by Eponina's perspective, but at the end the narrator's distance from her is decisive. While fiction is often presented as a space for imagined access to other minds, many of Ocampo's stories capitalize on our foraging for affective satisfactions only to send us away hungry.

Narrative Ambiguity and Estrangement

The ambiguous framing apparent in both "El retrato mal hecho" and "Los funámbulos" extends also to stories narrated in the first person such as "El vestido de terciopelo" [The velvet dress]. Like "El retrato mal hecho," "El vestido de terciopelo" ends with a death, although in this case the victim is a grown woman and the narrator is an unnamed child. Accompanying a seamstress named Casilda to deliver a dress to a wealthy Buenos Aires society lady, the narrator describes in detail the difficulty the client experiences when she tries to put on the dress for the final fitting. When the seamstress and the girl finally succeed at getting the woman into the dress, the situation deteriorates rapidly; by the story's end, she lies dead on the floor. Over the course of the narrative, the black dress accumulates a number of potentially sinister attributes. For example, when the señora asks the speaker, "te gustará llevar un vestido de terciopelo, ¿no es cierto?" [you might like to wear a velvet dress, right?] the narrator reports feeling that "el terciopelo de ese vestido me estrangulaba el cuello con manos enguantadas" (La furia 146) [the velvet of that dress was strangling my neck with gloved hands]. This impression recalls her earlier observation of the woman's efforts to pull the dress over her head: "algo lo detenía en el cuello" (144) [something held it at the neck]. The speaker also describes the dragon sequined onto the dress as if it were animate: "La señora cayó al suelo y el dragón se retorció" (147) [The woman fell to the floor and the dragon twisted]. These details appear to attribute a kind of agency to the dress itself, activating expectations associated with fantasy tales in which objects with mysterious powers act upon the characters, as in Julio Cortázar's "No se culpe a nadie" [No one is to blame] (1956).[32] Like "El vestido de terciopelo," "No se culpe a nadie" centers on a character's disastrous encounter with a garment that appears intent on suffocating him.[33] In both stories, the quotidian activity of dressing, which would normally be passed over as too obvious to require narration, receives exhaustive attention. The mundane activity loses its predictability, and the garments take on a sinister aspect.

In Cortázar's story, the strange hand and sweater attack until the character is driven to seek "alguna parte sin mano y sin pulóver, donde solamente haya un aire fragoroso que lo envuelva y lo acompañe y lo acaricie y doce pisos" (29) [a place without hand or pullover, where there is only a rough breeze that might envelop him and accompany him and caress him and twelve stories]. The final sentence shifts abruptly from the subjunctive that marks the relief he seeks – "un aire fragoroso que lo envuelva" – to the interrupting fact of what he finds: the fall from a height of twelve stories, which calls to mind the conclusion of "Los funámbulos." Taken literally, the story's title appears to set aside the notion of responsibility, and yet the phrase echoes the suicide note Emma leaves in *Madame Bovary*: "Qu'on n'accuse personne" [Let no one be blamed].[34] While the title and much of the story remains open to interpretation, the speaker frames the experience as a struggle with a supernatural force that renders part of his own body monstrous and unrecognizable: "el dedo tiene un aire como de arrugado y metido para adentro, con una uña negra terminada en punta" (25) [the finger has a sense of being wrinkled

---

[32] "No se culpe a nadie" was published before Ocampo's "Vestido de terciopelo"; nevertheless, as the examples of "El retrato mal hecho" and "Los funámbulos" (from *Viaje olvidado*, 1937) demonstrate, Ocampo developed her narrative approach significantly earlier. Gamerro credits Ocampo for beginning a project that was continued, with far more acclaim, by Cortázar (62). See also Ulla's conversation with Ocampo regarding the influence of her style on Cortázar and others (*Encuentros* 137). Frequently comparisons between Ocampo and Cortázar give greater importance to Cortázar, as in *Le fantastique argentin*, an edited collection on the two Argentine writers that downplays the direction of influence by positioning the section on Cortázar's fiction first, despite the fact that the Ocampo stories that "anticipate" his work were published earlier. Similarly, Amícola describes "Las dos casas de Olivos" as a precursor to Cortázar's "Lejana" (1951).

[33] The suffocating garments can be read as symbolizing social strictures. In "El vestido de terciopelo," the wealthy woman describes velvet as "una carcel" [a prison]; Cortázar's speaker mentions his impending engagement before trying to put on the sweater. For an elaboration of this possibility in "No se culpe a nadie," see Malva Filer's essay.

[34] Cortázar, who taught briefly as a professor of French literature, would likely have known Flaubert's work well.

and curved inward, with a black fingernail shaped to a point]. By contrast, in "El vestido de terciopelo," the speaker remains outside the fatal encounter, and her description is more ambivalent. It is not possible to determine whether the supernatural impinges on events or is imagined by the child narrator as an alternative to other causes. The final lines of the story reflect this ambiguity:

> La señora cayó al suelo y el dragón se retorció. Casilda se inclinó sobre su cuerpo hasta que el dragón quedó inmóvil. Acaricié de nuevo el terciopelo que parecía un animal. Casilda dijo melancólicamente:
> –Ha muerto. ¡Me costó tanto hacer este vestido! ¡Me costó tanto, tanto! ¡Qué risa! (147)

> [The woman fell to the floor and the dragon twisted. Casilda bent over the body until the dragon remained immobile. I caressed the velvet again which seemed like an animal. Casilda said sadly,
> "She is dead. It cost me so much to make this dress. It cost me so, so much." What a laugh!]

Ocampo's narrators demonstrate a frequent incapacity – or refusal – to provide the links between events, particularly when it seems to matter most, as at a turning point in the narrative or in the recounting of a death. Even as the simple sentences of the story's conclusion seem to conceal nothing, they offer neither commentary that would indicate motives nor causal connections to help readers knit events together into a coherent sequence. The personification of the dress, particularly the speaker's sense that she can feel its gloved hands around her own neck, might be construed as indicating the dress's murderous intent, but perhaps the narrator's feeling of strangulation marks her displaced knowledge of a murder she cannot recognize as such. This would be one way of making sense of the most ambiguous line of the quoted section: "Casilda se inclinó sobre su cuerpo hasta que el dragón quedó inmóvil." Beyond a certain class tension rippling through the story,[35] there is little indication of a motive for causing the death. Even if the dress perpetrates the crime, what do we make of Casilda's lack of response in the face of the woman's distress? This story, like many of Ocampo's, maintains these incompatible scenarios in uneasy tension.

When navigating this sort of textual ambiguity, we often look to tonal markers of emotion for guidance. Whereas the tone of "No se culpe a nadie" becomes

---

35 The *señora*'s offhand manner is far from endearing, and the narrator observes that she complains from the first moment she enters the room: "Quejándose, nos saludó" (143) [Complaining, she greeted us]. She insists, "Qué suerte tienen ustedes de vivir en las afueras de Buenos Aires" [You are so lucky to live on the outskirts of Buenos Aires], apparently unaware that living in the suburbs might be motivated by economic factors, not choice, and when asked to try on the dress, she protests, "¡Probarse! Es mi tortura!" (144) [Trying things on! It is my torture!]

increasingly panicked in tandem with the speaker's growing distress, marks of emotional response in "El vestido de terciopelo" are rare. Casilda's melancholy after the woman's death initially appears appropriate, but what she says – "¡Me costó tanto hacer este vestido! ¡Me costó tanto, tanto!" – immediately trivializes her initial "sadness" and reverses the apparent coherence of her response. Similarly, while the speaker aptly describes the scent of the *señora*'s perfume before she enters the room and the tactile quality of the velvet dress, her attentiveness to sensory detail finds no parallel in emotional sensitivity (145). Besides noting Casilda's "sadness" after the woman's death, the narrator's only reference to emotion is the refrain, "¡Qué risa!" [What a laugh]. This is her response when Casilda fumbles an aspirin and a glass of water, when the woman mistakes her for Casilda's daughter, when a handful of pins fall to the floor, when they cannot get the dress onto the woman, and when the *señora* struggles to breathe and dies. "¡Qué risa!" is particularly troubling in its opacity when it appears at the end of the story. Does the girl's laughter center on the squandered labor that the dress represents to Casilda or does she celebrate the death of a vain, wealthy woman? From the speaker's perspective, the closest thing to a crime committed by the woman might be her projection of cuteness, which is marked by her idealization of childhood ("¡Qué edad feliz!" [What a happy age]) and by the classic uninvited caress associated with elderly aunts and strangers: "me tomó del mentón" (144) [She took my by the chin]. The narrator's imposition of humor at the story's end seems to perform precisely the delight in the face of another's suffering that constitutes cruelty, yet the indiscriminate invocation of "¡Qué risa!" for events both trivial and tragic troubles the relationship between narrative performance and the ostensible emotions of the speaker.

Here and elsewhere in Ocampo's fiction, references to emotion often feel like labels crookedly affixed to situations.[36] "Emotion" in Ocampo's fiction turns out to create a point of estrangement from characters rather than a catalyst for imaginative identification with them. While Daniel Balderston suggests that Ocampo's narratives cause the reader to feel the horror of invented situations as if they were being suffered in his or her own body ("Los cuentos" 743), it seems more accurate to say that we *wish* to be oriented by feeling but find no such compass in her stories. The presence of everyday objects and the scenery of the petit-bourgeois sphere do not ensure any psychological realism or predictable relation to our experience. Instead, the frequent reappearance of a relatively small set of objects activates intertextual

---

[36] In "La casa de azúcar" the speaker explains his tears not in relation to his current crisis but rather as the consequence of a speck getting into his eyes on the train (*La furia* 57). Other characters rely on clichés to frame their feelings. Speaking of her close relationship with her mistress, the cook who narrates "La propiedad" brags, "¡Yo era su paño de lágrimas!" (100) [I was her shoulder to cry on] and another narrator describes a woman who "lloraba cuando reía" (70) [cried when she laughed], both using the sort of commonplaces that Victoria Ocampo objected to as out of place in a literary work.

connections between Ocampo's stories and primes us to "import" certain associations from one story into another. In this way, the deadly dress in "El vestido de terciopelo" reinforces the ominous character of the velvet dress received by Cristina in "La casa de azúcar." In the absence of emotional content associated with characters, objects (and the affective residues that accumulate on them) take on a greater role in our interpretative efforts.

What we *do* feel in response to Ocampo's fiction – feelings such as dismay, irritation, disgust, desperation, or fascination – is related more to our reading experience than to the feelings of characters or affective scenarios in the texts. In "El vestido de terciopelo," the point of difficulty is not so much the possibility of the characters' cruel indifference to the *señora*'s suffering nor what the girl narrator thinks or feels in response to events. Rather, readers' recoil comes down to a certain sense of propriety: the conviction that she (or Ocampo) ought not *narrate* in this fashion. We resent being exposed to this narrative misbehavior, namely, the narrator's failure or refusal to guide our feelings in response to the narrated events.

Dubious Propriety and Narrative Contamination

Whereas socially inappropriate responses are linked to cruelty in "El vestido de terciopelo," cruelty is just as prominent in stories narrated by speakers obsessed with propriety, as in "La casa de los relojes" [The clock shop] and "La furia" [The fury]. In "La casa de los relojes," the child narrator's close attention to social norms corresponds with an unwillingness or inability to register the cruelty that readers recognize with perfect clarity; once again, we encounter a child narrator who appears to describe an event that exceeds his understanding. The story describes a baptism celebration that leads to an inscrutable operation whereby a number of drunk men "iron out" the hump of the town's hunchback. A party celebrating a child's entry into the Christian community becomes the occasion for communal violence. Here as in other stories, religion is marked as fostering rather than restraining cruelty.[37] From the start of the story, a perfunctory notion of responsibility is invoked; as the teacher's favorite student, the unnamed

---

[37] Other instances of this tendency to present religion in a negative light can be found in "El verdugo" and "Los sueños de Leopoldina." In the fable-like story "El verdugo" [The executioner], the religious are among the cruelest witnesses to a bizarre event. In "Los sueños de Leopoldina" [Leopoldina's dream] the youngest women in a family obsessively desire to witness a miracle; they mention sightings of the Virgin Mary, but the narrator makes plain that they are primarily interested in an experience that will bring them fame and fortune (*La furia* 150). This is one of the rare instances in which cruelty is punished: in an ironic echo of Elijah's ascent into heaven in a whirlwind, Leopoldina and her dog are mysteriously raptured, leaving behind destructive consequences that reach well beyond the girls (the whirlwind "degolló, entre las piedras, los animales" [decapitated the animals against the stones]), once again figuring the vengeance that so often exceeds the offense in Ocampo's stories (155).

narrator (his letter is signed only "N.N.") acts on his promise to practice his composition skills by writing letters to his former teacher:

> Estimada señorita:
> Ya que me he distinguido en sus clases con mis composiciones, cumplo con mi promesa; me ejercitaré escribiéndole cartas. ¿Me pregunta qué hice en los últimos días de mis vacaciones? ... Me divertí mucho en la laguna Salada, hicimos fortalezas de barro; pero más me divertí anoche en la fiesta ... para el bautismo de Rusito. (*La furia* 59)

> [Dear Miss: Now that I have distinguished myself in your classes with my compositions, I am keeping my promise; I will practice by writing you letters. You ask what I did on the last days of my vacation? I had fun at Salt Lake, we made mud forts; but the most fun was last night at a party for Rusito's baptism.]

Framed as a response to the bane of many a schoolchild's writing experience ("What did you do on your summer vacation?"), the apparently quotidian character of this narrative continues through much of the narrator's account. He enumerates party preparations and describes his friendship with Estanislao Romagán, the hunchback who runs a repair shop for clocks and about whom the narrator says, "lo quería mucho" (60) [I loved him a lot]. This invocation of normalcy is both perplexing and vexing given that the letter offers a retrospective account of an event that, as the narrator will reveal, has lead to Estanislao's "disappearance." While the speaker shares his friend's excitement when the hunchback is treated like "el rey de la fiesta,"[38] the violent character of the evening's end either does not register or does not deprive him of enjoyment (and therein resides the possibility of cruelty in the child's narration).

The greater knowledge of the teacher, whose position as addressee is shared by the reader, is highlighted in the boy's repeated appeals to the *señorita*'s judgment of various character's actions. He twice ventures a judgment of a breach of social decorum, each time appending the rhetorical question, "¿no le parece, señorita?" (60, 62) [don't you think so, miss?]. In the laundromat where the mutilation of the hunchback takes place, the various chemical smells make the speaker sneeze, but he reassures his teacher, "me tapé la boca, siguiendo sus enseñanzas, señorita" (63) [I covered my mouth, following your instructions, miss]. In the same scene that seems to him like "una operación quirúrgica" [a surgical operation] someone exclaims "cochino" [filthy] causing the narrator to parrot adult disapproval: "¡Qué ejemplo para un chico!" (63) [Such an example

---

[38] This description echoes Quasimodo's short-lived glory as the "king" of the Feast of Fools in the opening pages of Victor Hugo's *Notre-Dame de Paris*.

for a child]. He remains focused solely on social propriety and neither offers nor invites judgment of the actions that lead to Estansilao's unhappy end. As in "El vestido de terciopelo" the narrative turns opaque precisely where we wish for clarity:

Me detuve para mirar el lugar donde iban a planchar el traje de Estanislao.
–¿Me desnudo?– interrogó Estanislao.
–No–respondió Gervasio–, no se moleste. Se lo plancharemos puesto.
–¿Y la giba?– interrogó Estanislao, tímidamente.
Era la primera vez que yo oía esa palabra, pero por la conversación me enteré de lo que significaba (ya ve que progreso en mi vocabulario.)
–También te la plancharemos– respondió Gervasio, dándole una palmada sobre el hombro.
Estanislao se acomodó sobre una mesa larga, como le ordenó Nakoto que estaba preparando las planchas ... Todos los hombres tropezaban con algo, con los muebles, con las puertas, con los útiles de trabajo, con ellos mismos. Traían trapos húmedos, frascos, planchas. Aquello parecía, aunque usted no lo crea, una operación quirúrgica. Un hombre cayó al suelo y me hizo una zancadilla que por poco me rompo el alma. Entonces, para mí al menos, se terminó la alegría. Comencé a vomitar. Usted sabe que tengo un estómago muy sano y que los compañeros de colegio me llamaban avestruz, porque tragaba cualquier cosa. No sé lo que me pasó. Alguien me sacó de allí a los tirones y me llevó a casa.
No volví a ver a Estanislao Romagán. Mucha gente vino a buscar los relojes y un camioncito de la relojería LA PARCA retiró los últimos. (63–64)

[I paused to look at the place where they were going to iron Estanislao's suit. "Shall I undress?" asked Estanislao.
"No," responded Gervasio, "don't bother. We will iron it for you with it on."
"And my hump?" asked Estansilao timidly.
It was the first time I had heard that word, but in the context I understood its meaning (so you see that I am making progress with my vocabulary).
"We will iron it for you as well," responded Gervasio, giving him a pat on the shoulder.
Estanislao settled himself on the long table, as ordered by Nakoto who was preparing the irons ... All the men were tripping on things, the furniture, the doors, the tools, on each other. They brought damp rags, jars, irons. The whole thing seemed, though you wouldn't believe it, like an operating room. A man fell to the floor and tripped me so that I nearly lost it. Then, for me at least, the fun was over. I began to vomit. You know that I have a very healthy stomach and my schoolmates used to call me an ostrich because I could swallow anything. I don't know what came over me. Someone grabbed me and dragged me home.

I didn't see Estanislao Romagán again. Many people came to look for clocks and a van from the clock shop La Parca loaded up the rest.]

The boy makes plain that he can see what is happening and captures the drunken confusion of the scene, but beyond providing us with the ominous vision of Estanislao stretched out on a table like a patient awaiting an operation, he offers no access to the particulars of what follows. A certain callousness shadows the speaker's narration, particularly when he interrupts the grisly exchange about "'ironing'' the watchmaker's hump to inform his teacher about his increased ability to draw on context clues to understand new words. He describes being trampled by one of the men, an experience that "por poco me rompo el alma" and that marks the point when "para mí ... se terminó la alegría," but he makes no reference to the emotional impact of what is happening to the hunchback whom he claims to love. By underscoring the strength of his constitution, the speaker highlights the degree to which his vomiting must be attributed to something other than having had too much to drink, yet he refuses to consider its relation to what he has seen, persisting in his inability or unwillingness to narrate what occurs.

Are we meant to read the narrator's naive perspective as sincere and as a source of ironic distance from the depicted cruelty, or should we intuit a performative dimension to this limited vision?[39] If we knew the narrator to be innocent, we would have the consolation of locating the horror of the story in what is done to the hunchback and the consequences that witnessing it may hold for the child, whether now or at some later date when trauma will register as such. Alternatively, if we knew the narrator to be aware and complicit, we could identify his coy performance with a double cruelty: cruel indifference to what happens to Estanislao as well as a cruel exposure of his addressee to a vexingly oblique encounter with violence. The ambiguity of Ocampo's child characters reinforces the possibility that the speaker deliberately "infects" his teacher with this story, inciting her to imagine the dark recreations that ensue between "me llevó a casa" and "no volví a ver a Estanislao Romagán" (64). With the exception of his concern with social propriety, the narrator offers no judgment of the events he narrates, and the story disables our main strategies for exercising judgment from without. As Campra notes, the frequent absence of guilt or responsibility in the stories themselves means that the disquiet they provoke is "de exclusiva competencia del lector" (191) [the exclusive domain of the reader]. Like the teacher, readers must cope with the competing possibilities

---

[39] Balderston assumes the sincerity of this innocence ("Los cuentos" 748) whereas Espinoza-Vera argues that we suspect its falsity at least some of the time (*La poética* 214). Mackintosh notes the degree to which the child's letter illustrates that he is progressing, not only in vocabulary, but also "inexorably in terms of experience," gaining knowledge that implies a certain complicity (112).

of complicity and innocence without access to psychological insights that might resolve uncertainty, however provisionally.

In "La casa de los relojes," the possibility of an unwitting transmission of responsibility remains open; in "La furia," however, the link between pedagogy and cruelty, narrative and contamination, is underlined rather insistently. This retrospective account centers on the deadly consequences of an unnamed adult speaker's affair with a Filipina governess named Winifred. Before the speaker can accomplish the sexual consummation he hopes for, Winifred disappears, leaving behind the boy who is always in her company. Ostensibly this is the child she is paid to care for, but the narrative leaves open the possibility that he is her son. The events leading up to the story's murderous conclusion alternate between the speaker's awkward advances, the boy's obnoxious behavior (he incessantly plays a drum), and Winifred's stories of her childhood, which center on her cruelty to a classmate named Lavinia. She frames these abuses as acts of motherly "dedication":

> yo vivía dedicada como una verdadera madre a cuidarla, a educarla, a corregir sus defectos ... Para corregir su orgullo, un día le corté un mechón que guardé secretamente en un relicario; tuvieron que cortarle el resto del pelo, para emparejarlo. Otro día, le volqué un frasco de agua de Colonia sobre el cuello y la mejilla; su cutis quedó todo manchado ... Para combatir sus inexplicables terrores, metí arañas vivas adentro de su cama. Una vez metí un ratón muerto que encontré en el jardín, otra vez metí un sapo. A pesar de todo no conseguí corregirla. (*La furia* 116–18)

> [I lived dedicated like a true mother to caring for her, to educating her, to correcting her defects ... In order to correct her pride, one day I cut a lock of her hair which I kept secretly in a reliquary; they had to cut the rest of her hair to match it up. Another day, I spilled a bottle of cologne on her neck and cheek; her skin became splotchy ... To combat her inexplicable terrors, I put live spiders in her bed. Once I put a dead mouse that I found in the garden, another time a toad. In spite of everything I could not reform her.]

Winifred's idea of cruelty as a means of instruction echoes Nietzsche in *Beyond Good and Evil*: to correct society, the philosopher must possess "a certain level headed cruelty that knows how to handle a knife surely and subtly, even when the heart bleeds" (134). Lavinia's failure to respond appropriately to Winifred's instruction appears to necessitate more drastic measures; the girl catches fire during a Christmas pageant and burns to death inside her costume. Winifred frames the accident that kills her friend in ambiguous terms: "una de las alas de Lavinia se encendió en la llama del cirio que yo llevaba en mi mano" (115) [one of the wings of Lavinia's costume caught fire from the candle that I was carrying in my hand]. Relegating the introduction of "yo" to an adjective clause at the end of the sentence, Winifred attempts to distance herself from this final "lesson" despite her explicit claims to responsibility for Lavinia's other sufferings. Perhaps her reluctance to claim this act resides in the fact that it cannot be so easily recuperated as benevolent; until Lavinia's death, Winifred was able to disregard her victim's pain by imagining herself as "operating" on a patient for her own good. Winifred's ambiguous description of the day of Lavinia's death as the "más feliz y más triste de mi vida" (115) [the happiest and the saddest of my life] leaves open the possibility that the sadness of the day resides not in the girl's death but in the loss of a patient who could be made to absorb her cruel attentions.

In response to the speaker's comment, "Qué cruel fuiste con Lavinia" [You were so cruel to Lavinia], Winifred assures him of the democratic character of her cruelty: "Cruel soy con el resto del mundo. Cruel seré contigo" (119) [I am cruel to the rest of the world. I will be cruel to you.] This exchange occurs in the hotel room where the speaker hopes to accomplish the consummation of their relationship that has so far been thwarted by the boy's presence. Instead, Winifred abruptly requests that he find the boy, whom she has smuggled into the hotel under her raincoat and has then left to wander the halls unsupervised. Initially, it appears that she brings the boy along despite the speaker's reservations ("¿Y si alguien lo ve? ... No permiten traer niños" [And if someone sees him? ... they don't allow children]); only in retrospect do we recognize the possibility that she deliberately stages this scenario (119). The speaker finds the boy urinating against a tree in the courtyard and returns to the hotel room with him only to discover that Winifred has disappeared. Unable to extract any information from the child, the speaker succeeds only at upsetting him, and the situation rapidly deteriorates:

> —Si tocas el tambor, te mato.
>   Comenzó a gritar. Lo tomé del cuello. Le pedí que se callara. No quiso escucharme. Le tapé la boca con la almohada. Durante unos minutos se debatió; luego quedó inmóvil, con los ojos cerrados ... Siempre fui así: por no provocar un escándalo fui capaz de cometer un crimen. (121)

> [If you play the drum I'll kill you. He began to yell. I took him by the neck. I asked him to be quiet. He refused to listen to me. I covered his mouth with a pillow. For some minutes he struggled; then he became still, with his eyes closed ... I was always like that: so as not to cause a scandal I was capable of committing a crime.]

As in "La casa de los relojes," "La furia" brings propriety and cruelty into discomfiting proximity; in the place of the lovemaking he hoped for, the speaker executes the consummation of Winifred's cruelty or, perhaps, of his own cruelty. "La furia" is exceptional as a "cuento cruel" that directly names cruelty and criminality, both in the speaker's direct observation that Winifred's treatment of Lavinia was cruel and in his recognition of the murder he commits as "un crimen." In this respect, it contrasts sharply with the many stories in which cruelty is naturalized or unacknowledged. Still, although cruelty is named and judged, its precise source remains unclear. Should we conclude that the circumstances at the hotel merely activate the capacity for cruelty that resided in the speaker all along, which he himself seems to recognize in his observation that "siempre fui así"? Or does responsibility lie with Winifred? Having refined her methods over the years, does she prepare the speaker with narratives of cruelty and then maneuver him into a situation in which his obsession with propriety can be neatly translated into murderous violence?

The narrative framing of the story further complicates any effort at conclusive judgment of cruelty. Although the narrator of "La furia" is an adult, like the narrator of "La casa de los relojes," he directs his account to a particular reader, an individual identified in the story only as Octavio. Once again, the narrative finds its ostensible motivation in the illustration of a student's faithful attention to his teacher's lessons. In the place of illustrations of improved vocabulary and manners, the speaker in "La furia" marks himself as a student in part through his insistence that he always carries a textbook. More significant, however, are the speaker's parenthetical remarks to Octavio, which recall the questions and comments that the speaker in "La casa de los relojes" directs at his teacher. When the narrator in "La furia" notes that he fell in love with Winifred because she "pronunció un alejandrino," he adds, "(Octavio, me enseñaste métrica)" (114) [she recited an alexandrine (Octavio, you taught me poetic meter)]. This remark implicitly identifies Octavio as the ultimate source of the knowledge that awakens the speaker's desire for Winifred; were it not for Octavio's lessons, the speaker suggests, he would not have become enamored with her. Another aside frames his attempts at seduction in relation to instruction of a different sort: "(Recordé tus consejos, Octavio, no hay que ser tímido para conquistar a una mujer)" (115) [I remembered your advice, Octavio, one must not be shy in order to conquer a woman].

Ascertaining the place of Octavio as fictional addressee is further complicated by the fact that Ocampo opened the story with the following dedication "(Para mi amigo Octavio)" (113). Ocampo's dedication may have been in response to Octavio Paz's 1947 poem, "Arcos," which he dedicated to her.[40] The poem figures artistic creation as an inward movement toward an assignation with the self that is endlessly deferred, and yet the poem's opening line, "¿Quién canta en las orillas

---

[40]   For Octavio Paz's reflections on his friendship with Ocampo, see José Luis Perdomo Orellana's article, "Dos amigos, dos poemas." Klingenberg speculates that the asides might have been a "sly response to Paz's well-known *machismo*" (*Fantasies* 269, n. 9).

del papel?" [Who sings on the edges of the paper?], suggests the mystery not only of the self who sings in the text but also of those presences that sing from its margins (62). The Octavio of "La furia" is such a presence; marginal and mentioned only in the speaker's parenthetical remarks, the influence of Octavio nevertheless appears pervasive. The typographical similarity between the paratextual dedication – "(Para mi amigo Octavio)" – and the parenthetical remarks within the story – "(Octavio, me enseñaste métrica)" [Octavio, you taught me poetic meter] – suggests that the function of "dedication" might be doubled in the internal parentheses as well. By dedicating his actions to Octavio and marking them as consequences of his instruction, the speaker transmits responsibility to his mentor. As the story's implicit addressee, Octavio is made vulnerable to contamination via narrative much as we discussed in relation to the teacher in "La casa de los relojes." While the speaker explicitly links Winifred to "las Furias," the relentless, crone-like avengers of mythology, perhaps the pursuing spirit that is most central to the story – and Ocampo's fiction – is narrative itself. In the next and final section, we will explore the degree to which Ocampo's fiction intensifies the afflictive capacity of narrative and demands that readers reckon with the implications of their reading habits and interpretative procedures.

Refusing the Reader's Innocence

It often seems that Ocampo's stories will absorb any action, any scene, any plot, or any character, no matter how grotesque or potentially disturbing. This impression is evoked repeatedly in Ocampo criticism; while what critics see Ocampo carrying to extremes varies, the common element is the notion that she insists on "final consequences."[41] Declaring Ocampo's extremity is one way of accounting for the intensity of the discomfort her stories sometimes arouse. Nevertheless, as the stories discussed in this essay illustrate, often readers must draw the most unsettling conclusions in Ocampo's stories or are enticed to imaginatively elaborate the particular horrors that lead to a given outcome. The high index of cruelty in many of Ocampo's stories redefines the horizon of expectation we bring to her work, often priming us to anticipate or generate cruelty where it is only sketchily suggested. This is one instance of

---

[41]   Notice that these claims are formulated in strikingly similar terms: Martínez Cabrera writes that Ocampo's aesthetic carries Quiroga's narrative strategy of using commonplaces in bad faith "hasta sus últimas consecuencias" (136), a judgment that echoes Molloy's assessment ("Simplicidad" 248). Balderston writes that Ocampo questions "el énfasis en lo fantástico" by "llevándolo a sus últimas consecuencias" ("Los cuentos" 743), and Zapata asserts that "on détecte dans certains récits une application rigoureuse de la loi jusqu'á ses conséquences ultimes" [one detects in certain stories a rigorous application of the law all the way to its final consequences] ("Rire" 16). For Díaz, the quest for experience in Ocampo is often "llevado a sus límites" (95).

what Karl Schlegel imagined as the critical reader's "completion" of the artistic work or of what Jean-Paul Sartre has called "directed creation" (53). While Ocampo is not unique among authors in eliciting our participation, her fiction tends to render that participation problematic, particularly in relation to the cruelty of the stories. Rosario Castellanos argues that Ocampo's fiction opens up an abyss within the quotidian habit of reading, forcing our recognition that reading is not an innocent act (150). Ocampo herself insisted on describing the reader as collaborator, with all the dubious implications of that role (Ulla, *Encuentros* 121).

Faced with gaps between the events and the absence of character interiority as a source of coherence, we begin to imagine multiple scenarios that would connect the existing textual elements. We might think of the potential energy of a boulder poised at the edge of a precipice. Rather than pushing that boulder off the ledge and determining the particulars of its disastrous path, Ocampo often guides our hands to the inviting surface of the rock and directs our gaze to the emptiness through which it might fall. At other times, she seems to position us at the base of the cliff, peering up into the sun as though to discern what sequence of events generated the disaster we see below. Even when the initial narrative is unsettling, its sinister dimensions multiply once we begin to "write" between the lines of the text, burdening us with the status of co-authors of Ocampo's cruelty.

In addition to this "directed creation," encounters with Ocampo's narratives generate uncomfortable feelings of responsibility made all the more vexing by our incomplete awareness of *who* or *what* we are responsible for. "Informe del Cielo y del Infierno" [*sic*] [Report from heaven and hell] offers a compelling allegory of the dilemma of responsibility experienced in reading Ocampo. Part accusation, part instruction manual, part cautionary tale, "Informe" presents heaven and hell as twin warehouses crammed with objects that serve as the basis for an inscrutable examination to determine one's final destination after death. The story reflects the special role of objects in Ocampo's fiction, and the word "cosa" [thing] refers first to those things that normally are in the houses of the world and then expands to include cities, gardens, mountains, reflections, temperatures, tastes, perfumes, sounds, and "toda suerte de sensaciones y de espectáculos [que] nos depara la eternidad" (*La furia* 225) [all manner of sensations and spectacles that offer us eternity]. The first-person narrator addresses the narrative to an undefined "tú" as if to provide counsel regarding the particulars of the scenario that will unfold at his or her deathbed: "los demonios y los ángeles, parejamente ávidos ... llegarán disfrazados a tu lecho y, acariciando tu cabeza, te darán a elegir las cosas que preferiste a lo largo de la vida" (225) [demons and angels, equally avid, will arrive at your bedside and, caressing your head, give you a choice of objects that you preferred through life].[42] One of the final stories in *La furia*, "Informe del Cielo y del Infierno" recuperates the associations that objects have gathered across the collection; the "frutas abrillantadas" [polished fruit] shine like the too-bright cheeks of the baby born in "El cuaderno"; the miniature horse brings to mind the cardboard toys that appear in "Voz en el teléfono"; the *bombones* repeat the candies hastily offered and then denied at the end of "La furia"; and "ojos de hiena" [eyes of a hyena] directly recalls the speaker's description of Winifred: "sus ojos brillaban, ahora me doy cuenta, como los de las hienas" (113) [her eyes shone, I now realize, like those of a hyena]. These connections accumulate in us as readers, intensifying the sense that the encounter with each object – or each word as textual object – is a kind of obscure test for us as well.

Beyond the decisive role of one's selection of objects, the precise nature of the examination in "Informe del Cielo y del Infierno" is impossible to determine. There is no indication as to what characteristics identify an object with heaven or hell. As the speaker observes in the final lines, "Ten cuidado. Conozco personas que por una llave rota o una jaula de mimbre fueron al Infierno y otras que por un papel de diario o una taza de leche, al Cielo" (226) [Be careful. I know people who because of a broken key or a wicker cage went to Hell and others who because of a page of the newspaper or a cup of milk, to Heaven.] Correctly choosing "cosas del Cielo" is no guarantee that one will go to heaven, nor is the opposite true: "Si eliges más cosas del Infierno que del Cielo, irás tal vez al Cielo; de lo contrario, si eliges más cosas del Cielo que del Infierno, corres el riesgo de ir al Infierno, pues tu amor a las cosas celestiales denotará mera concupiscencia" (226) [If you choose more things from Hell than from Heaven, you may go to Heaven; and on the other hand, if you choose more things from Heaven than from Hell, you run the risk of going to Hell, since your love of celestial objects may denote concupiscence]. Even if one were to crack the code to identify objects with heaven or hell, an arbitrary law is in force; choosing more objects of hell *may* get one to heaven, but there is no guarantee. Further, in the report, the two destinations appear absolutely interchangeable; their representatives, the demons and angels, move with equal ease through this world and are described as "parejamente ávidos" [equally avid] (225). With no knowledge of how choices

---

[42] "Informe" recalls the connection between one's fate and one's relation to objects explored most directly in "Los objetos," in which the protagonist begins to find all the objects that she had lost over the course of her life only to enter "a través de una suma de felicidades ... en el infierno" (*La furia* 108) [through a number of happinesses ... to hell]. Borges's short story "Deutsches Requiem" (1946) offers yet another point of comparison. In it, the narrator observes, "Yo había comprendido hace muchos años que no hay cosa en el mundo que no sea germen de un Infierno posible; un rostro, una palabra, una brújula, un aviso de cigarrillos" (*Obras* 579) [I had understood many years ago that there is nothing in the word incapable of generating a possible Hell; a face, a word, a compass, a cigarette advertisement].

will be weighed nor any notion of the relative appeal of heaven or hell, the story's addressee is placed in a double bind, called to exercise care but unable to determine what that care might consist of (226).

Describing the objects in the warehouses, the speaker intensifies this dilemma by warning that "tú" is the source of any deformation or ugliness found therein:

> Si el viento ruge, *para ti*, como un tigre y la paloma angelical tiene, al mirar, ojos de hiena, si el hombre acicalado que cruza por la calle, está vestido de andrajos lascivos; si la rosa con títulos honoríficos, que te regalan, es un trapo desteñido y menos interesante que un gorrión; si la cara de tu mujer es un leño descascarado y furioso: *tus ojos,* y no Dios, *los creó así.* (225, my emphasis)

> [If the wind roars, *for you*, like a tiger and the angelic dove has the eyes of a hyena when you look, if the spruced-up man crossing the street is dressed in lascivious tatters; if the rose with honorific titles presented to you is a faded rag, less interesting than a sparrow; if your wife's face is a piece of peeled and furious firewood: *your eyes*, and not God, *made them that way.*]

Whereas I have discussed deformation first and foremost as a deliberate defensive strategy on Ocampo's part, here the speaker assumes the offensive by attributing deformity to the addressee's senses and feelings. We might stress the links between this perspective and Kant's analysis of perception: while we believe the characteristics we observe to inhere in the objects before us, in fact our ways of seeing define what we are able to see. Perhaps we are organically incapable of apprehending the neutrality of objects; nevertheless, the speaker insists that we are still responsible for the deformations caused by our affective impositions. Figuring perversity in terms of a pathetic fallacy that deforms all according to the viewer's state of mind, the speaker further suggests that any hostility or cruelty we attribute to the objects is a false projection of something within us. For our discussion, John Ruskin's most famous example of the pathetic fallacy, drawn from Charles Kingsley's *Alton Locke* (1850), is particularly apropos: "They rowed her in across the rolling foam – The cruel, crawling foam" (cited in Ruskin 205). As Ruskin curtly observes, "The foam is not cruel, neither does it crawl" (205); one can similarly imagine Ocampo's speaker insisting, "the wind does not roar," or imagine Ocampo herself offering a similar comment regarding cruelty's relation to narrative, "the *word* is not cruel, nor does it threaten." Extending the speaker's argument in light of the material fact of words as objects and the text as a thing in the world, we arrive at an insistence on the radical innocence of narrative and on our indisputable responsibility for our reading. We might think of "Informe del Cielo y del Infierno" as a final trap laid for the reader of *La furia*, a story intended to intensify the effects that have characterized readers' encounters with the stories in the rest of the collection.

As we have seen, Ocampo flouts expectations of identification and psychological depth, insisting instead that readers reckon with her characters and stories as the objects they are: pieces of text, verbal constructions. In contrast to the aesthetic of cuteness, which "annihilates 'otherness'" by refusing to allow its object to be "separate and distinct" from the beholder (Harris 181), Ocampo maintains the hard edges of her characters – and of her fiction – as barriers to our empathetic intrusions. For readers conditioned to use narratives as affective prostheses, the insistence on surface in Ocampo's stories can feel like a cruel deprivation from the ways of feeling that "belong" to fiction. Readers of Ocampo often feel like the narrator in "Voz en el teléfono," unsettled to discover cardboard horses and little plastic automobiles in the places where we expected to find "real" things; recalled to the artificiality of the texts, surface is all we have to work with. One could argue, of course, that this is always the case, that any mimetic claims of literature are only approximate. But whereas in much fiction the surface of narrative is folded so as to create the illusion of depth, Ocampo's narratives insist on their own superficiality.

This resistant aesthetic intensifies the abrasive dimension of thematic cruelty in Ocampo's work; victims placidly accept their fates, and victimizers not only go unpunished but garrulously relate their crimes. If at times we wish to turn away from Ocampo's fiction, I would argue that it has less to do with the content than with the disconcerting effects of her stylistic and narrative choices. Like the addressees of "Informe del Cielo y del Infierno," "La furia," and "La casa de los relojes," we are exposed to the fury of narrative, a presence that contaminates by making us the authors of our own illness. If there is a lesson that Ocampo's fiction teaches us, it might be that all the visions of cruelty we thought were "hers" are in fact our responsibility, and the apparent irrelevance of ethical questions within Ocampo's stories only intensifies our isolation with that responsibility. Ocampo's stories haunt us in part because they make us feel responsible for her textual world in all its difference from what we might choose, and in that impossible responsibility resides the most compelling ethical implication of cruelty in her fiction.

5

Eros and its Archetypes in
Silvina Ocampo's Later Stories

GIULIA POGGI

> Le fiabe sono vere
> *Italo Calvino*

The Never-ending Quest

Characterized by the postmodern techniques of parody and collage, Silvina Ocampo's extensive narrative production (1937–88) is often structured as a rewriting of well-known fairy tales. This rewriting is almost always anomalous because it derives from the superimposition of different narrative structures. For example, in "La casa de azúcar" [The house made of sugar] (from *La furia*, 1959), Hansel and Gretel's attractive house, as suggested by the story's title, contaminates the space inhabited by the newlywed couple and projects onto the protagonist Cristina the character of the witch.[1] The presence of a feminine double can be found in other stories from the same collection, such as "La continuación" [The continuation] or "Carta perdida en un cajón" [Letter lost in a drawer], in which the angel/monster dialectic appears, as Patricia Klingenberg has suggested in the figures of Snow White and her stepmother.[2] Years later it will be Artemia, the protagonist of "Las vestiduras peligrosas" [Dangerous dresses] (*Los días de la noche*, 1970), who will become a modern-day Cinderella, destined to find with her succession of increasingly indecent outfits, not love, as in Perrault's story, but rather a dramatic and violent death.[3]

The notions of beauty and ugliness, good and evil, the angel in the house and the dissolute woman, all form part of Ocampo's incessant quest to bring to

---

1   Cristina is also a double for Violetta in Giuseppe Verdi's opera *La Traviata*.
2   See "The Mad Double" and *Fantasies of the Feminine* 112–22.
3   See my article on "Las vestiduras peligrosas."

light feminine fantasies and unconfessed drives. This quest led to her last short story collections, *Y así sucesivamente* (1987) and *Cornelia frente al espejo* (1988), which are marked by an accentuated lyricism and an increasing sense of nostalgia.[4] It is in the context of this dense and distilled prose that the archetypes of the simplest (and most ancient) form of narrating will reappear. These stories are no longer about modern-day Cinderellas or resuscitated Snow Whites, and woman is no longer represented as a double, rival, and counter-figure. Ocampo's gaze now appears to direct itself at an intimate feminine subject, one pervaded by the insoluble mysteries of Eros. Thus it is no surprise that, along with a rewriting of the classics of fantastic literature, the author challenges herself to revive symbols from a well-known repertoire learned during childhood, a time when, as we know, she studied French and English before Spanish.[5]

Blue Beard (or the Forbidden)

The first archetype that I will analyze is the forbidden room, also known as the story of Blue Beard and his wives, revisited with an astonishing role reversal in "Jardín de infierno" [The garden of Hell]. According to Adriana Mancini,[6] the title refers to one of Hans Christian Andersen's stories, "The Garden of Paradise," but I believe it also refers to the place evoked by Cornelia, the enigmatic protagonist of the title story of the volume in which both stories appear, *Cornelia frente al espejo*. In her dialogue before the mirror, Cornelia laments more than once the difficulty of finding keys that will allow her to enter prohibited spaces such as the house she remembers and describes in detail:

> No sabes el tiempo que tardé en conseguir las llaves de esta casa, nadie tiene confianza en mí ... ¡He vivido tanto tiempo en esta casa! Tengo un inventario mental de las cosas que me gustaban: el *jardín de invierno* donde me escondía, me fascina, el cuarto que era el cuarto de plancha, y que sirve ahora de depósito, también. Todo se ha transformado en salón de modas. Este salón era una sala ... Yo me asfixiaba cuando entraba aquí. Las manos de todos los retratos que me miraban me estrangulaban ... ¡Por no verlos hubiera vivido en el infierno! (*Cuentos completos* II 265, my emphasis)[7]

---

[4]   Graciela Tomassini also reads these last two volumes as a kind of synthesis of Ocampo's previous work, with a particular aesthetic of their own. See "La paradoja" and *El espejo*, chapter 5. For details on their style see Orecchia Havas.

[5]   Among these literary references is Henry James, evoked in "El diario de Porfiria Bernal" (*Las invitadas*, 1961); on this point, see Klingenberg's observations in *Fantasies* 82–93 and my article, "Dalla parte delle bambine."

[6]   Especially 275–89.

[7]   All quotations from the stories are taken from *Cuentos completos*.

[You cannot imagine how long it took me to get the keys to the house, nobody trusts me ... I have lived for so long in this house! I have a mental inventory of the things that I used to like: the *winter garden* where I would hide, fascinates me, the room used for the ironing, and that now also serves as storage. Everything has been transformed into a dress shop. This shop used to be a parlor ... I could not breathe when I would enter here. The hands of all the portraits that looked at me, would strangle me ... *In order to not see them, I would have lived in hell!*]

Later, another forbidden space is the room where Cornelia finds her lover in the arms of her rival:

Cuando llegué a la casa, la puerta de la calle estaba cerrada con llave. Me trepé a un balcón, encontré la puerta del balcón abierta y entré. En puntillas me dirigí al cuarto de Pablo. No había nadie. Después recorrí la casa, cuarto por cuarto, hasta que llegué al de Elena Schleider. *Eres lo único que tengo en la vida*, susurraba la voz transformada de Elena Schleider. En la penumbra primeramente no vi nada, luego, como la mujer de Barba Azul cuando entró al cuarto prohibido, retrocedí espantada. Pablo y Elena Schleider, como un monstruo mitológico, estaban abrazados, sobre la cama. (284)

[When I arrived home, the door was locked. I climbed up to the balcony, found the balcony door open and entered. I tiptoed over to Pablo's room. Nobody was there. Afterwards I wandered through the house, room by room, until I arrived at Elena Schleider's. "You are the only thing I have in my life," whispered Elena Schleider's transformed voice. In the darkness, at first I did not see anything; later, like Blue Beard's wife when she entered the forbidden room, I backed away frightened. Pablo and Elena Schleider were embraced on the bed like some mythological beast.]

Cornelia's obsession with the keys as well as her association of winter/hell (invierno/infierno), reappears with sinister premonitions in Bárbara's words to her husband. As Adriana Mancini notes, the protagonist's name (Bárbara) in "Jardín de infierno" is by no means accidental:[8]

Aquí te dejo las llaves de la casa. Esta es la del sótano, ésta la de la bohardilla donde están los dibujos, ésta la del cuarto de roperos, ésta es de la despensa, ésta la del cuarto de plancha y esta chiquitita, mírala bien, la del cuarto que está junto al *jardín de invierno*, que *llamo, no sé por qué, de infierno*. No

---

8   The name "Bárbara" plays on two sets of connotations not readily available in English: first, it is associated with "bárbaro," meaning barbarous or uncivilized; and second, it contains the word "barba," Spanish for "beard." (translator's note)

entres en este cuarto, no abras la puerta por nada, aunque te parezca, cuando llueve, que hay goteras o un incendio. Este cuarto te está vedado y darte su llave demuestra la confianza que te tengo. (315, emphasis added)

[I am leaving you the keys to the house here. This one is for the basement, this one for the attic where the drawings are, this one for the walk-in closets, this is for the pantry, this for the ironing room, and this little one, look closely, for the room next to the *winter garden* which *I call for some unknown reason "the garden of hell."* Do not enter that room, do not open the door for any reason, even if you think, when it rains, that there may be a leak or a fire. This room is forbidden to you and by giving you the key I am showing my trust in you.]

Silvina Ocampo submits Blue Beard to a parodic (and ironic)[9] inversion, which grows out of a progressive approximation to the symbols (the house, the key, the forbidden room) around which Perrault's story develops. Here is the detailed description of the keys Blue Beard hands to his wife before leaving on a trip:

Voilà, lui dit-il, les clefs des deux grands garde-meubles, voilà celles de la vaisselle d'or et d'argent qui ne sert pas tous le jours, voilà celles des mes coffres-forts, où est mon or et mon argent, celles des cassettes où sont mes pierreries, et voilà le passe-partout de tous les appartements. Pour cette petite clef-ci, c'est la clef du cabinet au bout de la grande galerie de l'appartement bas: ouvrez tout, allez partout, mais ce petit cabinet, je vous défends d'y entrer, et je vous le défends de telle sorte, que s'il vous arrive de l'ouvrir, il n'y a rien que vous ne deviez attendre de ma colère. (Perrault 124)

["Here," said he, "are the keys to the two great wardrobes, wherein I have my best furniture. These are to my silver and gold plate, which is not for everyday use. These open my strong boxes, which hold my money, both gold and silver; these my caskets of jewels. And this is the master key to all my apartments. But as for this little one here, it is the key to the closet at the end of the great hall on the ground floor. Open them all; go into each and every one of them, except that little closet, which I forbid you, and forbid it in such a manner that, if you happen to open it, you may expect my just anger and resentment.][10]

---

9   In reference to the rhetorical irony in Ocampo's discursive narrative see Tomassini, *El espejo.*

10   Translation by Andrew Lang, "Blue Beard," from *The Blue Fairy Book* (London: Longmans, Green, and Company, c. 1889), available online at http://www.pitt.edu/~dash/perrault03.html. (translator's note)

An analogous description appears in "The Bloody Chamber," Angela Carter's long short story which reconstructs Blue Beard's tale from the wife's perspective. In contrast to Ocampo, who omits many of the narrative passages from the French story, the American author faithfully reconstructs them, even adding to them by means of a slow narrative rhythm and rich dialogues and digressions. The ceremonial handing over of the keys is characterized by a hyperbolic catalogue based on various shapes and forms – "key after key, a key, he said, for every lock in the house. Keys of all kinds – huge, ancient things of black iron; others slender, delicate, almost baroque" – which ends by highlighting the only forbidden one (Carter 19).

However, in spite of incorporating many of Perrault's passages, Carter clearly deviates from the ending by introducing an unprecedented figure: the mother. "The Bloody Chamber" begins in effect with the mother's doubts about her daughter's impending wedding ("Are you sure you love him," she asks her daughter about the future husband) and it ends with her life-saving intervention. Thanks to that "maternal telepathy" and not, as in Perrault's story, the intervention of her brothers, the protagonist manages to save herself and erase forever the horror of the bloody chamber. This is a sharp contrast to the ending in "Jardín de infierno" in which Bárbara/Barba Azul [Blue Beard], who has recently returned from a trip, cannot prevent her husband's suicide in order to escape his perversions:

> Se oyó el coche que traía a la mujer. Ella entró como siempre, y con el mismo ímpetu pidió las llaves. Pero su marido no estaba. Alarmada fue al cuarto, donde las encontró. Abrió la puerta. En un papelito pegado a la pared pudo leer: "Aquí estoy. Colgado entre otros jóvenes. Prefiero esta compañía. Tu último marido." (II 318)

> [One could hear the car that brought the woman. She entered as always, and with the same impetus she asked for the keys. But her husband was not there. Alarmed she went to the room where she found them. She opened the door. On a slip of paper stuck to the wall she read: "Here I am, hanging among other young men. I prefer their company. Your last husband."]

In line with the fragmented enunciation of the story, which oscillates between a first-person narrator and a third-person omniscient narrator, this ending expresses a moral far from the happy ending in Perrault and from the utopian development in Carter. However, be it the baroque prose of Angela Carter or the bare prose of Silvina Ocampo, both emphasize a fundamentally important motif in Blue Beard's story: it is impossible for the transgressor, male or female, to clean the bloodied key. As Bettelheim has indicated, this is the only supernatural motif in a story characterized by its scarcity of fantastic devices and its proximity to legend and history.[11] This motif coincides, in Perrault, with the moment of maximum suspense when the curious wife, after having entered the forbidden room, attempts to wash the key which has fallen because of her fright:

> Ayant remarqué que la clef du cabinet était tachée de sang, elle l'essuya deux ou trois fois, mais le sang ne s'en allait point; elle eut beau la laver, et même la frotter avec du sablon et avec du grès, il y demeura toujours du sang, car le clef était Fée, et il n'y avait pas moyen de la nettoyer tout à fait: quand on ôtait le sang d'un coté, il revenait de l'autre. (Perrault 124)

> [Having observed that the key to the closet was stained with blood, she tried two or three times to wipe it off; but the blood would not come out; in vain did she wash it, and even rub it with soap and sand. The blood still remained, for the key was magical and she could never make it quite clean; when the blood was gone from one side, it appeared again on the other.]

Ocampo quickly sums up this scene by attributing to Bárbara's husband the same actions as Blue Beard's wife, and she almost paraphrases Perrault's text, though avoiding the detail about the enchanted key:

> Dos vueltas dio la llave. Abrió la puerta. En la oscuridad no vio al principio nada. Luego seis cuerpos de varones colgados en el cielo raso. Temblaba tanto que de la mano se le cayó la llave, que se manchó de rojo. A partir de este momento trató de quitarle la mancha a la llave. Fue imposible: ni arena, ni querosén, ni nafta pudo limpiarla. (II 318)

> [She turned the key twice. She opened the door. At first she did not see anything in the darkness. Then six male bodies hanging from the ceiling. She trembled so much that the key fell from her hand; it became stained with blood. From that moment on she tried to remove the stain from the key. It was impossible: neither sand, nor kerosene, nor gas could clean it.]

The bloodstained key also brands forever the protagonist of "The Bloody Chamber." After trying in vain to clean the key in the bathroom ("Crimson water swirled down the basin but, as if the key itself were hurt, the bloody token

---

[11] Bettelheim 299–303. For more information regarding the historical identification of Blue Beard as Gilles de Rais, the aristocratic murderer of the fifteenth century who Huysmans evokes in *Là-bas*, I refer the reader to the *Notice* by Rouger in Perrault 119–21; see also the conclusive chapter by Mancini (285–89) and her observations on George Bataille; and Vargas Llosa's introduction to the historical character. In reference to the inversion of the Blue Beard figure, see Klingenberg, *Fantasies* 234 and footnote p. 271 where she cites Silvina Ocampo on this tale in which "two sins struggle: curiosity and cruelty."

stuck ... I scrubbed the stain with my nail brush but it still would not budge," Carter 33), she has no other recourse but to return it to her husband. After having suggested she kneel, he brands her forehead "like the cast mark of a Brahmin woman" (36), as if to leave an eternal sign of transgression, a sign that neither the death of her husband at the hands of her mother, nor the peaceful cohabitation with her mother and the piano tuner who helped in her salvation, will manage to erase:

> No paint, nor powder, no matter how thick or white, can mask that red mark on my forehead; I am glad he cannot see it – not for fear of his revulsion, since I know he sees me clearly with his heart – but, because it spares my shame. (41)

With these words, Carter's story ends. We do not know if Silvina Ocampo read the story, nor to what point, more or less consciously, she tried to imitate it. What is certain is that Carter's parody of the Blue Beard story, as well as its re-elaboration by her South American counterpart, reflects a shared will to subvert the fundamentals of patriarchal culture. On the one hand, this culture prohibits woman's curiosity, while on the other it allows man to hide his darkest, innermost thoughts.

Beauty and the Beast (or Transformation)

The prohibition that marks the destiny of Blue Beard's wife and her modern heirs is strictly connected to her married status. According to the taboos that the culture of the father brings, matrimony is, in effect, the rite through which woman accesses that world. It is no coincidence that the beginning, not only of "Blue Beard" but also of many other fairy tales, coincides with a wedding; or, conversely, that a wedding (impeded by obstacles) is the final objective. Marriage, in effect, combines negative associations related to prohibition, as we have seen, but also positive ones, since it presupposes a transformation. The story of Beauty and the Beast revolves around this meaning, a story whose diffusion through Western literature has been traced in a brilliant essay by Marina Warner.[12] From its classical roots (the Cupid and Psyche myth as told by Apuleius in *Metamorphosis*), the story had been re-elaborated numerous times since the seventeenth century (for example, in *Le piacevoli notti* [The facetious nights] by Giovanni Francesco Straparola and *Lo cunto de li cunti* [The Pentamerone] by Giambattista Basile) up to the present day (one need only recall the theatrical adaptation by Jean Cocteau and one of its Italian versions, *Bellinda e il mostro* [Bellinda and the monster] included by Italo

---

12 See also Bettelheim 303–09.

Calvino in his collection). But the principal conduit for transmitting this tale dates from the start of the eighteenth century, when Madame de Villeneuve gave it a title (*La Belle et la Bête*) and, at the same time, the form of a fairy tale. Subsequently, Madame de Villeneuve's plot (that is, the meeting of a beautiful woman and a monstrous creature) was picked up by Madame de Beaumont.[13] Published in 1756 in *Le Magasin des enfants* (*Young Misses Magazine*), her version of Beauty and the Beast would be the starting point for adaptations, such as two of Angela Carter's stories, "The Courtship of Mr. Lion" and "The Tiger's Bride" (from *The Bloody Chamber*), and one of Silvina Ocampo's stories, "Miren cómo se aman" [See how they love each other] from *Cornelia frente al espejo*. However, Carter respects, as always, the sequences from the French story: a rich merchant, with economic woes, hands over his daughter to the mysterious and monstrous owner of a palace. Carter at the same time foregrounds the more fantastic traits – the enchanted palace, the disagreeable Beast, the innocent and beautiful Belle – while the Argentine author simply revisits the nucleus of the archetype and subjects it, once more, to an inversion.

The most interesting aspect of "Miren cómo se aman" is its elaboration of a previous story, "Paisaje de trapecios" [Scenery with trapezes], from the author's first short story collection, *Viaje olvidado* (1937).[14] The protagonist of this early version is Charlotte, a trapeze artist, who has a friendly rapport with Plinio, her monkey and partner, in the spectacular act:

> Plinio entraba anunciándole la mañana con una corrida balanceada de piernas torcidas, como si cada uno de sus brazos llevara colgado el cansancio de muchas personas, de muchos baldes de agua o de muchos canastos de frutas. Sus ojos eran tristes de malicia e imitación. Charlotte lo sentaba sobre sus faldas desnudas y le daba terrones de azúcar todas las mañanas de su vida. A veces se preguntaba si no era precisamente gracias a él que había entrado en esa compañía de circo o bien si era gracias a ella misma y a sus números de acrobacia. Pero las exclamaciones de admiración la perseguían

---

[13] An English version, "Beauty and the Beast," from *The Young Misses Magazine, Containing Dialogues between a Governess and Several Young Ladies of Quality Her Scholars*, 4th ed. (London: C. Nourse, 1783), is available online at http://www.pitt.edu/~dash/beauty.html. (translator's note)

[14] "Curiosamente en los dos últimos libros publicados por la autora … la escritura vuelve sobre sus pasos y refleja como un espejo la impronta de *Viaje olvidado*" (Tomassini, *El espejo* 25–26) [Curiously, in the last two books published by the author … her writing returns to a previous path and reflects like a mirror the imprint of *Viaje olvidado*]; later, after affirming "la familiaridad de estos nuevos cuentos con la primera escritura de la autora" [the similarity of these new stories with the author's first writing], Graciela Tomassini defines "Miren cómo se aman" as a new version of "Paisaje de trapecios," "cuyo desenlace se ha modificado con la incrustación de una recreación paródica del cuento de la 'La Bella y la Bestia'" (112) [whose ending she has modified with a graft of a parodic recreation of the story "Beauty and the Beast"].

a lo largo de los viajes, en los barcos, en los andenes, en las ventanilla de los trenes donde le llegaban las voces asombradas de "¡oh, miren la chica con el mono!" Todo esto no iba dirigido a ella ni a su gorro de lana rojo, ni a sus anchas espaldas. (I 34)

[Plinio would enter in the morning running, balanced on crooked legs, as if each arm hung with the fatigue of many people, from many buckets of water or many baskets of fruit. His eyes were sad with malice and imitation. Charlotte would sit him on her naked lap and give him sugar cubes every day of his life. Sometimes she would ask herself if it were not precisely because of him that she had gotten into that circus or if it had been thanks to her and her acrobatic numbers. But the cheers pursued her throughout her travels, on ships, platforms, train windows when she would hear surprised voices saying, "oh, look at the girl with the monkey!" All of this was not directed at her, nor her red woolen hat, nor her wide shoulders.]

It would serve no purpose to continue with the quotation, and in particular to compare it to the corresponding fragment from "Miren cómo se aman." If we exclude the name change that transformed Charlotte of 1937 into Adriana of 1988, the narrative continues identically both at the level of the plot and regarding the most detailed descriptions. The introduction of an extraordinary occurrence that will change Charlotte/Adriana's life is also identical: a man falls in love with her, unleashing a crisis in her relationship with the monkey. It is from this unexpected occurrence that the later story changes direction and transforms into a parody of fairy tales, giving rise to a brief dialogue between Adriana and her boyfriend: "Voy a concluir por ponerme celoso. "¿De quién?" Preguntó Charlotte. "De Plinio" (II 368) ["I will end up getting jealous." "Of whom," asked Charlotte. "Of Plinio"]. The motif of transformation introduces the theme of "Beauty and the Beast," that of the conflict between apparently opposing forces, like instinct and virtue, that the force of Eros will construct. Like Beauty of Madame de Beaumont's version, to whom the Beast addresses the same words each evening – "La Belle, voulez-vous être ma femme?" (48) [Belle, will you be my wife?] – Adriana is confronted with Plinio's imaginary question:

A veces cuando Adriana volvía a su habitación, y lo encontraba a Plinio esperándola, creía oír su voz que decía: "¿No te casarías conmigo?" Ella, asombrada, creyendo que había soñado esa voz y esa pregunta, vacilaba y luego le contestaba avergonzada: "Te quiero, pero no lo bastante como para casarme contigo." (II 368–69)

[Sometimes when Adriana would return to her room and she would find Plinio waiting for her, she believed she heard his voice say, "Won't you marry me?" She, astonished, believing that she had dreamed that voice and the question, would waver and then answer in embarrassment: "I love you, but not enough to marry you."]

Very similar to Belle's response to the disappointed Beast, and almost a direct quotation ("je voudrais pouvoir vous épouser, mais je suis trop sincère, pour vous fair croire que cela arrivera jamais" (49) [I wish I could consent to marry you, but I am too sincere to make you believe that will ever happen], Adriana's response obeys the clichéd repetition found in fairy tales ("estos diálogos repetidos empezaron a parecer naturales a Adriana" [these repeated dialogues started to seem natural to Adriana]), although, unlike those tales, it will not have a happy ending. This is because, with regard to the evolution that the archetype presents (once she has returned to her father's house with her sisters, Belle forgets her promise to the Beast and only when he is near death does she save him, thus causing his transformation into a prince), the Argentine story introduces the psychological motif of jealousy and competition between animal and human Eros. Without elaborating on what happened before (which can be easily deduced from the preceding dialogues), Silvina describes Plinio not only, as in the French story or in Angela Carter's versions, as dying of love, but also with an open wound in the middle of his chest which barely lets him utter the same question as always:

> "¿Te casarías conmigo?" Adriana le contestó con el mismo asombro, pero decidida: "Te amo y me casaré contigo." Al oír estas palabras, Plinio se incorporó y salió de su piel para transformarse en príncipe. Adriana extasiada lo miró y se abrazaron. (369)

> ["Will you marry me?" Adriana answered him with the same amazement, but with resolve: "I love you and I will marry you." Upon hearing those words, Plinio sat up and came out of his skin, transforming into a prince. An ecstatic Adriana looked at him and they embraced.]

But the transformation does not resolve in the familiar edifying ending of fairy tales, nor, as its naive ethic would presuppose, with the re-establishment of a balance thanks to love's victory over difference. Disappointed by Plinio's new appearance, Adriana starts to yearn for his previous identity:

> "Extraño tu piel, tus ojos, tu modo atrevido de mirar."
> "¿Te atraía más antes?"
> "Creo que sí."
> ["I miss your skin, your eyes, your bold way of looking at me."
> "Was I more attractive to you before?"
> "Yes, I think so."]

Thus the story ends when Plinio, incited by the public, recaptures his animal form, and Adriana takes him into her arms. This ending's closing words shed a new light on the return to the realm of instincts:

> Se oyó, también, la potente voz de un domador, que hizo el papel de maestro de ceremonias. "Señoras y señores, verán un espectáculo nuevo: el príncipe vuelve a ser mono en los brazos de su amada. *Miren cómo se aman.*" Los aplausos fueron atronadores. El público gritó: "Mono no, príncipe sí. Mono no, príncipe sí. Mono sí, príncipe no. Mono sí, príncipe no." (370, emphasis added)

> [One could also hear the potent voice of a trainer, who performed the role of master of ceremonies, "Ladies and gentlemen, you will see a new spectacle: the prince turns back into a monkey in the arms of his beloved. *Look at how they love each other.*" The applause was deafening. The public yelled: "No to the monkey, yes to the prince. No to the monkey, yes to the prince. Yes to the monkey, no to the prince. Yes to the monkey, no to the prince."]

Rhythmically amplified by the voice of the audience, the dialectic between the idealized figure of the man and the animal (traditionally associated with ugliness, as is the monkey), between instinct and its sublimation, projects a sinister light on the transformation as a typical recourse in fairy tales. Thus we are faced with one of the many ambiguities through which Ocampo disorients and displaces her readers.[15] By converting a plausible situation into a theorem impossible of solution, Ocampo melds two different, though not completely opposite, narrative statutes. Traces exist at the discursive level that connect the initial realist impetus of the story with its development, which vacillates between the absurd and parody. In fact, the phrase the trainer pronounces toward the end ("Miren cómo se aman" [Look at how they love each other]) is the same one that the narrator used at the start to introduce the strange pair ("¡Oh, miren la chica con el mono!" [Oh, look at the girl with the monkey!]). Similarly, the sentence that describes Plinio's gaze ("Sus ojos eran tristes de malicia y de imitación" [His eyes were sad with malice and imitation]) justifies the disappointment with which Adriana greets his transformation into a human ("extraño tu piel, tus ojos, tu modo atrevido de mirar" [I miss your skin, your eyes, your bold way of looking at me]).

This speaks of imperceptible symmetries, small hints that the narrative was first conceived as detective fiction (in the 1937 version, the boyfriend becomes Plinio's killer, causing Charlotte to demand, through a newspaper advertisement,

---

15 Patricia Klingenberg comments on this ambivalent ending: "One idea that emerges from this absurd ending is that the public has no idea what it wants, is both embarrassed by and addicted to romance" (*Fantasies* 153).

that he pay with his life) which later switches to another narrative mode. This deviation ends necessarily by contracting narrative passages of the fairy tale model and by eliminating figures that, like that of the father (perhaps substituted for the boyfriend?), gave momentum to the entanglement. Even so, the descriptions of the Beast's mysterious and enchanted palace, which occupies a great deal of space in the various versions of the story, are supplanted by those of anonymous and somewhat squalid urban spaces (hotel rooms, taxis, cafes). In addition, there seems to be no reason to include the typical magical objects, such as the rose Belle's father takes from the Beast's garden, which unleashes his ire and prompts the proposition of handing over his daughter. One may read, however, the distorted memory of this evident symbol of beauty in the flowers that decorate the trapeze artist's costume at the start of the Argentine story: "Adriana dejó caer su mirada hacia sus pechos. El vestido era de lana gruesa bordada con flores" (366) [Adriana's glance fell upon her breasts. The dress was made of thick wool with embroidered flowers]. And a detail of dead flowers appears at the close of the first part:

> Una risa breve los envolvió dentro del baile. Hacía mucho frío afuera esa noche y el interior del bar alemán abrigaba con olores espesos a gente, a cerveza, a frituras. En el medio de las mesas había florecitos de metal angostísimos y altos con tres flores muertas. (368)

> [A brief laugh enveloped them in the dance. It was very cold outside that night and the inside of the German bar warmed them with the thick odor of people, beer, and fried food. In the center of the tables there were thin, tall metal vases with three dead flowers.]

The Blue Bird (or Love Eternal)

The third story that we will analyze is one of the shortest of *Cornelia frente al espejo*. Its title, "Color del tiempo," refers back to an invocation uttered by the protagonist of "The Blue Bird," a story that Madame D'Aulnoy included in her *Le Cabinet des fées*. The story is well known: the widowed king's daughter, the beautiful Florine, is under her stepmother's power. In an attempt to keep Prince Charming away from Florine so that he will marry her daughter (the ugly Truitonne), the stepmother locks up Florine in a tower with the help of the evil fairy Suissio. The prince is then transformed by Suissio into a blue bird which allows him to fly up to Florine's window every night; the two fall in love and communicate with one another until their enemies, helped by the evil Suissio, manage to separate them. Transformed back into his human form, Prince Charming is on the verge of marrying Truitonne when Florine, disguised as a beggar, gains access to the royal palace. The prince recognizes her and learns the truth. Once they are reconciled, the two lovers marry, and thus put an end to their long period of separation and many vicissitudes.

As one can deduce from this brief summary, Madame d'Aulnoy uses all the characteristic ingredients of fairy tales (a stepmother, an evil fairy, beauty and ugliness, animal transformation, disguise) in order to affirm that true love is timeless and that nothing can impede its triumph. As always, Silvina Ocampo concentrates on the central and most lyrical part of the story, foregoing altogether the complication that articulates it. Conceived as a monologue in the first person that leads into a brief final dialogue, "Color del tiempo" seems more like an impassioned confession in which love and death alternate, and in which passion wears the wings of the prince transformed into a blue bird:

Estoy enamorada: eso reemplaza la belleza ... Soy capaz de morir en otros brazos, aunque me maten cien veces las alas azules, afiladas ... Debajo de mi camisa tengo plumas azules, tan azules como el mar, que no conozco. (II 371)

[I am in love: that replaces beauty ... I am capable of dying in other arms, although the sharp, blue wings may kill me a hundred times ... Under my shirt I have blue feathers, as blue as the sea that I do not know.]

These words remind us of the first encounter between Florine and the prince transformed into a blue bird, as described by Madame d'Aulnoy:

Adorable Florine, merveille de nos jours! pourquoi voulez-vous finir si promptement les vôtres? Vos maux me sont point sans remède. –Hé,! qui me parle? s'écria-t-elle, d'un manière si consolante? –Un roi malheureux, reprit l'Oiseau, qui vous aime et n'aimera jamais que vous. – Un roi qui m'aime! Ajouta-t-elle. Est-ce ici un piège que me tend mon ennemie? Mais au fond qu'y gagnera-t-elle? Si elle cherche à découvrir mes sentiments, je suis prête à lui en faire l'aveu. –Non, ma princesse, répondit il, l'amant qui vous parle n'est pas capable n'est point capable de vous trahir. En achevant ces mots, il vola sur la fenêtre. Florine eut d'abord grande peur d'un oiseau si extraordinaire, qui parlait avec autant d'esprit qui s'il avait été homme, quoqu'il conservât le petit son de voix d'un rossignol; mais le beauté de son plumage et ce qu'il lui dit la rassura. (39)

["Adorable Florine," he said, "the wonder of our days, why do you want yours to be so soon ended? Your misfortunes are not without a remedy." "Ah! who is it who speaks to me with words of comfort?" she cried. "An unhappy king," replied the bird. "He loves you, and will never love anyone else." "A king who loves me?" she said. "Is this some snare my enemy has laid for me? But in the end what would she gain by it? If she seeks to find out what my feelings are, I am ready to make them all known to her." "No, my princess," he answered, "the lover who now speaks to you is not capable of betraying you;" and so saying he flew on to the window-sill. At first Florine was very much afraid of a bird so strange, that spoke as sensibly as a man, though in the gentle notes of a nightingale. But the beauty of its plumage and the words it said reassured her.][16]

Precisely within the framework of these nocturnal encounters, Florine utters the triple invocation, "Oiseau bleu, couleur du temps/ vole à moi promptement" [Blue Bird, the color of time, make haste to return to me], that the narrator of "Color del tiempo" will pick up:

> Un ruiseñor o tordo me llama. Fue mi amante. Se llama *ruiseñor azul* y en una ventana abierta de noche, hablamos hasta que el sol nos despertó. ¿De qué hablábamos? No podría decirlo. Decía inolvidables cosas ... He perdido la vida pero no sé si él la perdió. Tan solitario era su canto. *"Pájaro azul del color del tiempo* vuelve a mis brazos. ¡Oh inmortal! Vuelve." (371)

> [A nightingale or thrush calls me. He was my lover. His name is blue nightingale and through an open window at night, we talked until the sun woke us. What did we talk about? I wouldn't be able to say. He would say unforgettable things ... I have lost my life but I don't know if he lost his. His song was so lonely. *"Blue bird, the color of time,* return to my arms. Oh immortal! Return!]][17]

As the quotation marks and italics indicate, this is a quotation or, better yet, a faraway memory of some words that have remained impressed on the imagination of the writer, and which Madame d'Aulnoy has already highlighted as authentic ("Ce sont là ses propres paroles, auxquelles l'on n'a rien voulu" [These are her own words, which it has been thought best to keep unchanged]). The narration suddenly changes from first to third person: "Huí de su lado. Huyó el ruiseñor. ¿Sería un ruiseñor? Hace tanto tiempo que existen" (372) [I fled from his side. The nightingale fled. Was it a nightingale? They have existed for a very long time]. It then transitions to a quick final sequence:

> El hombre vino a buscarme. Lo seguí. Me acerqué a la jaula, vi una pelambre oscura. Era un mono diminuto pero precioso. Medía cincuenta centímetros.

---

[16]   English translations are from Miss Annie Macdonell and Miss Lee's translation of "The Blue Bird," in *The Fairy Tales of Madame D'Aulnoy* (London: Lawrence and Bullen, 1892) which is online at http://www.surlalunefairytales.com/authors/aulnoy/1892/bluebird.html. (translator's note)

[17]   Regarding the importance and significance of the color blue in Silvina Ocampo's stories, see chapter 6 of Galeota Cajati.

Cantaba, para siempre lo oiría, para siempre porque fue el primero de mis santos. (372)

[The man came for me. I followed him. I approached the cage, and saw the dark skin. It was a small, but beautiful monkey. He measured fifty centimeters. He sang, I would forever hear him, forever because he was the first of my saints.]

From the blue bird to the dark monkey: what clearly emerges is the same dialectic as that which ended the story previously analyzed ("mono no, príncipe sí"), and also the mix of different animal attributes which profoundly relate to the realm of human emotions. In fact, the repetition of the syntagm "forever" projects the monkey's song toward eternity, that is, that of the bird/nightingale, whose antiquity the narrator has already mentioned: "¿Sería un ruiseñor? *Hace tanto tiempo* que existen" (emphasis added [Was it a nightingale? They have existed for a *very long time*]). The affirmation, "fue el primero de mis santos" [he was the first of my saints], also refers back to a distant past which motivates the purchase of the caged animal and the narrator's contact with the anonymous vendor. As always, an ordinary event, even a commercial one, marks the return to reality. But it is a painful reality that, contrary to what happens in the corresponding story by Madame d'Aulnoy, does not prepare for a happy ending, but instead for the certainty of an unforgettable, comforting memory:

Pagué y me fui llevando el corazón en mis brazos.
Si alguien lo quiere, yo tengo una grabación intacta. Gracias. Está grabada en mi corazón y esta grabación sirve. (372)

[I paid and I left carrying my heart in my arms.
If someone wants it, I have the recording intact. Thank you. It is recorded in my heart and this recording is enough.]

This is the last temporal gap in a story that continually oscillates between past and present, an oscillation that cancels the distance of the narrator's evoked memory at its beginning ("Desde la mañana oí el canto de aquel pájaro" [From morning on I heard the singing of that bird]) and in the updated ending has a movement opposite to that which governs the French story.

The Price of Silence

The brief study of love's power that we have reviewed above shows Silvina Ocampo's fondness for the better known fairy tales and her tendency to mix and superimpose them. The oscillation between bird and nightingale and the consequent creation of the syntagm "blue nightingale" suggest that in conceiving her story, Ocampo thought not only about Madame d'Aulnoy, but also about the no less famous tale by Hans Christian Andersen which exalts a nightingale's song that saves the emperor of China. Nor is this the only reference to the Danish writer that surfaces in *Cornelia frente al espejo*. The symbology that surrounds the Snow Queen, protagonist of one of Andersen's celebrated stories, may have inspired "El sillón de nieve," a short narration without temporal coordinates nor proper names that seems more like a narrated dream, almost an Oedipal nightmare.[18] In addition, the final attack on the narrator by the cats transformed into wolves harkens back to another cult figure, Red Riding Hood,[19] and ends by converting this very brief story into a late revisiting of childhood fears.

An ironic interpretation of a celebrated Hans Christian Andersen character also appears in "Permiso de hablar," a story that concentrates once more on an impossible relationship, similar to, as the ending points out, the little mermaid with her prince. This same relationship, however, had been evoked in a story, "Y así sucesivamente," published a year earlier in the homonymous collection from 1987. Characterized by the usual discursive fragmentation, the story is comprised of two parts, the first of which is dominated by the present:

> Amar a alguien no es bastante y tal vez por previsión, para no perder nunca lo amado, se aprende a amar todo aquello que lo rodea cuando se está con él. La bufanda que tenía puesta, la camisa, el pañuelo ..., el jardincito abandonado con una estatua de Baco, *o una sirena maltrecha* que no arroja agua, sino barro de su boquita de serpiente. (II 236, emphasis added)

> [To love someone is not enough and perhaps by anticipation, so as to not lose the beloved, one learns to love all that surrounds him when one is with him. The scarf he had on, the shirt, the handkerchief ... the small garden with the abandoned statue of Bacchus, *or a battered mermaid* that spouts, not water, but mud from her serpent mouth.]

Included in the litany of memories enunciated by this anonymous voice, the figure of the mermaid takes form in the second part of the story, marked by an unexpected temporal change and by the introduction of two young protagonists. Here is the passage where one of them, pushed to enter the sea because of tedium and sadness, finds the strange creature:

---

[18]   Graciela Tomassini (*El espejo* 120) discusses Ocampo's recurring use of snow symbolism in the titles and its connotations of death.

[19]   With regard to this interpretation, see Bettelheim 166–83.

Penetraba en el agua como los pájaros acuáticos, siguiendo la línea del volado de agua, que trazaban las olas. De pronto vio lo que no podía creer que fuera cierto: un cuerpo semiacostado en la arena donde se deshacía la última curva de la última ola. Ahí, sumergido hasta la cintura en el agua cuando avanzaban las olas, se veía la parte del torso con el pelo suelto, que podía ser un montón de algas. (238)

[He penetrated the water like the aquatic birds, following the line of the ruffled water that the waves traced. Suddenly he saw what he could not believe was true: a semi-reclined body on the sand where the last curve of the last wave was breaking. There, submerged up to the waist in water when the waves would advance, one could see part of the torso with loose hair that could be a mass of seaweed.]

Fascinated by the young woman, whose curled hair shines under the sun's rays and whose eyes reflect the colors of the sea, the young man realizes that she does not have feet: "Miró para todos lados buscando su toalla, pero no había toalla, ni siquiera vio las huellas de sus pies" (239) [He looked everywhere for her towel, but there was no towel, he did not even see her footprints]. Nonetheless, he falls madly in love with her, which, unlike in Andersen's tale, manages to break her silence: "¿Cómo hará ahora para olvidarla? Estos ojos que está viendo, uno azul y otro verde, nunca se olvidan. ¿Dónde tendrá que huir para olvidarlos? ¿Dónde para oír este silencio? Pero habló" [How will he be able to forget her? These eyes that he is seeing, one blue and the other green, can never be forgotten. Where can he go to hear this silence? But she spoke.]

At every sunset the pair engage in brief and uncertain dialogues. Surprising as always, the end sees the faithful lover disappear in the tide:

Contempló el mundo que lo rodeaba. Se inundó de sal, de yodo, de amor ... Se compró una cámara fotográfica. Retrató a su amada. Conservó el retrato. Se sintió amado, ineludiblemente fiel. Durmió con ella en el agua. No es tan difícil. Ni siquiera imposible, declaró el enamorado. ¿Y ella? Que alguien del fondo del mar conteste. (240)

[He contemplated the world that surrounded him. He was inundated with salt, iodine, love ... He bought a camera. He took a picture of his beloved. He kept the portrait. He felt loved, inescapably faithful. He slept with her in the water. It is not so difficult, nor impossible, declared the lover. And she? May someone from the bottom of the sea answer.]

Projected onto the same fantastic setting in which Andersen had placed his mermaid (a derivation, in turn, from the romantic character of Ondine), these suggestive descriptions from "Y así sucesivamente" disappear completely in

"Permiso de hablar." A modern parable about the impossibility of communication between man and woman, the story published the following year demonstrates rather the analogy between silence and pain. Upon verifying that not even her boyfriend, Teodoro Mudo, manages to understand her, nor is she capable of hearing his miraculously recovered voice, Romina turns into another pained mermaid at the close of the story: "A Romina acabaron por llamarla la Sirena de Andersen, que, al hablar y al moverse, sentía que le clavaban cuchillos en los pies y que nunca pudo declarar su amor al príncipe" (361) [They ended up calling Romina Andersen's Mermaid, who, upon speaking and moving, felt that knives were piercing her feet and that she could never declare her love to the prince]. A few words synthesize the curse pronounced by the witch, whom Andersen's creature consults in order to change her tail into a woman's legs:

> Then your tail will divide in two and shrink into what humans call "pretty legs." But it'll hurt: it'll be like a sharp sword going through you. Everyone who sees you will say you are the loveliest human child they have ever seen. You will keep your graceful movements – no dancer can glide so lightly – but every step you take will feel as if you were treading on a sharp knife, enough to make feet bleed ... Every step she took, as the witch had foretold, was as though she were treading on sharp knives and pricking gimlets; but she gladly put up with that ... Still she went on dancing, although every time her foot touched the ground it felt as though she were treading on sharp knives. (Andersen 150–52, 156–57)

Symbolized by the repetition of the one syntagm ("the sharp knife") at the narrative level, the mermaid's decision to surrender to suffering runs parallel to the witch's demand for the loss of her voice in exchange for her help. This loss also characterizes the strange creature in "Y así sucesivamente," and the protagonist in "Permiso de hablar" replaces it with tears and sighs, the clichéd notion of love's suffering that affects the animal species as well as the human one:[20]

> El llanto nunca fue considerado como palabra: hubo un conflicto porque nadie se ponía de acuerdo sobre este tema ... Hasta los perros habían comprendido que no tenían que ladrar. Acostados sobre la pata derecha inclinaban la cabeza y de vez en cuando silenciosamente suspiraban ...

---

[20] Andersen had already expressed this as a trait of his Little Mermaid. Upon learning that the prince loves another woman she can only sigh: "'I saw the pretty girl he loves better than me' – and the mermaid sighed deeply, for she didn't know how to cry" (160–61). But in the moment of her final transformation she will manage to cry: "And the little mermaid raised her crystal arms towards God's sun, and for the first time she knew the feeling of tears" (169).

Romina trató de decir algo. Ningún sonido salió de su garganta, sólo se oyó un suspiro. El suspiro que marca la época en que desapareció esa costumbre de anunciar el derecho de hablar y del silencio. (360–61)

[Weeping was never considered a word: there was a conflict because no one could agree on this topic … Even the dogs understood they were not supposed to bark. Lying on top of their right paw they would tilt their heads and every once in a while sigh silently … Romina tried to say something. Not one sound came out of her throat, only a sigh. The sigh marked the era in which that custom of announcing the right to speak and to remain silent disappeared.]

The alternation of silence and words which inspires the story ends up radicalizing the conflict elaborated by its archetype.[21] No longer developed in open settings, but instead in enclosed spaces (cinemas, theaters, conference halls) distinguishable through the intermittent lighted signs, the exemplary story of Romina and Teodoro Mudo questions one of the most persistent commonplaces in patriarchal culture: identifying woman with silence and suffering.[22] In contrast to the characters in Andersen's story and "Y así sucesivamente," those in "Permiso de hablar" acquire an identity, even an everyday quality that extracts them from the timeless world of magical heroes and heroines. The question remains, however, whether the anagrams of Romina (Marino means "marine") and the boyfriend's surname (Mudo means "mute") are not clues the author left in order to have us remember the magical tale that precedes the modern short story.

In the Manner of a Fairy Tale

From the aforementioned analyses, it is clear that in the short stories (very short on occasion) in which Silvina Ocampo revisits motifs befitting the classification of folklore,[23] there is a constant contamination between different narrative strategies. The frequent and sudden changes from first to third person, the oscillation between mythical past and quotidian present, the fluctuation between direct and indirect discourse, generate, in these last experiments by Ocampo, a fragmentary and uneven structure, which disregards the fundamental uniformity

21   The same alternation is found in the posthumous story "Silencio y oscuridad," published in *La repeticiones y otros cuentos* 50–53.

22   See Warner, chapter 23 "The Silence of the Daughters: The Little Mermaid" in dialogue with chapter 20 "The Silence of the Fathers" in relation to Blue Beard.

23   At least three of the examples analyzed can be traced back easily to the types Aarne and Thompson proposed: to C 611 (a variant of 311) the forbidden room; to 425 Beauty and the Beast; and to 432 the prince transformed into a bird.

of fairy tales. It is significant that not one of the four stories analyzed starts with the classic incipit, "Once upon a time," but rather they begin *in medias res*, at times directly introducing the protagonist by name:

Se llama Bárbara. No comprendo por qué me casé. ("Jardín," II 315)

[Her name was Barbara. I don't know why I married her.]

Adriana dejó caer su mirada sobre sus pechos. ("Miren," II 366)

[Adriana let her gaze fall to her breasts.]

Desde la mañana oí el canto de aquel pájaro. ("Color," II 371)

[From morning on I heard the song of that bird.]

Las voces se comunicaban por medio de una maravillosa distribución de colores. ("Permiso," II 359)

[The voices would communicate by means of a marvelous distribution of colors.]

Another significant detail is the almost total lack of assistants and opponents, that is, in Vladimir Propp's words, of characters whose function is to obstruct or facilitate the path of the hero or heroine. On the other hand, strongly symbolic characters such as Belle or Blue Beard's wife (also anonymous in Angela Carter's rewritings) acquire a name (Charlotte/Adriana in the first case, Bárbara in the second), just as a name and a precise identity characterize Romina ("our neighbor"), the modern mermaid of "Permiso de hablar." Ocampo's reduction of pre-existing complications to the most minimal terms is resolved in a quick, choppy, and paratactic prose – a prose, careless because of the urgency of contingent, even autobiographical subject matter, which nevertheless shows discursive traces and reminiscences, and at times direct quotations, taken from the most celebrated fairy tales.

One story, however, from *Y así sucesivamente*, appears to refute what has just been asserted. I refer to "El secreto del mal," the story of an empress who becomes ill and whose malady nobody seems able to cure. This story deals with a folkloric motif that Ocampo develops, ostensibly without ignoring the stages that her treatment presumes. After a formulaic incipit ("Once upon a time there was an empress who mysteriously became ill"), the story proceeds with the entrance of a wise man (another standard figure), and his decree that her illness derives from her subjects and that her cure consists in summoning each one of them for a test. Unfortunately, none of her subjects gathered in the plaza guesses the secret of the infirmity, until a boy (who later turns out to be a dwarf) runs

into the room where all the wise men are gathered to announce that the cause
of the evil is a ring the empress wears on her finger. After taking it off the
empress while she sleeps, the dwarf puts it near his ear and "respectfully" listens
to its pronouncement: so that the empress may be cured, it is necessary that her
subjects become ill. It is at this point that the story deviates toward the absurd.
Taking advantage of the people's devotion, which makes them quickly obey the
public health minister's orders – "'¿Ya se enfermaron?' gritó impaciente ... '¡Sí,
sí!' respondieron los súbditos" ["Have you gotten ill?" he shouted impatiently
... "Yes, yes!" the subjects responded] – the empress regains her health:

> Despertó curada, con muy buen apetito. No le bastó el desayuno habitual, le
> sirvieron también una manzana del color de su cara. Al ver que le faltaba el
> anillo se enfureció y ordenó que mataran a los sospechosos, hasta encontrar
> al culpable. Muchos murieron, pero no el enano. (II 200)

> [She awoke cured, with a very good appetite. Her usual breakfast was not
> enough; they also served her an apple the color of her face. When she saw
> that her ring was missing, she became furious and ordered that they kill the
> suspected parties, until they found the guilty one. Many died, but not the
> dwarf.]

Given the expectations created by its quickly succeeding actions, the motif of
the magical ring, and the rigorous past tense, the narration of this apparent fairy
tale ought not deceive us. Despite the folkloric motif that it engages, and the
dialectic between collectivity and power that it presents (similar to the dialectic
in Andersen's "The Emperor's New Clothes"), the story of the dwarf who saved
the empress refers back to another archetype. Behind this strange pair lurks the
celebrated episode of voyeurism from *Orlando Furioso* (that of the queen and
the dwarf, XXVIII, 34–5) which, in turn, was inspired by Scheherazade's story
that frames *The Thousand and One Nights.*[24] Unlike the preceding stories,
characterized by superimposed narrative strategies which at times are openly
in conflict, this one presents a singular homogeneity and uniformity of plot.
The rapid succession of its actions and, above all, its ironic ending ("Many died.
But not the dwarf") suggest, once more, an inversion of the foundational roles
in fairy tales: it is not the emperor now, but rather the empress who exercises
her authority, derived from her unsatisfied sexual drives, on the anonymous
mass of subjects.

---

24   This is according to Cesare Segre's commentary in *Orlando Furioso* (Ariosto 1365).

The Permanence of Eros

In accordance with the circularity that characterizes all of Silvina Ocampo's narratives, the stories analyzed here constitute the fruit of a progressive approximation to a theme or to an archetypal nucleus that was already established. In fact, as we have witnessed, there is a continuity between them, whether they belong to the same collection, as is the case with the closed room which is present in "Cornelia frente al espejo" and in "Jardín de infierno";[25] or to different collections, such as the mermaid in "Y así sucesivamente," destined to reappear in "Permiso de hablar"; or even if they are chronologically far apart, as is the emblematic case of "Paisaje de trapecios," reworked more than thirty years later into "Miren cómo se aman." The "I" which blossoms through the fragmented and repeated diegesis is a kaleidoscopic "I," a product of a changing feminine identity, continually called into question depending on what role she plays in the couple. These roles end up subverting the rigid separation between heroes and heroines, the elemental logic on which fairy tales are founded.

Thus Bárbara/Barba Azul [Blue Beard] converts the prohibition topos, traditionally attributed to men, into an instrument of power in a woman's hands; and the questioning of the beneficent effects of transformation that mark the ending of "Miren cómo se aman" suggests a demystification of the feminine fear of her masculine counterpart's "bestial" instincts. Even in the stories with a more lyrical tone, in which Eros is expressed through evocations and invocations, one can perceive Ocampo's tendency, if not to subvert sexual roles, at least to interchange and sublimate them. The anonymous narrator of "Color del tiempo," for example, identifying herself with Princess Florine from "The Blue Bird," exalts song as the purest form of dialogue between two beings – though not necessarily man and woman – entangled in an eternal passion. And it does not matter if, according to the familiar technique of displacement, the bird's song becomes, at the end of the story, that of a "diminutive monkey" (the least poetic and most human of the animals): what is most important is that it stay recorded in her heart so as to justify the permanence, beyond the concept of time, of every type of Eros. In this sense "Color del tiempo," emphasizing the poetic nucleus of the French story (whose happy ending is completely omitted),

---

[25] A motif that already exists in the last story ("El cerrajero") of *Y así sucesivamente*. The dialogue between the protagonist and the man called upon to open the iron box that contains his stories and poems ends with a clear reference to the murdering husband ("Ya sé que su trabajo es importante, más importante que el mío. Cuando Barba Azul agita sus llaves, al volver a casa, el corazón le palpita" [I know that his work is important, more important than mine. When Blue Beard rattles his keys, upon returning home, his heart beats.]) and with a note of fear ("Para terminar me pidió un cuchillo filoso. ¿Será para matarme?" [In order to finish, he asked me for a sharp knife. Shall it be in order to kill me?]) (II 256–57).

represents an archetype opposite to that of "The Little Mermaid" and Ocampo's double re-elaboration of it. In fact, the anonymous couple of "Y así sucesivamente," as much as Romina and Teodoro Mudo of "Permiso de hablar," participate in the same desire for silence that contradicts the most peculiar (and least erotic) desire of the human condition: communication through words. "Por algo los animales no hablan" (359) [There is a reason why animals do not speak], the narrative voice of "Permiso de hablar" affirms. Faced with the silence to which Romina gradually becomes accustomed, to the point of forgetting the meanings of words and her transformation into a mermaid, her deaf boyfriend, who never spoke, unexpectedly learns to talk. However, it is a useless transformation since no one (least of all Romina) is able to hear his voice, lost "en el ruido ensordecedor de la gente" (360) [in the deafening noise of the people]. On the other hand, the progressive assimilation of Romina into Andersen's fabulous creature suggests the impossibility of dialogue between woman and man, even when, by ironic luck, he manages to surpass his limits.

It is worth noting that all the couples in the stories examined are based on a manifest anomaly. The monkey and the trapeze artist, the blue bird and the female narrator, the deaf mute and the mermaid, the mermaid and the young lover, the empress and the dwarf are all examples of relationships between unequal partners, even different species. These relationships are found frequently in fairy tales but, unlike what happens in these traditional tales, Ocampo's never seem normal; instead they reaffirm, even emphasize, the disparity that characterizes them. So, while in "The Blue Bird" the metamorphosis of the prince/bird is yet one more test for the lovers who recuperate perfect parity and harmony at the end of the story, in "Color del tiempo" the metamorphosis constitutes an immutable condition, or rather mutable within the same natural framework. Similarly, Adriana's disillusionment when she sees her Plinio transformed into a prince reflects the conflicted manner in which women recognize their own instincts. And finally, the gradual slide toward the ocean's depths by the protagonist of "Y así sucesivamente" represents a paradoxical response to the impossible coexistence of the earthbound world with the aquatic one, as Andersen decreed in "The Little Mermaid."

It is as if, on the one hand, Silvina Ocampo allows herself to become fascinated with the animated and indistinct nature that surrounds the hero and heroine in fairy tales, and on the other, refuses to adopt the denouements that restore a disturbed order. On the contrary, her stories always opt for an open, ambiguous, even decidedly shocking ending. One only need think of the brief words of goodbye that the suicidal husband leaves for Bárbara/Blue Beard ("Tu último marido" [Your last husband]); the mechanical alternation at the end of "Miren cómo se aman" ("Mono no, príncipe sí; mono sí, príncipe no") [No to the monkey, yes to the prince; yes to the monkey, no to the prince]); the message

("Y esta grabación sirve" [And this recording serves]) with which the female narrator of "Color del tiempo" reveals *in extremis* her painful absence. If these unexpected endings serve to update and redirect the fragments of a timeless discursive narrative (rhythms, syntagms, reminiscences taken from the most celebrated fairy tales) toward a realistic dimension, they also bear witness to the presence, throughout the author's entire body of work, of phantasms and personal mythologems.

The equation of Eros and animal instinct that Silvina Ocampo focuses on repeatedly in her later writings can be detected from the first: for example, the desire of three friends for a dark horse which dominates a story dated 1937;[26] the hare that the dogs never reach in "La liebre dorada" (*La furia*, 1959); and Miss Fielding's metamorphosis into a cat which closes "El diario de Porfiria Bernal" (*Las invitadas*, 1961). Similarly, the exaltation of the color blue in "Color del tiempo" is a result of the incremental approach to a motif, that of feminine clothes, already addressed in previous stories such as "Las vestiduras peligrosas" (1970), or the even earlier "El vestido verde aceituna" (1937). Hidden on the breast of the mysterious female narrator ("Debajo de mi camisa tengo plumas azules, tan azules como el mar que no conozco" [Under my shirt I have blue feathers, as blue as the sea that I do not know], the feathers of the blue bird thus represent the lyrical and, I would say, metaphysical synthesis of two opposite tendencies present in Ocampo's narrative universe: the insistent attention to the most ephemeral and transient manifestations of daily life and their projection onto a symbolic level. The color blue, like the color green (it is worth mentioning that the mermaid in "Y así sucesivamente" has eyes of two different colors), conjures the mysteries of the marine abyss that Ocampo evoked many times in her stories (from "El mar" in 1937 to the much later "La nave" of 1988), just as other stories refer to the land (for example, "En el bosque de los helechos," 1987). And the land as much as the sea (but also the air, in all its meteorological variations, including fire) form part of an archaic and disintegrated cosmos, an enchanted space that Ocampo cyclically traverses, propelled by her phantasms and by questions that she never manages – even less so in her later writings – to answer.

Translated by Fernanda Zullo-Ruiz

---

[26] I am referring to "El caballo muerto," a story from *Viaje olvidado* that represents, in my opinion, another ironic inversion of a trope – that of the prince on a white horse – proper to fairy tales.

6

In Memory of Silvina Ocampo[*]

Noemí Ulla

> Me gusta el azul, me gustan las uvas, me gusta el hielo,
> me gustan las rosas, me gustan los caballos blancos. Yo
> comprendí que mi felicidad había empezado, porque en
> esas preferencias podía identificarme con Paulina.
> *Adolfo Bioy Casares, "En memoria de Paulina"*

Silvina Ocampo and I became friends immediately, almost by instinct. She discovered this first. More reserved, I was timid at first in showing affection. She, on the other hand, when we had seen each other only once or twice, called me a few days after the death of her sister Victoria to ask if I knew about it. Later I understood the friendly hand she had extended.

4. Silvina Ocampo and Noemí Ulla, 1981.

[*] This essay was originally published as part of a special issue of *Cuadernos Hispano-americanos* in 2002 and later expanded for the new edition of the author's *Encuentros con Silvina Ocampo* (2003). The latter is the version translated here. (translator's note)

I remember her voice and the question, "How are you?" which arose not just from courtesy. If the answer "Fine" failed to convince her – she had a kind of truth detector in her attentive listening – she would reply, "No, you are not fine." It was useless to hide any worries; we already knew each other very well.

Silvina Ocampo was born in Buenos Aires in 1903 at 550 Viamonte, youngest daughter of Manuel Ocampo and Ramona Aguirre. She married Adolfo Bioy Casares in 1940, the year of the publication of the *Anthology of Fantastic Literature*, which they prepared with Borges, their mutual friend, who also served as witness at their wedding. She died in Buenos Aires on December 14, 1993.

In the living room of their house we used to sit and talk among the beautiful jars filled with eucalyptus branches that the mirror on the chimney mantel allowed to reign with grace. There she made me aware of the mystery of those branches, squeezing some of the leaves: "only the male plants produce such a pleasing aroma." We had in common a love of plants and trees. The two of us, in different cities and different times, had grown up playing in gardens along river banks, she in San Isidro on the River Plate and I in Rosario on the Paraná. We knew the names of an infinite number of flowers, but she had studied trees and plants in more detail. Both Silvina and her sister Victoria were proud of their expertise. Many references to nature appear in Silvina's stories and poems. Among them, "Todos los árboles" [All the trees] and "Todos mis metros a la naturaleza" [All my verses to nature], and "Los árboles de Buenos Aires" [The trees of Buenos Aires], included in *Amarillo celeste* (1972).

Around 1980 I was working with Borges on the correction of some poems and we used to linger together through the afternoon. Many times the Bioys would invite us to dinner and Silvina would be happy to see us; if it was summer she would be dressed in a lightweight shirt belonging to Adolfito – as we called him – and since at this time she was translating Emily Dickinson, she would ask Borges questions about English words whose exact meaning in Spanish gave her doubts. She trusted him completely and it was a pleasant scene where two friends shared opinions, argued, searched for the right semantic fit for the word to be translated. However, during the meal Silvina was almost always quiet while the rest, Bioy, Borges, and I, talked, until at some point her energetic voice would rise and she would object to something. I still have in my ear the murmur of those conversations when the friends aimed their comments at some literary curiosity of the moment. Interested in "dejà vu," Borges was talking one night with Bioy during dinner, digging into the depths of the topic, conjecturing about its possibilities with reflections that brought new questions to the fore. Silvina seemed abstracted even though she had many times addressed the same issues, in poems and stories.

What pain Silvina felt at the news of Borges's death! I remember especially one afternoon in which we were united in our grief by silence. Her daughter

Marta observed us, providing care and attention to our sadness, our diminishment, at the table set for two where Silvina and I could scarcely talk, tears interrupting any attempt to speak. Her poem about her love for Borges, written in 1973 (now included in *Poesía inédita*) and called "Homenaje a Jorge Luis Borges," demonstrates all that he meant as poet and as friend, in the memory of their discussions of Rossetti, de Quincey, Lope, Darío; their disagreements about Shakespeare and Baudelaire, Emerson, Wilde, Poe, Almafuerte. In the poem's conclusion she clarifies the difference between them for those whose laziness tended to lump them together or to compare with excessive preference one or the other. Certainly they were poets who have stylistic elements in common and a certain contextual similarity by way of their shared cultural habits. These might deceive on a first reading. But Silvina defined their difference with modesty and firmness:

> Nunca te ha empalagado la poesía
> y ella como una lumbre te acompaña;
> a mí me suele dejarme en las tinieblas.

> [Poetry has never irritated you/ and she ac-
> companies you like a torch;/ as for me she
> usually leaves me in the dark.]

I think that of the literary genres she utilized, it is in poetry, more than in the stories, where she bares her most intimate self. Line, meter, rhyme, both assonant and consonant, seem to give free rein – as contradictory as that may sound – not to her imagination, which never abandoned her, but to the need to show her intimate fabric and to contradict what the classical tradition expects. Obeying various verse structures throughout her long poetic production, she dares to mock the "literary institution," since in that way and under the pretense of respecting and continuing it, she develops themes, motifs, and original scenes both forbidden and almost forbidden, scenes with the intensity that discursive revelation demands. It would be repetitive to provide examples of these assertions, but the best samples are in *Lo amargo por dulce* or *Amarillo celeste*, the latter of which acts as a hinge within her generous poetic work, since in it she begins a partial withdrawal from rhyme. I will name a few poems from both books which represent her intimate discourse as well as classic meter: "Acto de contrición" [Act of contrition], "Morir" [To die], "La casa natal" [Birthplace] (from *Lo amargo por dulce*); "Amor con amor" [Love with love], "Amor," "A mi infancia" [To my childhood], "El duelo" [The wake], "El jabón" [Soap], among others of *Amarillo celeste*; and the sonnet "A España" that I included in *Poesía inédita y dispersa*. With free verse, "El caballo blanco" [The white horse] presents a curious evocation of childhood in the company of her sisters. The first-person voice does not play with autobiographical illusion, but fully embraces the biographical element. If in this poem it is clear that the subject doing the writing (*enonciación*) coincides with the subject of the narrative (*enunciado*), in other poems both the third-person and first-person voices express a greater embodiment of emotion than one finds in the stories.

On just a few occasions did she speak of her father or write about him. The most frequent character in her poems is her mother, as in the "Sonetos del jardín" [Sonnets from the garden] (*Enumeración de la patria*), "La sombrilla" [The parasol] (unpublished but included in *Poesía inédita*), and "Los árboles de Buenos Aires" (*Amarillo celeste*), where the desire to remember and idealize her is most evident and clearly linked to the notion of "mother" nature. However, the father appears as a strangely solitary figure in "Muerte de mi padre" [Death of my father], which I thought indispensable for *Poesía inédita*. With her habitual taste for enumeration and pleasure in description, an element that Philippe Hamon relates to the didactic,[1] Silvina Ocampo embellishes and distinguishes her most intimate poems, and in this one she speaks of the pain that filled the family home because of the suffering of her father:

> El caluroso enero entre persianas frías
> mostraba con pasión su filo iluminado
> y miré con asombro sintiéndome una extraña
> las plantas, los espejos, los retratos, las sillas,
> los ancestrales géneros, las frescas esterillas,
> la lustrosa quietud trémula de la araña
> como si yo a mí misma entre objetos me viera
> desertando lo humano. Sin duda me enajena
> de un modo misterioso, imperioso, la pena
> y me vuelve insensible como un mármol cualquiera.

> [The hot January behind cold blinds
> passionately revealed his lit profile
> and I looked with surprise feeling myself a foreigner
> at the plants, the mirrors, the portraits, the chairs,
> the ancestral fabrics, the fresh cane floor mats
> the lustrous, trembling quiet of the chandelier
> as if among objects I could see myself
> deserting the human. Surely pain distances me
> in a mysterious, imperious way,
> and makes me unfeeling as common marble.]

---

[1]   On the use of enumeration as a device in Silvina Ocampo, see also my study, "Construcción de una poética en la exaltación de la patria: Sara de Ibáñez y Silvina Ocampo."

The paternal figure also appears with all the force of strong feeling in the story "Autobiografía de Irene" and in the poem of the same name. Are the classic eleven-syllable rhyming pairs, used by Lope and Alarcón, what allow her to escape the motif of the longed-for mother? In contrast to the majority of her works, the mother in this magnificent poem appears a bit blurred, and the clarity is carried by the father.

In her later years she began to leave behind the conventions of classical poetic tradition. The sonnet, for instance, is a form she had used frequently despite having called it a "cage" because of its structural restrictions. "Como siempre" [As usual] is a poem in free verse from this period in which she explores the story of an old argument with her sister Victoria. The contradictions of emotional distance and happy memories of childhood sibling intimacy, and the intellectual mentoring which Victoria had offered her since her baptism, are visible here. In part, the difference of age – Victoria was thirteen years older – and, to some extent, the admiration Silvina had for her older sister both impeded an expression of the fondness that she might have wanted to show more openly:

> Aunque no vivamos en un cuento de hadas
> llegaste a mi bautismo,
> y llegaste con un regalo que nadie regala:
> un misterioso amor lírico.
>
> [Although we may not live in a fairy tale
> you arrived at my baptism
> and you arrived with a gift which no one gives:
> a mysterious lyrical love.]

The reproach which Silvina levels at herself is at having procrastinated in mailing a letter written to Victoria. Again, distance triumphed over the show of affection. Once, while a musician of my acquaintance, Simón Blech, directed "The Prince Igor Overture" at a concert that took place in the Plaza San Martín de Tours, just outside the windows of the Bioys' apartment building, Silvina made the following remark: "I never think about Victoria, you know, but when I listen to this piece it makes me sad and I remember her; Victoria was always playing it on the piano." These open-air concerts were performed in the summer of 1987, and Silvina had really liked the one conducted by Simón Blech. Undoubtedly, it had resonated profoundly in evoking the memory of her sister with whom she was united both by trees and plants and by music.

When the years began to slowly fence her in to the point of persuading her to remain at home all the time, it was Bioy who facilitated the possibility of watching videos in order to stimulate her imagination. "See how she reacts to these?" he asked me one day with tenderness, "lots of ideas have come to her; now she is writing something about animals." Without doubt Bioy was the object of Silvina's love, of her most intense passion; the claims of abandonment, the question about the meaning of all things, the doglike happiness at seeing him return at night, are themes that appear in the following poems: "Sonetos de la imaginación" (*Los nombres*), "Amar" [To love], "Qué es amar" [What is to love], "Espera" [Wait] (*Amarillo celeste*), "La llave maestra" [The master key] (*Poesía inédita*). The five poems dedicated to the imagination from *Los nombres* were written in those years in which politically committed literature was declared to have replaced fantasy. In contrast to that dominant critical opinion, her sonnets declare loyalty to the muse, the imagination, and intellectual and loving loyalty to Bioy Casares, to whom they are dedicated:

> En sus efímeras y abiertas manos,
> le entregaré, le entrego el corazón,
> que es de cristal y de adivinación.
>
> La seguiré hasta el fin de los veranos.
> La seguiré por largas galerías
> con la belleza y el horror por guías.
>
> [In her ephemeral and open hands
> I place, now and in the future, my heart
> that is made of crystal and prediction.
>
> I will follow her to the end of all the summers
> I will follow her through long galleries
> with beauty and horror as guides.][2]

More than journeys through space, Silvina was attuned to journeys of the intellect, to which she returns constantly, as in the sonnets mentioned above, asking herself about the origin of things, about abstract and religious motifs, about human and animal behavior. Of these I remember a beautiful poem, "Los delfines" [The dolphins] from *Amarillo celeste*, and an eloquent remembrance of her dog Catriel: "Extraño su discreción, su silencio, sus ladridos, esa manera espontánea que tiene de ser" [I miss his discretion, his silence, his barks, that spontaneous manner]. Meditations, philosophical studies, the process of painting and sketching, the problem of the image and the copy, all these related themes develop from conjecture to affirmation in an unfolding which supplants and corrects ideas continuously. The

---

[2]   The reader should understand that the pronoun references to "her" are to the imagination of the title, mentioned by Ulla a few lines above. (translator's note)

paradigmatic poem "Los diseños" [The designs] (*Los nombres*) uses rhyming twelve-syllable lines which nakedly reveal the power of argumentation and an obvious and fertile ambivalence. To love and not to love, to be present or not, to be abandoned or to abandon, are ambiguous and opposing feelings which the sonnet "El balcón" [The balcony] exemplifies, where Silvina sings to her two countries, France and Argentina, choosing in the end the difficult identity of a kind of exile:

En el verano de un balcón, en Francia,
mirábamos los cedros extranjeros
y un demasiado azul en la distancia
lago, lleno de ceibos y jilgueros.

Nos gustaba una patria más vacía:
No hay aquí una palmera, yo decía.
¡No nos despierta el canto de las aves
con las aguas barrosas, con las naves!

¡Ah! yo prefiero el Río de la Plata.
Fiel a la ausencia y todavía ingrata,
soy a veces aquí una forastera:
falta ahora el balcón, no la palmera,
faltan cedros, y no costas barrosas.
¡Ah, qué azul era el lago y había rosas!

[In the summer of a balcony in France
we watched the foreign cedars
and an impossible blue in the distance
a lake filled with ceibo trees and goldfinches.

We liked a more open country:
There are no palm trees here, I would say
Bird song does not wake us up here
with muddy waters and ships.

Ah! I prefer the River Plate.
Faithful to absence and still ungrateful,
I am here at times a foreigner.
Now I miss the balcony, not the palm tree,
I miss the cedars, not the muddy coasts.
Ah! how blue was the lake and there were roses.][3]

---

3   For a more extensive interpretation of the poems of "Sonetos del jardín," including this one, see my essays in *Invenciones* (2001).

The love for two countries, so present in her work, appeared again with regard to a trip I made to France when I was invited by the University of Toulouse-Le Mirail, at the suggestion of the writer Mario Goloboff. Because of my essay "Tango, rebelión y nostalgia," on tango lyrics, I was invited to participate in the international colloquium in honor of Carlos Gardel. From the moment she found out about this, Silvina started asking me, even more than usual, about what I was going to write for the occasion, about the places I planned to visit, what coat I was going to pack, and she presented me with a beautiful umbrella as a gift. She gave the impression that she herself was the prospective traveler, so much anxiety did she show about what would be my first trip to Europe. Then she asked me to read to the gathered writers, professors, and researchers her poem, "El zorzal insistente" [The insistent thrush], dedicated to Gardel; Milagros Ezquerro and I did a joint reading in Spanish and French that autumn of 1984.[4] She always remembered Gardel with emotion, in contrast to Bioy and Borges who were less enthusiastic.

One day she surprised me with a portrait she had done of me, not for the first or the last time, since she liked to draw her friends. But this one was different. When I saw it, the head surrounded by colored flowers and butterflies, I realized that she had interpreted what I had felt about going to France, a dream of mine since my adolescent studies of French. Years later I chose that portrait for the cover of my book *El ramito*. Silvina wanted to know if I wrote fiction, "You have so much imagination but you don't give yourself time to write and life taught you to be this way. You don't have time for yourself; your hours are taken from you." She lamented that I didn't have enough time to write more in the midst of the mad mixture of activities that absorbed my attention and from which she would have liked to free me. She worried a lot about those around her, that they might not be able to realize their dreams; often she lamented Borges's illness and the impossibility of his being able to recover his sight. "Can you imagine, poor Georgie, what he must suffer?" she used to say. She spoke often of my story collection *Ciudades* and she wrote a poem based on one of her favorites.[5] I was pleased especially by one comment she made, "You have such freedom in your writing!" Her observation certainly stemmed from the rigorous traditional literary forms which had been demanded of her and which only later was she able to abandon, especially in her last two volumes of stories, *Y así sucesivamente* and *Cornelia frente al espejo*.

---

[4]   "El zorzal insistente" was included, without its French translation, in the volume published following the conference: *Le tango: Hommage a Carlos Gardel*. Toulouse: Université Toulouse-Le Mirail: Eché, 1985, 9. (translator's note)

[5]   This poem, "Éxtasis," was included in my book's French translation (1994) and later the original Spanish version was included in *Poesía inédita* (2001).

The special, vacillating sound of her voice, as if she were creating the mystery and the joy of telling a story, is still present in my memory. Today, the importance of what she wrote is beginning to be appreciated, even by her past detractors, whose criticism, based on the ideological prejudices that censured her imagination because of a lack of political commitment, forgot that both the literature of witness, of denunciation, and that of the imagination can coexist in a civilized society. Undaunted by fads, and without actively planning it, Silvina Ocampo has imposed herself as required reading. Her talent, the special innovation of her writing, her translations of poetry, her personal imprint on the arts, require an undisputed place in universal literature which few writing in Spanish from her day so amply deserve.

Translated by Patricia N. Klingenberg

7

Classical Reference in Silvina Ocampo's Poetry*

FIONA J. MACKINTOSH

Silvina Ocampo's work abounds in classical references. Many of her best-known stories are peopled by curious *cursi* or mundane modern incarnations of furies, fates, seers, and sibyls, as well as by quirky characters bearing weighty names such as Ulysses, Isis, Athropos, Rhadamanthos, The Three Fates, and The Three Furies.[1] Her peculiar genius is to be found in the ways in which, as Noemí Ulla has observed, Ocampo makes the meanings of this classical mythology resonate with her own network of myths, and also in her ability to integrate the world of Greek and Latin culture and mythology into the everyday (*Invenciones* 80–81, 182). Ocampo's poems, even more so than her short stories, make repeated reference to classical mythical figures, yet this important dimension of her work has not yet been fully explored by critics.[2] I therefore propose to present an overview of classical references in Ocampo's poetry, examining the various ways in which she draws upon classical mythology. I shall argue that Ocampo obliges the reader to consider her chosen classical references in a new light, whether by virtue of geopolitical repositioning or metapoetic reflections. I will then focus in the final pages of the chapter on the mythical character to whom she affords the most extended treatment, namely Narcissus.

*   I am greatly indebted to my colleague Professor Isabel Torres at Queen's University Belfast, for her careful reading of, and extensive feedback on, an earlier version of this article, as well as for numerous pointers to specific classical sources.

1   For an example of the work done on classical reference in Ocampo's stories, see Brenda Sánchez. In my discussion I will use the English transliterations of the classical names, but when quoting directly from Ocampo's work, I will obviously retain the Spanish versions. All translations are mine, unless otherwise indicated.

2   Noemí Ulla makes many important observations regarding Ocampo's classical heritage in both *Encuentros* (1982) and *Invenciones* (2000), but this topic was not the main focus of her studies of Ocampo's poetry.

Context: Ocampo's Acquaintance with the Classics

Ocampo was home-schooled with French and English governesses, and – as far as I can ascertain – for her, as for many of her contemporaries, much of her acquaintance with classical references was, at least initially, mediated through other literature (Campuzano 325). It is therefore to Ocampo's extensive reading of English, French, and Spanish poetry that we must turn first in order to appreciate an important dimension of her acquaintance with the classical world. First, we can see a rich mine of classical allusions and references in those anglophone poets that Ocampo translated for publication in her sister Victoria's influential cultural journal *Sur*, and those she translated and published alongside her own poetry in *Lo amargo por dulce* (1962). These poets include Shakespeare, Donne, Pope, Wordsworth, Byron, Keats, Walter de la Mare, David Gascoyne, Kathleen Raine, Graham Greene, Stephen Spender, Vita Sackville-West, Edith Sitwell, and Edwin Muir.[3] Further possible sources of classical references are the anglophone poets she translated and/or introduced in the 1949 volume *Poetas líricos ingleses* [English lyric poets], edited by Ricardo Baeza, for which she wrote an extensive introductory essay.[4] Baeza says of the collection: "Los autores reunidos son ... los cimientos mismos de la cultura occidental y de una u otra manera, cada uno de nosotros halla en ellos el eco de sus propias ideas y sentimientos" (vii) [The authors gathered here are ... the very foundations of Western culture and in one way or another, each of us finds in them the echo of his/her own ideas and feelings]. Perhaps such an echo operates for Ocampo when she passionately defends Milton's use of mythological characters or when she waxes lyrical about Keats's works inspired by his love of Greek mythology, such as *Endymion* (which, as well as familiarizing Ocampo with Endymion and Cynthia, brings in Venus and Adonis, Clauco and Scylla, and Arethusa), and *Hyperion* (which references Hyperion, Saturn, Apollo, and Moneta), and when she extols his "Ode on a Grecian Urn" (Baeza xxx). Of Poe, she admires "To Helen," "Ulalume," and "Eulaly" (xxxii), while she praises Tennyson for *Ulysses*, *Tithonus*, *The Lotus-Eaters*, *Œnone*, and *Hero to Leander*, among others (xxxiii). In Swinburne she favours *Laus Veneris*, *Atalanta in Calydon*, and *The Garden of Proserpine* (xli). She describes how we absorb certain lines of poetry subconsciously, and for her, the poets whose lines she remembers include Garcilaso, Ronsard, San Juan de la Cruz, Góngora, Quevedo, Donne, Milton, Bécquer, and Darío

---

3   For a discussion of Ocampo's relationship to British poetry, see my 2004 article, "My Dreams are a Field Afar."
4   "Ingleses" [English] is here used by Baeza in a general way to mean "writing in English," so the term includes Poe and others.

(xxxv–xxxvi), all of whom are heavily steeped in the classical tradition, albeit in response to highly differing aesthetic imperatives.

As we turn, secondly, to her absorption of classical references through French poetry, we know from Ulla and Bioy Casares that she read and liked Valéry, whose many works dealing with Narcissus may well have had a bearing on her own fondness for this particular figure. Valéry wrote a poem entitled "Narcisse parle," a title which, if literally rendered into Spanish, is also coincidentally the title of Ocampo's longest poem on the subject of Narcissus, "Habla Narciso" [Narcissus speaks], an analysis of which will be the focus of the final section of this chapter. Valéry also wrote "Fragments du Narcisse" as well as a cantata on the subject of Narcissus. Ocampo translated many French poems with classical references, a selection of which are included in her *Poemas de amor desesperado* (1949). For example, her translations of Ronsard sonnets include references to Crete, Theseus, the Aegean sea, Helen, and Cassandra; she translated Nerval's "El desdichado" [The unhappy one] which references Orpheus. Her own poems "A Francia" and "Tarjeta postal" [Postcard] (*Espacios métricos*) willingly confess the magnitude of her cultural debt to France, and her published translation of Horace's Ode V appears (according to the slightly ambiguous editor's note) to have been translated through the French, not directly from Latin (*Poesía completa* I 287). This reinforces the impression that Ocampo's acquaintance with the classics was initially mediated, whether by reading classical authors in translation, or reading imitations of, and homages to, classical figures in later works.

Turning thirdly to Ocampo's knowledge of Hispanic Golden Age poets, for whom classical imitation and homage are key aesthetic impulses, we see that her reading in this area was also considerable, Garcilaso de la Vega and Luis de Góngora being key points of reference. For example, "La abandonada" of *Espacios métricos* takes an epigraph from Garcilaso. As Juan Alfonso Carrizo puts it, "La madre patria fue para América la puerta por donde entraba Europa y, con ella, toda la cultura greco-latina" (20) [The mother country was for America the doorway through which came Europe and with it, the whole of Greek and Latin culture], visible in everything from legal structures such as the senate to literary epics in the classical manner.[5] Ocampo also had various important classically inspired Latin American poetic precursors such as Leopoldo Lugones, a key figure in the *Antología poética argentina* (1941) which Ocampo edited with Bioy Casares and Borges, and – almost inevitably for any twentieth-century Latin American poet – the founder of Latin American *modernismo*, Rubén Darío. Darío's four poems "Los cisnes" [The swans], from his 1905

---

5   For an overview of the general history of classical culture in Argentina, see Assis de Rojo and Flawia de Fernández.

collection *Cantos de vida y esperanza*, include a sonnet on Leda and the swan in the light of which Ocampo's sonnet "Leda y el cisne" (*Los nombres*) can productively be read as a kind of gendered Bloomian revisionary movement from the strong precursor (Bloom 10). Her version of the myth, rather than replaying the scene as a rape or a seduction, focuses on the reflection in the water of both woman and bird, making them equals.

In addition to her absorption of classical sources mediated through modern anglophone, French, and Hispanic texts, Ocampo's immediate domestic environment, which even included pet dogs rejoicing in nobly classical names such as Diana and Áyax, contributed to the impact of the classical world on her poetic production. Bioy Casares's exhaustive memoir *Borges* (2006) testifies to the fact that the classical world and classical literature were among the topics of conversation when Borges dined (almost daily!) with him and Silvina. Take for example the entry for 2 November 1963, where Bioy records that they discussed Rome and Athens, looking up the dates of Homer, Hesiod, Socrates, Cato, Virgil, Juvenal, Livy, and Darío in Webster's Biographical Dictionary (Bioy Casares, *Borges* 971). Clearly part of their knowledge of the history of classical literature was gleaned from browsing such dictionaries, and Rubén Darío was viewed by them as a logical continuation of this tradition. In the entry for 15 June 1957, Bioy notes their discussion of the *Odyssey* and the *Iliad* (290), which included commenting on Eugenio de Ochoa's Spanish translation of the *Aeneid*, Pope's translation of the *Odyssey*, and Tennyson's translation of fragments of the *Iliad*, implying that in their appreciation of classical literature, an awareness of issues of translation was paramount. That Ocampo was equally sensitive to these questions can be seen in the multilingual production of *Narciso/Narcissus* (1987), which contains not only her poem "Habla Narciso" in her own Spanish and English versions, but also Ovid's Latin version of the Narcissus myth with a Spanish verse translation of it alongside.[6]

The final significant piece in the contextual jigsaw of Ocampo's interest in the classical world is found in Juan Rodolfo Wilcock, her close friend and collaborator. They co-authored a play, *Los traidores* (1956), which is set in Rome in the year AD 211 and bases its main characters and events on Roman history. Septimus Severus's sons, Caracalla and Geta, appear alongside assorted Eumenides, minor characters, and ghosts. Other classical references abound in Wilcock's own work; for example, his 1953 volume *Sexto* contains "Hae puellae" [These girls] (9–10) which links classical muses to a decadent contemporary Argentinian cityscape. So overall, Ocampo's cultural context – both at the macro level of Latin American literary culture through Lugones, Darío, et al., and at

---

6   References to Ovid's *Metamorphosis* are to the Latin Library online. Citations in the text are given by book in Roman numerals then line numbers. (editor's note)

the micro level of her own immediate circle, her readings and translations – demonstrates a rich and active engagement with classical tradition, the poetic manifestations of which this chapter seeks to explore.

Ocampo's Poetry: General Classical Traits

Turning now to Ocampo's own poetry, right from her first collection, *Enumeración de la patria* (1942), this sense of engagement with classical tradition, particularly epic conventions, is apparent. Helena Percas (*La poesía femenina* 627) and Noemí Ulla (*Invenciones* 21) draw attention to the classical accent in formal and metrical terms of both *Enumeración...* and *Espacios métricos* (1945). There are clear classical precedents for the act of a poet charting his or her relationship to the (home)land, such as Virgil's *Georgics* or Hesiod's *Works and Days*, as well as more recent Latin American precedents in the classical manner, such as Rubén Darío's exuberant *Canto a la Argentina* (1910), which celebrates the centenary of Argentine independence, calling Argentina a pupil of the Musagetes and praising its Homeric voice. Ulla notes a classical precedent in Ocampo's use of anaphoric and asyndetic structures in *Enumeración* (*Invenciones* 44) while Borges, in his review of this same collection, likens her use of catalogues to Virgil. Indeed, such epic-style catalogues recur throughout her poetic production, for example the explicitly entitled catalogue of trees in "Los árboles de Buenos Aires" from *Amarillo celeste* (1972), which has classical precedents in Book II of Virgil's *Georgics* or Book X of Ovid's *Metamorphoses*. She favours the title "Dialogue" for various poems, for example "Diálogo de Narciso" (*Espacios métricos*) or "Diálogo de la diosa" [Dialogue of the goddess], and references Plato's *Dialogues* in "La belleza" [Beauty] (*Poemas de amor desesperado*), remarking archly that Plato's extensive discussion of beauty in his Dialogues was in vain. It is interesting that Borges's review of *Enumeración de la patria* likens Ocampo to Walt Whitman, whose "After all, not to create only" (1871) calls on the Muse to "migrate from Greece and Ionia" to a "better, fresher, busier sphere"; Borges also likens her to Virgil. As Fiona Cox has noted, "Virgil is integral to the American ambition to transport the authority and glory of Rome into a new continent" (10–11). Ocampo's enumeration of her homeland is ambiguous in its ambition, not so much nation building as quirkily individual invention. Typical of this quirkiness is her staging of a classical atmosphere through the literary topos of a landscape of statues, but statues frequently in ruins. For example, "Lamentos del vano amor" [Laments of vain love] (*Lo amargo por dulce*) is dedicated to a broken statue. Such images may indicate a reaction to Darío's subservience to the classical world in his *modernista* gardens, since as Ulla notes with reference to Ocampo, "los jardines del Modernismo con sus cisnes y sus hermosas estatuas han quedado atrás ... sus estatuas aparecen rotas y así es como las admira' (*Invenciones* 22–23) [the gardens of *modernismo* with their swans and their beautiful statues have been left behind ... her statues appear broken and that is how she admires them]. But this aesthetic appreciation of ruins in Ocampo's poetry could also be placed within a wider framework of ruins as reminders of both tradition and transience.

Ovid's *Metamorphoses*: A Tradition of Transformation

The poet within the classical tradition to whom Ocampo's work is most directly indebted is Ovid. As Isabel Torres has noted, the first Spanish translation of Ovid, by Jorge Bustamante in the mid-sixteenth century, was entitled *Transformaciones* rather than the more obvious cognate *Metamorfosis* (*Rewriting* 8), and the preponderance of the verb "transformar," together with the overwhelming importance of the process of transformation in Ocampo's poetry (which Ulla identifies as a classical inheritance, *Invenciones* 73), clearly singles out Ovid's *Metamorphoses* as a key point of reference.[7] Indeed, Ovidian transformations are one of the most constant features of Ocampo's poetry. In "Sueña con su muerte una prostituta" [A prostitute dreams of her death], the poetic voice claims she could transform herself into many other things, ranging from sounds, "una lejana música" [a distant music], and sights, "un rostro reflejado en una miniatura" [a face reflected in a miniatura], to experiences, such as "una noche de mayo" [a night in May] (*Poesía completa* II 330).

Ocampo's anthropomorphic treatment of trees and plants further reveals her underlying sympathy with the world of Ovid's *Metamorphoses*, where humans can be rendered into plants at the whim of a jealous god.[8] Indeed, the opening poem of *Árboles de Buenos Aires* sets a mythic scene in which, at closing time in the Jardín Botánico, trees and statues dance, and the poet insists that it is neither an illusion nor the wind as they join hands and bathe in the fountain. The poet tries to imagine what the plants say (as so often in *Metamorphoses*, the human who has recently been turned into a tree or plant or animal tries vainly to speak). She imagines that some confess to being hermaphrodites, as if, like in the myth of Salmacis and Hermaphroditus (*Met.* IV.285–388), their bathing in the fountain had turned them into such creatures. The poet herself would like to have been a tree, thereby desiring the kind of metamorphosis that in Ovid may save vestal virgins from the amorous designs of rapacious gods.

---

[7]   Jorge Monteleone gives it a different twist, however, linking Ocampo's fondness for transformation to an instinctive avoidance of autobiographical revelation (2).

[8]   This kind of sympathy is also present in some of her more fantastic fiction, for example "Hombres, animales, enredaderas" [Men, animals, vines] (*Los días de la noche*), or "Sábanas de tierra" [Sheets of earth] (*Y así sucesivamente*). Both are newly available in English translation in Balderston's *Thus Were Their Faces*.

Yet as well as projecting herself into the tree through desire, she also maintains her external view of the situation, imagining what the plants hear as the one who loves them walks away (*Poesía completa* II 209). The poet thus performs a delicate balancing act, desiring to be the tree yet regarding it as other (in contrast to, for example, the Pablo Neruda of "Entrada a la madera," who finally enters into a kind of ecstatic oneness with the tree).[9] She maintains control of the trope of metamorphosis, here exploiting it solely in the hypothetical realm and thereby implicitly making it a metapoetical comment on poetic freedom.

Within *Poemas de amor desesperado*, there is a whole series of poems which revolve around transformation or metamorphosis: "El maleficio" [The curse], "Castigo" [Punishment], "Canto" [Song], "La metamorfosis," "Anáfora" [Anaphora], "Transformación," and "Fantasmas de las glicinas" [Ghosts of the wisterias]. In later volumes, we have "Alquimia traslúcida" [Translucent Alchemy (Weiss)] (*Lo amargo por dulce*),[10] "Metamorfosis" (*Árboles de Buenos Aires*) and "Lecciones de metamorfosis" [Lessons in metamorphosis] (*Poesía inédita y dispersa*). These poems of transformation range from brief quatrains to extended tripartite narrative poems, and the changes are sometimes narrated in poems which also dramatize an audience reaction to the transformation, as Ovid does in some of his nested episodes where another tale is told to explain the back history to the current tale (for example, the interpolated tales in the Orphic account across *Met.* X–XI). I will analyse in detail some of these transformatory poems, in order to give specific examples of the varied ends to which Ocampo uses transformation.

"La metamorfosis" is a narrative poem with a concrete dramatic turning point. The female poetic voice seeks to know the truth about her unfaithful lover by spying through his window. Even at the outset this poem promises revelation on various levels, since it seeks "la múltiple verdad" [the multiple truth] – implying the existence of different truths from different perspectives, or wider philosophical truths in contrast to the narrow circumstantial truth. The quatrains consist of three *alejandrinos* [fourteen-syllable lines] followed by one heptasyllabic line, with the rhyme scheme ABAB. This construction of the quatrain has clear parallels with the classical Sapphic ode, which also has three long lines followed by one short, with the ABAB rhyme scheme. In the fifth of these quatrains comes the moment of truth, when having seen what she most dreaded, "Cambió toda mi vida" [My whole life changed]. From this point onwards, as if catalysed by the verb "cambiar," the poetic voice goes through a giddying series of vengeful transformations:

---

9   Published as one of "Tres cantos materiales" in *Residencia en la tierra II*.

10   Jason Weiss has published a selection of Ocampo's poetry in translation (*Silvina Ocampo* 2015), and all quotations from this are marked "Weiss."

Fui la sombra, el obstáculo, fui un abismo infinito
donde el perfume pérfido del jazmín se elevaba.
En un furioso mar, fui el no escuchado grito
de un hombre que me amaba.

Fui veneno y cuchillo, lepra en una mejilla,
fui el ladrido del perro, en mi desolación,
la muerte numerosa y en su lejana orilla
fui sólo un corazón.

(Poesía completa I 222)

[I was the shadow, the obstacle, an infinite abyss
where the jasmine's perfidious perfume rose up.
In a furious sea, I was the unheeded shout
of a man who used to love me.

I was poison and knife, leprosy on a cheek,
I was the bark of a dog, in my desolation,
numerous death and on its far shore
I was just a heart.]

In each incarnation, the poet effectively imagines her participation in the unfaithful lover's downfall, but in doing so, entangles herself in his imagined pain, as when she becomes his drowning cry for help which is ignored. The idea of transforming into a dog, here in order to bark pain and aggression (presumably in a more visceral way than words could express), is a particular *leitmotif* in Ocampo's poetry, as we shall see later with reference to "Espera" and "Habla Narciso."[11] The poet then tries to knock on the lover's window, but cannot, as her hand had transformed into a bunch of feathers. She desperately asks love what she is now, only to then supply the answer herself:

Ave, piedra o araña, uno de los cipreses
o nada, tal vez hoy. (222)

[Bird, stone or spider, one of the cypresses
or nothing, perhaps today.]

These various transformations into bird, stone, spider, or cypress tree all have well-known Ovidian precedents (Ino's companions, the Theban women, are changed into rocks and birds; Arachne becomes a spider, Cyparissus a cypress),

---

[11] The *leitmotif* is shared with her prose, and to some extent with that of Bioy Casares. See my essay, "Bioy, Ocampo and the Photographic Image" 143.

and the characteristic Ovidian suddenness of such transformations appears to underlie the poet's final observation, made just before turning into a creeper: "Morir es transformarse en lo que no se espera" [To die is to transform into what one does not expect], as if to say that what we usually refer to as death is not to be feared, since it is (merely) an *expected* transformation – into a corpse; what really hurt are the *unexpected* and therefore cruelly abrupt transformations as a result of amorous catastrophe or jealous revenge which strike us in the midst of life. They are the real definition of dying. So Ocampo uses Ovidian metamorphoses to underline the violent shattering of sense of self occasioned by betrayal in love. But reading a metapoetic dimension to the outcome is also possible, in that we could see the list of transformations which have clear Ovidian precedents as also being *expected* poetic transformations, expected by virtue of poetic tradition and *imitatio*.[12] In this scenario, dying – which is always unique (following Derrida, "Chaque fois unique, la fin du monde") – breaks with poetic imitation.

In the second of the "Sonetos de amor desesperado" we have a reference to Attis, shepherd of Phrygia, in which the poet, suffering unrequited love, wishes for what Attis suffered as a punishment (being turned into a pine tree), in order that she may finally achieve indifference to the object of her affection.

> Atis, con tu follaje, noblemente
> podría al fin ser yo la indiferente.
> (*Poesía completa* I 208)

> [Attis, with your foliage, I could nobly be
> at last, indifferent as he.]

Here, the intertextual reference activates a model of excessive desire which is excessively punished. In Ovid (*Fasti* IV), Attis broke his vow of chastity to the goddess Cybele with a Naiad; in revenge, Cybele killed the Naiad by wounding her tree; at this, Attis went mad with grief and castrated himself, and then (as the story goes in *Met.* X.103–5) was turned into a pine tree. What is interesting about Ocampo's appropriation of this story is the gender dimension: her poetic persona invokes a self-castrated male to overcome desire for a man, thus introducing – albeit by negation – a homoerotic touch, as she will later in her short story "Amada en el amado" [*Los días de la noche*] where by entering her male lover's dreams of other women, the female narrator becomes a lesbian. In the fifth of these sonnets we have the "Helíades," who in Ovid (*Met.* II.340–66) wept so for the loss of their

12 See Torres (*Love Poetry* 11–16) for exemplification of Golden Age poets' "desire to exceed the achievements of Classical and Renaissance vernacular models" (xii).

brother Phaeton that they were turned into poplars. The poet's apostrophe to these poplars initially appears to imply sisterhood, addressing them as "hermanas en la pena" [sisters in grief], yet in the first line of the two tercets we realize that she is in fact setting herself apart from these possible co-sufferers: "¡Fraternales follajes!, yo estoy sola" (209) [fraternal foliages!, I am alone]. So the potential for achieving sibling sympathy by the poetic gesture of aligning herself to these female classical figures of suffering is enacted and simultaneously negated, intimating that her grief is greater, since it is not shared. Thus here the classical model is invoked and rejected, in order to dramatize both the extent of her suffering (a way, as she put it in defending Milton, of versifying our pain [Baeza xvii]) and also, metapoetically, to illustrate the Bloomian struggle of the belated modern poet with the twin poles of imitation and individual expression.

Having thus far seen Ocampo's use of transformation to explore love betrayed, unrequited, indifferent, and lamented, we move in "Castigo" to the transformatory punishment which love can inflict. This pithy poem (threat or prophecy?) consists of a single quatrain, again reminiscent of the pattern of the Sapphic ode, which activates the world of classical mythology through reference to Minerva, Roman goddess of wisdom, and Medusa, snake-haired Gorgon of Greek mythology who would turn to stone anyone who gazed into her eyes. The poetic "I" addresses an unspecified "you" who occupies the position of Medusa in the equivalent Ovidian passage (*Met.* IV.791–801). Given its brevity, I quote "Castigo" [Punishment] in full:

> Transformará Minerva tus cabellos
> en serpientes y un día al contemplarte
> como en un templo oscuro, con destellos,
> seré de piedra, para amarte.
> > (*Poesía completa* I 217)

> [Minerva will transform your locks
> into snakes and one day as I look at you
> as if in a dark temple, with flashes of light
> I will be stone, to love you.]

What is so compelling about this body blow of a poem is the sense of an evolving transformative process projected into the future: Minerva will transform the lover whose gaze will then petrify the speaker. Its brevity assumes knowledge of the mythical intertext; it omits accusation or details of the offence for which this transformation is the punishment, even leaving us in doubt as to the speaker's feelings about the situation. Is it bitter, triumphant, perverse? Yet the speaker has already performed the ultimate act of transformation by turning the projected event into a poem, the poetic agency thus undercutting the tone of willing submission. In this way, Ocampo appears to be using the well-known mytheme not only to underline the poet's freedom to transform any subject, but also to express her characteristically ambiguous view of love, summed up in the title of the work she had co-authored with Bioy Casares only a couple of years previously, *Los que aman, odian* (1946) [Those Who Love, Hate].[13]

The "lover who is turned to stone" mytheme recurs in "El maleficio" [The curse]; this retells the story of poor Eumetis who has turned into a statue outside the door of the lover who cruelly abandoned her. The poem is constructed with an internal framing narrative: the first stanza introduces Eumetis, in whose dead hand there is a manuscript in which she has written her story in the form of a letter-poem addressed to her faithless lover. This literary sub-genre points to a possible classical precedent in Ovid's *Heroides*. The rest of the poem presents her story as read aloud by her lover (the shift in voice indicated visually by the use of italics), who presumably discovered the paper in Eumetis's dead hand. We are thus allowed to "overhear" a secret communication: "De los remotos labios de su amado/ esuchad el secreto revelado" [From the remote lips of her lover/ hear the secret revealed] (*Poesía completa* I 211). The use of the *vosotros* form, "escuchad," rather than *ustedes*, is unusual for Ocampo, though she also uses it in "Fantasmas de las glicinas" and in the Helíades sonnet discussed earlier, giving the declaration an oratorical feel of addressing an audience. This theatricality is further emphasized by the deliberate scene-setting of the opening lines, which give us the backdrop and plot summary in succinct headline format: "Antros de oscuridad. Elaborada/ venganza del amor enamorada" (211) [Dark haunts. Elaborate/ revenge of love in love]. Eumetis exacts her revenge by foretelling her lover's consignment to oblivion, where – she exclaims maliciously – "ah, todo, todo te será vedado" (214) [ah, all, all will be forbidden to you], while she will live on in these lines of poetry. So, she may have become a statue, a monument to her living self, but she also has a second avatar in her written self.[14] Once again, Ocampo uses the classical mytheme as a way of dramatizing the poet's ultimate power of transformation, triumphing over petrification through the written word.

There is a very interesting parallel between this poem and "Canto" [Song], which features transformation. In "Canto," the poet uses a very similar line structure to that of Eumetis's vengeful phrase previously quoted. But here, rather than *everything* being *forbidden* to the faithless lover, *nothing belongs* to the poetic voice: "¡Ah, nada, nada, es mío! (*Poesía completa* I 218) [ah, nothing, nothing is mine!]. This parallel between the two poems, whether

---

13   Thanks are due to Isabel Torres for pointing out a classical precedent for this title in a two-verse Catullus poem: "Odi et amo, quare id faciam, fortasse requires? Nescio, sed fieri sentio et excrucior" [I hate and I love. Perhaps you wonder how this is so? I don't know. I only feel it and it is excruciating.]

14   Thanks are due to Isabel Torres for the observation that rivalry between sculptural and written memorials for poetic immortality has its *locus classicus* in Horace *Odes* 3.30.

conscious on the part of Ocampo or not, is pertinent, since one is the flip side of the other. In "El maleficio," the whole world has been rendered beyond the cursed lover's reach; in "Canto," the poetic voice can be like the whole world, she can even *be* the whole world, but none of it belongs to her. In a tacit allusion to Narcissus and Echo, the poet figures herself as secondary to the natural world, the emphasis on repeated 'e/o' vowel sounds underlining the echo effect:

> Soy como los reflejos de un lago tenebroso
> o el eco de las voces en el fondo de un pozo
>
> (218)

> [I am like the reflections of a gloomy lake
> or the echo of voices at the bottom of a well
>
> (Weiss 55)

Then she goes on to inhabit, or transform herself into, various different shapes and forms:

> Soy el lebrel que huyó en la lejanía
> la rama solitaria entre las ramas
>
> (219)

> [I am the greyhound that fled in the distance,
> the solitary branch among the branches
>
> (Weiss 55–56)

But as she laments, there is always an unbridgeable gap between this protean poetic self and any sense of ownership. They are like so many guises, temporary masks, and ultimately the poet owns nothing.

> Mas todo es inasible como el viento y el río...
> Soy todo, pero nada, nada es mío
>
> (219)

> [But everything's elusive like the wind and the river...
> I am everything, but nothing, nothing is mine]
>
> (Weiss 56)

Here once again Ocampo exploits metamorphosis for what Torres calls, speaking of Ovid, its "metapoetic potential ... as a figure for the processes of artistic creation" (*Rewriting* 8), though the idea of owning nothing is not necessarily to be read in a negative fashion. It is, after all, within the context of a song rather than a lament, and the twice-repeated phrase "Todo lo he recibido" [I have received it all (Weiss 55)] could point to a positive celebration on Ocampo's part of an inherited poetic tradition, and of what Stephen Hinds calls "the echoic element in discourse itself" (16).

This leads us to the fact that Ocampo sits very comfortably within a tradition of rewriting, palimpsest, imitation, myths with no "original" source, and apocryphal versions – "apócrifo" being another of her key words, like "transformar," "previsto" [foreseen], and "predestinado" [predestined]. A typical example of Ocampo's relaxed (and somewhat Borgesian) attitude to authorship and originality is the note she appends to her poem "Los días perdidos" [The lost days] (*Lo amargo por dulce*), where she confesses to not knowing whether the poem is originally hers or a translation from English; whichever, the poem has gone on growing and has become hers (*Poesía completa* II 38). Likewise the relationship of her classical references to the "originals": the whole cast of classical characters scattered across her poetic oeuvre is largely, to borrow Hinds's phrase about tradition, "mobilized ... for the particular purposes of particular poems, and even for the particular purposes of particular moments in particular poems" (123). These purposes in Ocampo, when not exploring the many facets of love, are frequently metapoetical. To take one example, in "Promesa" [Promise] (*Espacios métricos*), a kind of poetic farewell to life, great mythical lovers are mobilized for the purpose of representing inescapable ephemerality; Pyramus and Thisbe, Cassandra, Leda and the swan, all vanish, but their passing allows the poet to offer metapoetic commentary on the way such references to mythical and historical figures move allusively from poem to poem:

> las sombras de Marius y Yugurta
> en un poema inglés se alejan juntas,
> entran en la elegía de Propercio
> mezclándose a los metros de otros versos
> > (*Poesía completa* I 96)

> [the shadows of Marius and Jugurtha
> in an English poem retreat side by side,
> they enter Propertius's elegy
> mixing into the metres of other lines.]

Here she is presumably referring to Ezra Pound's "Homage to Sextus Propertius," an "English" poem in a broad sense.[15] Her poem sees the enemies retreating together, joined by the metrical pull of poetry.

---

15   Marius and Jugurtha fought against one another in the Jugurthine war of 111–104 BC. Pound's "Homage" is part translation, part interpretation of some of Propertius's love elegies. See Tryphonopoulos and Adams 147–8.

In "Tácita" (*Espacios métricos*) Ocampo mobilizes the silent goddess Dea Tacita for the purpose of representing another important metapoetic dimension, that of the value of silence. "Tácita" weighs up the potential of silence to be both blessing and curse in a bipartite poem addressing the goddess in the second person. The two parts are emphasized by parallel lines with opposing meanings, and the goddess's nature is determined not by herself, but by the contradictory human emotions which colour the poet's attitude towards her. For example, part one opens with the exclamation "Qué horrida es tu llegada si vanamente he hablado" (*Poesía completa* I 90) [How horrid is your arrival if vainly I have spoken], whereas part two exclaims equally fervently, "Qué dulce es el silencio después de haber hablado" (91) [How sweet is silence after having spoken]. In part one, silence has a negative charge of words withheld: "qué perversa es la voz de los labios callados" (90) [how perverse is the voice of silent lips] and furthermore, the cruel avenging Eumenides are linked to this callous world of Tacita, being described as "born of silence." However, the equivalent phrase in part two repeats precisely the image of closed lips, using anaphora to give greater relief to their now positive charge: "Qué dulce es el acuerdo de los labios callados" (91) [How sweet is the accord of silent lips]. The contrast of positive and negative which holds sway throughout the two parts gives way in the final couplet to an impassioned plea on the part of the poet, asking Tacita to give back what she never said, in retrospective anguish at lost opportunities. Ocampo thus makes use of this female mythical figure to exemplify and examine the contradictory nature of our human experience, and the ways in which passion colours our memories.

"Euterpe" (*Enumeración de la patria*) similarly engages with a particular mythological figure, but in addition continues Ocampo's ongoing speculation on the wider implications of mythological reference. Initially the poem presents itself as a kind of eulogy to this muse of music, who – the poet acknowledges – has guided her. The poet's description of Euterpe's physical appearance evokes (neo-) classical statuary with the folds of a tunic, but the reverential tone of the first four stanzas is then humorously undermined by a kind of frank admission of self-interest:

> ¡Ah! si pudiera yo esculpir tu estatua
> sobre algún pedestal de fuego. *Fatua*
> y arrodillada te dedicaría
> una oración que *me* perpetuaría.
> (*Poesía completa* I 65, emphasis added)

> [Ah, could I but sculpt your statue
> on some plinth of fire. *Fatuous*
> and kneeling I would offer you
> a prayer which would grant *me* eternity.]

The poet appears to be poking fun at the whole (neo-)classical tradition of high-flown eulogies to the muses, which may require authors to abase themselves through some variant on the *topos humilitatis*, but which ultimately all seek to glorify the poets themselves as much as the ostensible object of adoration, the muse. As in "Castigo" and "El maleficio," the poetic voice's triumph is predicated on the word being more lasting than stone. Nevertheless, despite its somewhat flippant tone, the poem does actively raise the perennial question of the *Ars poética* and of how poets have to negotiate their relationship with the imagery they inherit from poetic tradition. It is pertinent at this point to turn to the preliminary remarks Ocampo makes to Ricardo Baeza's collection of *Poetas líricos ingleses* where, regarding the image of the rose, she says that in "primitive" poetry it is simply a rose, rather than a miniature labyrinth, but that subsequent poems are doomed merely to repeat it with increasingly elaborate layers of symbolism (Baeza ix). This observation helps us to read the first stanza of the second section of "Euterpe," in which the poet had deliberately linked the rose to none other than this labyrinthine image:

> Oh rosa laberíntica del verso,
> verso que juntas lo que está disperso,
> imagen meditada largamente,
> cielo del estudioso, ambigua fuente.
>
> (*Poesía completa* I 66)

> [Oh labyrinthine rose of verse,
> verse which brings scattered things together,
> image long pondered,
> heaven for the studious, ambiguous source.]

The poet here cannot escape her belated position (Bloom 12) in a long poetic tradition stretching back to what she quaintly terms "primitive poetry." The image of the rose is no longer just a rose; it symbolizes lyric poetry and what poetry brings together. It is an image which has been much studied, it provides rich pickings for the student of such images, and as an ambiguous source with so much prior cultural baggage it is perfect for foregrounding ambiguous models.[16] Yet in the following three stanzas, the poet admits that she has only known pleasure, pain, and love thanks to the muse/poetry – a phenomenon

---

16   Thanks are due to Isabel Torres for the observation that this cultural "baggage" includes Ausonius's "De rosis nascentibus," which mediated the rose into the Western tradition; the rose also features heavily in amorous lyric and *carpe diem* poetry, as well as mystical and religious poetry with the Virgin Mary as rose.

which Ocampo had reiterated in her justification of Milton's use of classical mythological figures, saying that we need the distancing effect of these universal figures in order to put into poetry our personal feelings. The third and final section of the poem subtly digs at the muse, implying that the muse is as dependent on the poet as the poet is on her. Where will the muse be without someone to praise her? And this question could apply equally to the classical world in general. Where would these ancient mythological figures be, were they not continually reinterpreted by poets and others in every generation?

With this metapoetic dimension in mind, it is pertinent to mention the poem "Anáfora" (*Poemas de amor desesperado*). The title invokes a poetics of repetition. In a literal sense the phrase "Tendría que" [I would have to] is repeated four times in the same prominent place at the beginning of different tercets. In a broader sense the title refers to a literary history of repetition: the poem harks back both directly to classical sources in its reference to Mars as intrusive lover, to the transformation of Arethusa into a fountain, and to the labyrinth, and to the common Ovidian mytheme of flight and transformation; but it also engages with the stylization of tropes as later encapsulated by the metaphysical poets – such as the idea that before the poet would cease loving, the sun will melt like wax and the ocean will boil (*Poesía completa* I 227–28). Thus the poem embodies the idea of a living tradition of ongoing classical allusion and interpretation. I shall therefore turn now to the significance of Ocampo's self-positioning as an American and Argentinian poet within this tradition.

From Europe to America: Geopolitical Considerations

Ocampo's relationship to this living tradition of classical allusion is frequently linked to her own sense of identity as an American, and specifically Argentinian, poet. Nowhere is this more obvious than in one of Ocampo's very few poems which have a definite and significant political and historical context, the poem "Esta primavera de 1945, en Buenos Aires" [This spring of 1945, in Buenos Aires] (originally published in the magazine *Antinazi*, 29 November 1945, included in *Poesía completa* I 165–67). In this, the only classical reference is to Clio, the muse of history, and the poet expresses her own sadness and pain at historical events through a visual evocation of Clio ashamedly hiding her face behind her arm. The events which cause Clio such shame can be identified as the 17 October demonstration in the Plaza de Mayo demanding the release of Juan Domingo Perón from prison, and his subsequent triumphal speech from the balcony of the Casa Rosada. By invoking Clio and characterizing her reaction to this mass event as one of shame, Ocampo is effectively lamenting a lack of political decorum, a reaction typical of those of her immediate circle to incipient Peronism.[17]

In the earlier "Plegaria de una señora del Tigre" [Prayer of a lady from Tigre] (*Enumeración de la patria*), in which the poet explicitly lays claim to the classical world, a geopolitical reading of the broader relationship between American poetic creation and European tradition suggests itself. A woman addresses the Tigre delta in the province of Buenos Aires, declaring her lifelong loyalty to the place, and asserting its superior worthiness as a backdrop or setting for the classical and Shakespearean figures, the Ophelias and Narcissuses she has seen pictured elsewhere in books. As Andrés Bello in his 1823 "Alocución a la poesía" [Allocution to poetry] and Walt Whitman (as previously cited) call on the muse of Europe to come to America, so too this poetic voice sees the landscape of the Tigre delta as a kind of new nautical *locus amoenus* worthy of these mythical figures. Indeed, she has listened to the call of "las sirenas del barro acaudalado" [the sirens of the silt] (*Poesía completa* I 23). Yet she is not equally welcoming of all classical elements: Leda's swans, which the Tigre brings to her in dreams, are approved, but Tigre is also warned not to invent labyrinths (25).[18] And classical mythology has to share space with the Teutonic mythology of Lohengrin, thus reducing its pre-eminence. So the relationship of New World poet to Old World sources is one of careful appropriation.

Similar but more creative strategies are at work in her poem "Buenos Aires" (*Enumeración de la patria*), where she invents a classical pedigree for her city, positing it as already imagined by the ancient Romans. However, this fantasy has a typically saucy twist, in that she imagines Buenos Aires as seen secretly by Tiberius among his copies of the fabled erotic books of the first-century BC Greek poetess Elephantis, thus exoticizing Buenos Aires by association. This "fake," imaginary classical origin is juxtaposed with an eclectic mixture of other characters who, in Ocampo's flights of fancy, also imagined Buenos Aires before its "official" founding(s)[19] – characters who metonymically represent Chinese, Japanese, British, and also biblical culture. In this way, the primacy of the classical heritage is once again reduced and relativized in what could be construed as a characteristically eclectic *porteño* take on appropriating the classical and other cultural heritages to the New World.

---

17   Bioy and Borges, through their joint writing persona of Bustos Domecq, similarly made their reaction to Peronist populism clear in the short story "La fiesta del monstruo" (1947). Cited with the works of Borges.

18   Isabel Torres suggests a possible Ovidian reading (see *Met.* VIII.166–8) where the labyrinth emblematizes the constraints of the artist's confrontation with tradition, since it almost becomes the space of confinement for its own creator, Daedalus.

19   Buenos Aires is famous for having been founded twice, and Ocampo acknowledges this by including both the founders, Solís and Mendoza, in her poem.

The potential for such geopolitical readings is heightened when the classical world is taken metonymically to represent Europe as a whole. The poem "Ausencia" [Absence] (*Poesía inédita y dispersa*) seems initially to idolize Europe, utilizing an anaphoric structure over its six quatrains to build up a picture of all the things the poet values there, and by which she swears, repeating the word "Por" [by] at the beginning of every successive phrase (*Poesía completa* II 311). Gothic and Roman churches, painting, music, literature, all great European culture is there, and the culmination of the catalogue is the classical world, invoked by reference to Diana and her hounds with their fabulous eyes. Yet there is a sting in the tail of this apparently subservient homage to the pre-eminence of Europe and its classical heritage. To what purpose is the poet invoking this culture? To what does the absence of the title refer? Ocampo reserves the answer to these questions for the final (punch) line: the poet is swearing by all of European culture from her current position in America – where she has, shock horror, forgotten it all! Apparently, mere distance and absence is sufficient to erase all of European culture from her memory. Temporarily, of course, and not really, since it is present in the poem, but the powerful rhetorical effect is to put European culture firmly in its place, dramatically downplaying its immediate importance from the standpoint of the New World. The "fabulous eyes" of Diana's hunting hounds thus become, retrospectively, fabulous in more ways than one: still to be admired, yet also acknowledged as (mere) fable. And with this interpretation in mind, we can consider stanza 5, which swears by "todos los poetas que en el tiempo se imitan" (311) [all poets who in time imitate one another]. This appears to sum up the whole (post)classical world of *imitatio*, emphasizing the inescapability of classical reference within the Western literary system. In this poem, then, Ocampo demonstrates her easy familiarity with European culture as a whole, viewed from outside; she can cast a critical eye over it, but from within a poetic structure that implicitly offers homage to it, through adhering to a traditional poetic form (ABBA quatrains of *alejandrinos*).

Most interesting regarding the ambiguous relationship to classical and by extension all European culture is the post-colonial twist given to Homer's sirens' song (found in Book 12 of the *Odyssey*) in the poem "Descubrimiento de América" [Discovery of America] (*Los nombres*). The poetic voice is Argentinian, yet the first stanza shows us that this voice is both situated in, and addressing, Europe. We are told that the poem was written in Paris in 1951. "Quién oye aquí mi voz" [Who here hears my voice] ask the opening lines; "Es y no es castellana" [It is and is not Castillian] (*Poesía completa* I 357), yet the lack of a question mark hints that the question is purely rhetorical, the answer is implicitly "no one."[20]

---

[20] Ocampo observes somewhat wryly in a letter sent in 1970 from Paris to her sister Angélica in Argentina that Buenos Aires appears not to exist in Europe. In Princeton University Library, Fraga and Peña Collection.

Europe is addressed as "tú" [you, familiar form], and the voice imagines how Europe must have been before it knew of America. We note the double quotation marks – for all of the poem apart from the opening frame stanza, giving us the transatlantic context, the poetic voice "quotes" its own voice which acts as a goad and inspiration. We are thus made to listen to her voice, since it is highlighted by this poetic frame. So, in a poem whose title we might initially and normatively interpret as "Discovery of America," swayed by the force of historical narratives, and backed up by the image of Columbus's eyes searching for land, what the voice in fact relates is America's gradual "discovery" of Europe, irresistibly drawn by its siren call (358). This ambiguity is present in the title, which could be alternatively construed as "America's Discovery." From imagining an insular Europe, unaware of America in waiting, the poem then focuses more on the siren calls of Europe to an unsuspecting America of Indians, plains, birds of the Paraná, and even to the poet herself in her invisible pre-natal kingdom. We thus, implicitly, get the colonized's view of its difficult relationship to the colonizer; we see Argentina's perennial problem of being drawn towards European "delights and knowledge" at the possible expense of its own "American" identity, which may founder on European shores. The dark intricacies of that relationship are hinted at; we note that the siren is described as thirsty, as if Europe too were eager to drink in knowledge – and no doubt material wealth. In the final stanza of the poem, we are returned to Argentina and to a final defiant reassertion of Argentine difference (and superiority?) with the mention of the unusual River Plate, unusual for being broader and longer than the European rivers mentioned in the previous stanza.

The Atlantic space opened up between these two distant shores is another area ripe for geopolitical interpretation. The ocean offers a no-man's land in which identity can become fluid and transitional. In her poem "Imprecación al mar" [Curse on the sea] (*Los nombres*), the poet at first desires this freedom from self which also holds the possibility for metamorphosis or transformation:

> En tu fulgor, ...
> quiero dejar de ser, no ser humana,
> dejar mi vestidura cotidiana, ...
> ser piedra apenas, piedra o caracol,
> presa en tus vidrios como en un crisol.
> (*Poesía completa* I 369)

> [In your glitter, ...
> I want to stop being, not be human,
> leave my everyday clothing, ...
> be barely stone, stone or shell,
> prisoner in your glass as if in a crucible.]

She goes on to accord the sea its classical heritage, referring to its attraction for Andromeda, Aeneas, Ulysses, and the sirens, yet then undercuts this by saying that the powerful attraction of death inherent in the water renders any sense of history and time lifeless. Perhaps the fact that this is a curse to the sea, rather than an ode, is because the poet is at once attracted and repelled by this potential of the sea to eliminate time, identity, and life itself. Ocampo is perhaps also attracted and repelled by the inescapable classical associations, which provide a framework for interpretation and invention, but also threaten to drown originality in a watery labyrinth.

This metapoetical reading of drowning links us to the first of her "Sonetos de la opuesta ribera" [Sonnets from the opposite bank] (*Enumeración de la patria*), a nicely ambiguous and relational title. The opening sonnet is entitled "Palinurus insomne" [Palinurus sleepless],[21] and it bears an epigraph from the *Aeneid* V.871. Singling out the figure of Palinurus, who was the pilot of Aeneas's ship and who drowned without receiving proper burial, Ocampo imagines his perpetual state of sleeplessness. His never-ending weariness is voiced by choruses of sirens tired of singing (lines 4–5), as if he and they are kept perpetually in exhausting limbo by their timeless mythical presence, condemned to repeat their mythical actions. Linking this poem back to "Imprecación al mar," we see again how in Ocampo's appropriation of classical mythology, the sea as image is double-edged, having the potential to become an infinite closed mythical circuit.

Narcissus

This notion of a watery closed circuit brings us to Narcissus, the classical figure most extensively reincarnated within Ocampo's poetry, and thus deserving of particular focus within a consideration of her use of classical references.[22] There are many individual references to Narcissus scattered throughout Ocampo's poetry.[23] For example, in several poems from Árboles de Buenos Aires, trees are likened to Narcissus, either explicitly – for example, the rubber tree is described as the Narcissus among trees (*Poesía completa* II 213) – or implicitly – for example, the palm tree is referred to as one of those trees that tend to look at their own reflection in ponds (222). Sometimes Ocampo appears to extend this to implicitly include Echo, after Ovid. For example, the *ceibos* (Argentina's national tree) are seen trying vainly to embrace the narcissi flowers (native to

---

[21] I take the English title "Palinurus sleepless" from the excellent translation of this poem by Timothy Adès.

[22] For some discussion of the sirens, which also feature prominently in Ocampo's poetic imagery, see my essay "'Tales eran sus rostros'" 65–67.

[23] The relevant passage of Ovid is *Met.* III.339–510.

Europe), which in turn are drinking in their own reflections (243); the potential geopolitical reading here is self evident. Ocampo also frequently delights in multiplying these narcissistic images, for example in "Palmeras del lago" [Lakeside palms], where not only are the palm trees reflected in the lake, but she also presents us with the idea of love as a double Narcissus, created by the reflection of a statue of two lovers kissing. The ambiguous view of love that this implies is consonant with that expressed in Ocampo's *Poemas de amor desesperado* or indeed in much of her short fiction. Lovers may be merely seeking an other who is like themselves, or the couple together simply desire the image of themselves as a couple, and as soon as they part that image is lost.

The evocation via poetic techniques of Narcissus and his image is key to the portrait given in "La cara" [The face] (*Lo amargo por dulce*). In this poem, the poet constructs an elaborate portrait of the eponymous face by comparison with other experiences and other faces.[24] In order to emphasize the beauty of the face described, the poet names Narcissus, famed for his irresistible beauty, only to make him suffer by the comparison:

> más fugaz, más hermosa que la cara
> frente a **Narciso** atento de **Narciso**
> (*Poesía completa* II 69) [my emphases]

> [more fleeting, more lovely than the face
> bent to **Narcissus** of attentive **Narcissus**]

His fatal obsession with his own image is emphasized by the construction of the second line, which sends us back and forth from face to reflection, using mirrored hemistichs in a similar way to Ovid (see, for example, *Met.* III.446–7).[25] The words "frente a Narciso atento" are effectively in parentheses, but this awkward grammatical logic is far less strong than the irresistible pull of the stressed syllables of the hendecasyllabic lines. These neatly split the second line, with Narcissus on one side and his reflection on the other, giving a hypnotic rhythmic and visual reflection. Our attention is drawn to the internal rhyme of the first and sixth syllables, which has the effect of making the mythical voice of Echo audible in the line (an effect we saw earlier in "Canto"), and to the strong and parallel positionings of the name "Nar-**cis**-o" at the end of each half of the line. The effect of this closed circuit between gaze and reflection is

---

[24] For a discussion of the importance of the face in Ocampo's work more generally, see my "'Tales eran sus rostros.'"

[25] Ovid's "dazzling sequence of mirroring effects" in the Narcissus passage is noted by Mandy Green (31).

claustrophobic, and serves to highlight by contrast the poet's preference for a face which is more fleeting, not always fatally identical to itself.

The unwelcome nature of the Narcissus double reappears in a different guise in "Sinmí" [WithoutMe] (*Amarillo celeste*), a poem about the poet's ghostly absent self, who is likened to a stupid and unexpected Narcissus. The poem revolves around the poet's neurotic imaginings of what the places she frequents are like in her absence, to the extent that this absence of self is paradoxically given substance in the proper name "Sinmí" or WithoutMe, and becomes a kind of perverse love object. A Narcissus, but – as she puts it – an unexpected and pointless one: pointless, because like Narcissus (whose reflection "comes and stays with you, and leaves with you, if you can leave!" in *Met.* III.435–6, trans. Kline), the poet cannot know "Sinmí," cannot simultaneously be absent and yet present to experience that absence; and unexpected, because one does not expect such strong feelings to be provoked by oneself rather than by another person.

The sonnet "El escenario" [The stage] (*Amarillo celeste*) returns to this "WithoutMe" idea, setting the scene for absence this time by reference to Penelope. However, the expected return of Ulysses is figured negatively as disillusionment. We are encouraged to view the scene as the poetic "I" did, from above, like gods in the classical world looking down on mere mortals: "Con los ojos de un dios cruel ese día/ como en un escenario me veía" [With the eyes of a cruel god that day/ I saw myself as if in a play] (*Poesía completa* II 164). Yet the final tercet does not provide the expected clarification about who is playing the absent Ulysses; rather, the emotional drama is complicated. On the one hand, the poet seems to pity herself at that earlier stage of her life for not yet being in possession of her (current) self, literally for lacking self-possession: "¡Pobre sin mí yo misma!" [Poor me without me!]. So here we return to the narcissism developed in "Sinmí," except that now the narcissistic desire is played out as a desire for the future self rather than the absent self, and this desire is only created in hindsight and projected backwards. Adding the dimension of time allows Ocampo to combine the Narcissus story with elements of that of Penelope, whose narrative looks forward to a future moment. Ocampo's poetic subject thus becomes a female Narcissus who in later life looks back and realizes that she had, Penelope-like, been waiting for the absent one who turns out to be none other than her future self.

"La cara apócrifa" [The apocryphal face] (*Amarillo celeste*) extends these meditations on self, bringing together the focus on the face which we have previously seen in "La cara" with the negative charge of "Sinmí," though in this case, the negativity is a lack of authenticity rather than a lack of presence. The poet's own face is experienced as radically at odds with the poet's sense of self, to the extent that it feels "apocryphal," and as in the two previously discussed poems, the myth of Narcissus is invoked to illuminate, albeit ironically, the poet's state of mind. The framework for a comparison with Narcissus is set up, since the poem revolves around the poetic persona's obsession with gazing at her own face. The poem is structured around a series of (mis)encounters she has had with her face, particularly intense in early adolescence when gazing in the mirror and trying by turns to become witty, cruel, or mysterious. However, her gaze is not motivated by love or desire for what she actually sees, as in the case of Narcissus, but for what she would *like* to see, and this urgent desire overrides both gender obstacles and conventional ideas of beauty. The faces she most desired to emulate were those of Bindo Altoviti[26] "(¡qué importaba que fuera un varón si parecía un ángel!)" [(what did it matter that he was a man when he looked like an angel!)] and of the dancer Pavlova as a swan "(¡Qué importaba que fuera fea si bailaba!")" [(What did it matter that she was ugly when she could dance!)] (*Poesía completa* II 126). The mismatch between desire and reflection generates feelings of frustration, incredulity, and desperation, which are only heightened by the fact that the desired reflected faces are "impossible" reflections of her, since one is a man (albeit angelic) and the other an older woman (ugly yet graceful), and both are named, famous Others. So the subsequent brusque interruption of a punishing adult voice which asks what she's doing and condemns as sinful too much staring at one's face in the mirror abruptly skews the poem's perspective, shifting it from an emphasis on how the girl is actually feeling as she gazes at herself, and what she is seeing with the eyes of fantasy and desire, to how the adult who is watching her gaze (mis)interprets her feelings. Only at this point is Narcissus invoked by name, but it is the poet's adult self with hindsight, together with the censoring parental voice, which are the ones to see Narcissus in this scene. If there is eroticism, it is an unknowing, naive eroticism. But there is another possible interpretation offered to us of this proto-Narcissistic scene:

> o tal vez ya iba urdiendo
> las líneas que después, mucho después,
> desearía ardientemente borrar. (126–7)

> [or perhaps she was composing
> the lines that later, much later,
> she would ardently desire to erase.]

Perhaps rather than erotic physical attraction for these desired reflections of the self, it is the intensely private attraction of writing which is the real narcissistic tendency here.

---

26 Presumably as famously represented by the artist Raphael, c.1515.

So far, then, we have seen Ocampo referencing Narcissus to a variety of ends: to comment on Argentina's relationship to Europe, to explore the contradictory nature of love, self-knowledge, and identity, and to highlight the impulse to write as a potentially narcissistic activity. Each of these instances has used Narcissus as a kind of intertextual shorthand to activate certain aspects of the tale as most familiarly told by Ovid. But there are two poems in which Ocampo focuses solely on the Narcissus myth, with Narcissus himself as character taking centre stage. The first is her poem "Diálogo de Narciso" (*Espacios métricos*), to which Ocampo places an epigraph from Valéry's "Étude pour Narcisse" [Study for Narcisse] alongside a line from Cicero, "*Sui amantes, sine rivali*" [Lovers of themselves without rivals], which is in ironic contraposition to the poem that it prefaces. In the dialogue, it is difficult to distinguish which is the voice of Narcissus and which the voice of his reflection, and this sense of two parts of an indivisible whole is the predominant image throughout. The relationship between Narcissus and his reflection is aggressively antagonistic, yet they are inescapably and triumphantly yoked together through the persistent *pareados* [rhyming couplets]:[27] "Yo que tanto sufrí por tu tristeza/ te hago sufrir ahora con destreza" [I who so suffered through your distress/ Now make you suffer with great prowess], yet "En nuestro amor el tiempo ya se extiende/ y comprendemos lo que nadie entiende" [In our love time is extended/ and we know what none has comprehended] (*Poesía completa* 1 103). What is this superior understanding? Does it stem from the truism that we can never fully know another person, yet in this case, when the other is the self, the knowledge is superior? Individual possession is dispossessed by duality: "Ya no me pertenece/ este amor que en nosotros sólo crece" [No longer do I possess/ this love which grows in us], yet this shared love is inextricably bound up with violent jealousy: "tus ojos a otros ojos se parecen/ y los míos por eso se oscurecen" [your eyes to other eyes liken/ and when my eyes see that they darken] (104). The constant spiralling of attraction and suspicion is summed up in the oxymoronic idea (again emphasized by the rhyme scheme) of the conflictive reasoning that has united them: "el argumento adverso y dividido/ que nos ha dócilmente reunido" [the adverse view which us divided/ our distance gently has elided] (105). The fact that "argumento" also means "plot" gives a metapoetical resonance to the lines, reminding us (if we needed any reminder) of the mythical "plot" that this poem recreates. We are also again reminded of the Ocampo "motto," "los que aman, odian."

This suspicious jealousy returns, as we shall see shortly, in Ocampo's second and most extensive direct treatment of the Narcissus myth, her poem "Habla

---

[27] I beg the reader's indulgence regarding my translations here. I have prioritized conveying the impact of the original rhymes at the expense of other factors.

Narciso," which was published separately from any collection in 1987.[28] Ocampo's poem is presented in the original Spanish, side by side with her own English version, and followed by Ovid (*Met.* III.316–510) both in Latin and in Rubén Bonifaz Nuño's Spanish translation. The book also serves as a catalogue of Duilio Pierri's paintings of Narcissus done on the walls of the publisher's house. Much could be said concerning Ocampo's poetic translation into English of her own poem. The original combines hendecasyllables and *alejandrinos*, whereas her English translation has no regular metrical pattern. The titles already differ slightly, "Habla Narciso" being translated by Ocampo not literally as "Narcissus speaks," but as "Narcissus's Voice," and the divergences are much more marked in individual lines of the poem; for example, "Enajenado por ti, igual a tí [*sic*]" (9) [Alienated by you, equal to you], in which the unusual placing of the stressed syllables in the hendecasyllable underlines the sense of alienation, is rendered by Ocampo as "Like you resembling me," the element of alienation being dropped and a pleasing blurring between subject and object created in its stead.

Narcissus's monologue to his reflection is initially wistful, saying how much the two together could have shared in "el verano de aquel tiempo" [Ocampo: "the summer of those days"], a suitably vague *in illo tempore/tempus amoenus*. Narcissus could have given to his reflection "mi doble identidad" (9) [Ocampo: "my double identity"] – an ironic observation since the reflection inescapably shares it. But soon the jealousy we saw previously in "Diálogo de Narciso" returns, as Narcissus asks his reflection "¿qué hacías aquel día en un momento de quietud/ en que estábamos sentados a orillas del agua/ diciendo secretos?" [Ocampo: "What were you doing that day in a moment of repose/ when we were sitting in [*sic*] the edge of the water/ with [*sic*] secrets?" (10). Narcissus, distracted, occupies himself watching the trees uniting themselves with their reflections, repeating Ocampo's trope observed in various poems of *Árboles de Buenos Aires*. Inevitably, his reflection, who is "distraído como yo mismo" [Ocampo: "distracted like myself"], fails to say words of love to him. Various interesting points of translation emerge as this jealous scene develops: the Spanish has "Con la boca entreabierta," which we would perhaps instinctively translate as "with his mouth open," supplying a possessive since Spanish routinely uses the possessive less than English. Until we are told otherwise, then, this could apply either to Narcissus or to his reflection, or indeed to both, since Spanish does not always pluralize parts of the body when referring to more than one person. Ocampo, however, opts for "Our mouth opened slowly," not the expected plural noun "our mouths." The effect of this plural possessive with a singular noun is

---

28   Mackintosh quotes from the original publication, listed in the Works Cited as *Narciso/ Narcissus*. It is also available in *Poesía completa* II 332–5. Ocampo's English version, however, is not included. (editor's note)

to underline the unity of Narcissus with his reflection, a "we" with one body, which is an effect also present in Ovid's original which refers to "our body:" "O utinam a nostro secedere corpore possem!" (*Met.* III.467). The unspoken words of love in Spanish emphasize the "I" (not) doing the loving: "no me decías, soy yo, soy yo que te amo" [you didn't say to me, it's me, it's me who loves you], whereas Ocampo's English shifts the emphasis on to the object of that love: "you didn't tell me 'You are the one I love, the only one'" (10). It is as if Ocampo were viewing the poem and its translation as Narcissus and his reflection; their simultaneous unity yet separation is operating visually at the level of the two-column layout on the page, and hermeneutically in terms of the mirrored relationship between her original and her translation.

In the section where the Spanish equates Narcissus's waiting with seeing, Ocampo alters the verb tenses in the English translation, bringing the waiting into the eternal present. The two versions read thus:

> esperarte, Narciso, *era* para mí verte (13) (my emphasis)

> [waiting for you, Narcissus, for me *was* seeing you] (my translation and emphasis)
> Waiting for you, Narcissus, *is* like seeing you (Ocampo's English; my emphasis)

The shift to present tense calls to mind Ocampo's poem "Espera" [Waiting] (*Amarillo celeste*) in which, in the Penelope-like situation of a woman waiting for her loved one's return, the poet also finds pleasure in the act of waiting or hoping: "Cruel es que todo sea precioso hasta el retorno/ de la espera, y el lento padecer del amor" (*Poesía completa* II 137) [It is cruel that everything should be precious even the return/ of waiting, and the slow suffering of love].[29] The masterful use of *enjambement* encapsulates the heightened tension of the waiting, which in both "Espera" and "Habla Narciso" is the supreme activity. Towards the climax of "Habla Narciso," Ocampo accumulates references to the paradoxical nature of Narcissus's identity. In a series of imperatives to his reflection, Narcissus demands "dame la fracción de tu mitad" [Ocampo: "give me the fraction of your half"] and "Sepárate de tí [*sic*] mismo, mi amado,/ que nadie te reclame, salvo yo/ o la mitad de mí mismo" [Ocampo: "divide yourself, my love,/ so nobody may claim for you, but me/ or the half of myself"] (14). This long and dramatic section culminates in a conceit on presence and absence worthy of

---

[29] I am resisting the facile temptation to read these two moments as semi-autobiographical, but on the subject of waiting, see Iglesias and Arias (90–1).

the metaphysical poets so beloved of Ocampo,[30] and which recalls the use Ocampo made of the theme of absence in "Sinmí" and "El escenario:"

> Mi ausencia será mi presencia siempre,
> todos viven de ausencia, yo, de presencia.

(14)

> [Ocampo: My absence will be my presence always,
> everybody lives from absence, I from presence.]

In the closing two stanzas, Narcissus is willing himself into an oblivion of darkness and silence, without hope, knowledge, or memory. Interestingly, where the Spanish says "Ninguna sílaba saldrá del eco" [No syllable will come from the echo], Ocampo's English version makes the mythical reference to the doomed character of Echo more explicit by dropping the definite article and capitalizing the E of echo: "No syllable will come from Echo" (15).

The closing passage of the poem is deliberately classical in tone, cataloguing the greyhounds of Arcadia – Melampus, Ichnobates, Dorcaeus, Oribasus, Poemenis, Ladon, Tigris, Harpalus, Agriodos, and Hylactor.[31] The poet expresses the desire to be Hylactor, "para aullar hasta la noche" [Ocampo: "to howl all the night of nights"] (16). Once again there is a correspondence with the poem "Espera." Here in "Habla Narciso" the (male) poetic voice of Narcissus wishes to be a dog in order to howl forth his grief until nightfall, though Ocampo's quasi-biblical "night of nights" gives the English version added lyrical poignancy. There in "Espera," the (female) poetic voice laments the impossibility of becoming a dog in order to express her delight at the loved one's projected return: "Y es cruel aún después tener que ser humana,/ no convertirme, al verte, en perro, de alegría" (*Poesía completa* II 137) [And it is still cruel afterwards having to be human/ and not change, on seeing you, into a dog, from happiness]. In both poems we are thus returned to the world of transformation where this exploration of classical reference in Ocampo began. Yet Ocampo defies her mythical predecessor, Ovid, by refusing the final metamorphosis of Narcissus into a flower, and instead leaving his grief and his love immortalized in the image of "mi corazón demorado para siempre" (*Poesía completa* II 335) ["like my heart that lingers

---

[30]   She translated John Donne's "Twickenham Garden," "Elegy X: The Dream," and "The Apparition," and Andrew Marvell's "To his Coy Mistress."
[31]   The list of Arcadian hounds occurs earlier in *Met.* III.206–7, when Actaeon is torn to pieces by his own hounds.

for ever"] (16).[32] This ending parallels "La metamorfosis," where after jealous rage is spent through transformations into flora and fauna, all that is left is "mi corazón" [my heart] (*Poesía completa* I 222). It also closely corresponds to the mood of Ocampo's prose writing at the time, where in the intimate and apparently autobiographical fragments of "Anotaciones" (*Cornelia frente al espejo*) which reference "A.B.C." [Adolfo Bioy Casares], she writes "Déjame mirarte, imagen de mi alma" [let me look at you, image of my soul] (*Cuentos completos* II 365). So at the very conclusion of her lifelong poetic engagement with Narcissus, love is what endures, surviving and defying all bodily transformations.

Conclusion

We have seen that reference to the classical world forms a core part of Ocampo's poetic universe. Through her extensive readings and translations of works in English, French, and Spanish which engage with the classical world, Ocampo amasses a wealth of mythological references, for the most part at second or third hand, on which to draw in order to articulate and enrich her poetic expression. Classical echoes are present stylistically in her use of catalogues and dialogues, as well as thematically in her predilection for (ruined) statues and classical characters. Key individual figures such as Narcissus provide a perfect vehicle for her to explore perennial themes of love, hate, and jealousy, and form an extensive intratextual network of references within her poetic corpus. The whole repertoire of the classical world and its mythology is metonymically summoned by Ocampo in order to rehearse geopolitical concerns regarding the always ambiguous relationship between Argentine literature and its European others, where the essence of Argentinian identity is that it is European yet not European, American yet not American, always gazing nostalgically across the Atlantic towards where one is not. The eternal metapoetic drama of any poet's relationship to tradition, as variously theorized in Ocampo's lifetime by Eliot, Borges, and Bloom among others, also emerges through Ocampo's indirect approach to her classical sources. But most of all, Ocampo utilizes giddying Ovidian transformations and metamorphoses to dramatize the contradictions and pains of love. As Monteleone astutely observes:

> el amor es, para Silvina, el reconocido tema de su poesía. El amor, donde nadie persiste en su ser ... ni siquiera en el amor hay fijación posible del yo. Este sujeto agobiado de objetos que infinitamente se transforman. (2)

[32] Interestingly, the final Spanish line, which I here quote from "Habla Narciso" republished in 2003, is missing in the original 1987 catalogue.

[love is, for Silvina, the recognized theme of her poetry. Love, where no one remains as they are … not even in love can the self be fixed. This subject overwhelmed by objects which transform themselves infinitely.]

Ocampo's biggest debt to the classical world, and to Ovid in particular, is her recognition that the dramatic changes wrought in us by love, jealousy, and despair can be most intuitively grasped and expressed through the protean world of metamorphosis, and through the transformative processes of poetry that actively transfigures traditional models.

8

Silvina Ocampo and Translation

MARÍA JULIA ROSSI

> El original es infiel a la traducción.
> *Jorge Luis Borges*

Silvina Ocampo's practice of translation is one of the least known parts of her work, overshadowed by her vast poetic and narrative production. However, Ocampo devoted many years to it: her translations of Emily Dickinson's poems are the most extensive examples of this practice, but they are not the only ones. In this essay, my objective is twofold: in the first half I offer a brief overview of the relationship Silvina Ocampo had with the English and French languages by way of a complete listing of her translations into Spanish and her own compositions originally written in those languages. I organize this part of my argument in three sections: one on translations of Emily Dickinson's poetry, a second on translations of other poetry and prose, and finally, on writing directly in languages other than Spanish and self-translation. Afterwards, I analyze one of Ocampo's original English poems and her own translation of it. "Dream of Death of a Harlot" is particularly important because it is the longest of her poems to be published in English and also because her translation illustrates the author's approach to translation as an intrinsic part of a broader creative process. Perhaps because it was initially published under a pseudonym (a name later given to a character in a short story), it has yet to be included in a book of Ocampo's poetry. Many years later, and under her own name, Ocampo published a Spanish version of the poem, "Sueña con su muerte una prostituta." The central thesis of this chapter thus proposes that languages were not only sources for Ocampo as a reader, but also formed a fruitful creative space for her as a writer. I claim that translation should be considered as one manner – among others – in which her relationship with languages expressed itself. In this same vein, I argue that in Ocampo's case, translation was not an isolated or episodic practice, but instead reveals a complex connection with languages that in turn sheds light on her literary practice more broadly.

Translation: Emily Dickinson's Poems

The most ambitious translation project embraced by Silvina Ocampo was that of Emily Dickinson's poems.[1] It was perhaps the only sustained project to last for so many years and the only one that has a unity of purpose. The translation of Dickinson's poems began around 1970, and it was not a response to any external request (Mackintosh, "A Happy Transmigration?" 24). Almost twenty years later, Ocampo described the beginning of her interest in Dickinson in an interview with Fernando Sánchez Sorondo:

> A mí me pasó algo raro con Emily Dickinson … Alguien me hizo llegar dos poemas suyos excelentes e iguales: uno, dedicado a un hombre y el otro, a una mujer. Según estos poemas, Emily Dickinson habría estado simultáneamente enamorada de sus dos destinatarios y sentiría lo mismo por los dos, el hombre y la mujer. Sospecho, sin embargo, que Emily Dickinson no conoció el amor físico. Habrá recibido, sí, el roce de una mano, una caricia, y tal vez no más. (quoted in Ocampo, *Dibujo* 352)

> [Something strange happened to me with Emily Dickinson. Someone showed me two excellent and equal poems: one dedicated to a man and the other to a woman. They suggested that she was simultaneously in love with her two addressees and felt the same for each. I suspect, however, that Emily Dickinson never experienced physical love. She may have received the brush of a hand, a caress, and perhaps nothing more.]

Ernesto Montequin, the curator of Ocampo's archive, points out the coincidence of a trip Ocampo took to Europe around the same time that an edition of Dickinson's complete poems was published in England; it is highly possible that she acquired this volume during her trip, a volume that Montequin describes as groundbreaking: "[A]l cuidado de Thomas H. Johnson, es la primera en ofrecer la totalidad de los poemas de ED en un *reading text* riguroso pero servicial con el lector común" (interview) [under the care of Thomas H. Johnson, it is the first (edition) to offer all the poems by ED in a rigorous reading text which is at the same time useful to the common reader]. Montequin clarifies that all of Ocampo's translations followed this edition, in which poems and fragments appear numbered from 1 to 1775.[2]

---

[1]   On other translations of Dickinson's poems to Spanish, see Mackintosh, "A Happy Transmigration?" 36, n. 1.

[2]   Quoted from an unpublished written interview from May 2013. Since it is unavailable to scholars it has not been included in the Works Cited. (editor's note)

In 1976 Ocampo was awarded the Guggenheim fellowship for this project. With regard to the fellowship and its circumstance, Montequin comments:

> Silvina gana la Guggenheim en 1976 con el proyecto de traducción de los poemas de Emily Dickinson. No creo que el proyecto fuese pensado *ad hoc* para la beca, sino que preexistía, al menos en la intención de traducir una cantidad importante de poemas. Pero me parece que primero apareció la posibilidad de la beca –traída por su amiga Francis Korn, que la había obtenido uno o dos años antes– y luego *se le ocurrió que era más factible que se la dieran con el proyecto de traducción que con el de la escritura de cuentos o de una novela.* (interview, my emphasis)

> [Silvina won the Guggenheim in 1976 with the translation project of the poems of Emily Dickinson. I don't believe that the project was planned *ad hoc* for the grant, rather that it was ongoing, at least in its intention to translate an important number of the poems. I think that the possibility of the fellowship appeared – by way of her friend Francis Korn who had obtained one some years earlier – and then *it occurred to her that it would be more feasible to get it for a translation than for the writing of short stories or a novel.*]

I think this speculation by the curator of the archive, underlined in the quotation, is worth noting since it reveals the singular relationship that Ocampo had with her work as a translator as well as with the rest of her literary production. The book, published by Tusquets, for which Ocampo was responsible, includes less than half of these translations.

Some of them were published in newspapers in Argentina, both before and after the appearance of the book. On February 19, 1978, *La Prensa* published three translated poems in a brief article entitled "Tres poemas de Emily Dickinson." Both the translation and the introductory note were attributed to Ocampo. In 1980, by way of a foretaste of the Tusquets edition,[3] the cultural supplement of *La Razón* published a selection of sixteen poems in a double-page article with a large central image of Dickinson.[4] In this vein, *La Capital*, a newspaper from Rosario, Santa Fe, published two poems of those sixteen on April 6, 1986; on the latter occasion the article not only included an image of Dickinson but also one of Ocampo, something the previous two did not.

---

3   Tusquets published the translations for the first time in Spain in 1985. The following year, the publishing house reprinted the volume and launched it in Argentina. This Argentine launch occasioned the articles I mention here.

4   The poems are numbers 50, 67, 70, 101, 188, 209, 214, 228, 249, 258, 305, 354, 370, 379, 520, and 827.

Being the longest and most visible of her translation projects, the Emily
Dickinson book has provoked the most critical attention. The prologue by Borges
which introduced Ocampo's translations in the first edition was perhaps one of
the most counterproductive paratexts for their reading, because in some instances
it seems to have had an overstated influence.[5] Twenty years after the first edition
of the translations and almost simultaneously, Fiona Mackintosh, Marta Dahlgren,
and Delfina Muschietti dedicated meticulous articles to Ocampo's work as
Dickinson's translator.[6]

Mackintosh's purpose was to examine Ocampo's translations in light of
Borges's affirmations, with respect to her supposed "literalidad" [word-for-word
approach]; however, Mackintosh's essay transcends this narrow objective. In a
careful reading of Ocampo's translations, Mackintosh presents successive
examples to support what she calls a "deforming tendency" – which lacks the
apparent negative connotation of the phrase and refers to the idea of "carelessness"
("A Happy Transmigration" 29) – as a productive phenomenon of Ocampo's
translation strategies. Mackintosh's assertions are cautious and intelligent,
besides being clearly and profusely supported by textual examples from the
poems themselves. Her essay considers intentionality, lexical, syntactic and
semantic levels, gender issues, personal relationships, word repetition, and key
syntagms (30ff.). Her reading takes Borges's comments seriously and includes
the examination of his metaphor of the body and the soul to think about issues
of translation in terms of the transmigration of souls: "His final phrase 'venturosa
transmigración' [happy transmigration] suggests that Ocampo's versions give
a sense of Dickinson's soul having passed into Ocampo's body" (27). Mackintosh
concludes with this suggestive invitation:

> Perhaps the way to interpret Borges's provocative prologue is therefore to
> read it as hinting that the transmigration of Dickinson's soul into Ocampo
> has been accomplished, but that in a new "body," the soul acquires
> different characteristics. This transmigration is inevitably accompanied
> by a transmutation, a shift of emphasis and effect in the nature of "faith"
> and of other key networks of signification within the poetry. The adjective
> "venturosa" may have to be interpreted as describing a serendipitously

5   Originally, Ocampo wrote two possible prologues, "Sueño de un prólogo" and "Emily
Dickinson," both unpublished but now included in *El dibujo del tiempo*. Regarding these texts,
Montequin points out: "Según las cartas conservadas en el archivo de Silvina Ocampo, la editora
Beatriz de Moura la instó a escribir una introducción para el volumen. El libro llevó, finalmente,
un prefacio de Jorge Luis Borges" ("Nota" 382). [According to letters preserved in the archive,
the editor, Beatriz de Moura, encouraged her to write an introduction to the volume. The book
carried, in the end, a preface by Jorge Luis Borges.]
6   A fourth study by Eduardo Paz Leston appeared in 2009, about which I will have more
to say later.

felicitous (and occasionally infelicitous) – but not unchanged – expression of Dickinson's soul. (35)

Dahlgren devoted her article to a comparative study of translations of Dickinson's poems with a perspective on their phonological, syntactic, and semantic aspects. In addition to Ocampo's work, she focuses on translations by Marià Manent and Margarita Ardanaz. Her comparative study reveals various mistakes – such as translation errors and language comprehension problems – in Ocampo's translations (1090, 1100, 1103) and celebrates what she considers a good choice (1104). She comes to a working conclusion that privileges closeness between poems in the source language and target language, in other words, between the English poems and their translations: "Ocampo, in spite of a few misunderstandings on the lexical level, is the one who follows the original most closely (paradoxically, as she is the acknowledged poet)" (1095). Dahlgren also notices Ocampo's search for a poetic diction, closely related to her own status as a poet (1095) and criticizes the translator's choice of a linguistic variant of Spanish (Rioplatense, from the region of the Río de la Plata), displaying her own openly Eurocentric perspective (1101). In sum, this article is an examination of explicit reach and descriptive depth.

Muschietti is perhaps the critic who aspired to the most ambitious characterization of Ocampo's work as Dickinson's translator. Despite her comparative strategy, she develops a different approach: it proceeds fragmentarily and considers isolated aspects, first via a comparison of the Italian translation of Amelia Roselli, who, according to the article, only translated eleven poems ("Traducción" 6), but mainly within the framework of her own project to found a school of poetic translation (1). After a long presentation of the theoretical postulations which orient the reading, the comparative examination is limited to three items: one example (four lines of the poem 443), one comment on another line from the same poem, and one comparison with other Spanish translations of four other lines (poem 505). Although detailed, complete, and encompassing multiple linguistic levels, the examination does not transcend a prescriptive approach. Muschietti's conclusions, however, are the most daring and the boldest. On the one hand she affirms that

além de la recurrencia en elegir lo sentimental-emotivo en lugar de lo concreto propio de Dickinson, Ocampo también en muchas de sus elecciones lleva el poema a un plano más íntimo ... y así le quita al poema de Dickinson el tono metafísico-filosófico que suele imbricarse con lo cotidiano. (21)

[besides the repeated selection of the sentimental or emotive over the material, characteristic of Dickinson's work, Ocampo also in many of her choices carries the poem to a more intimate level ... and thus removes the metaphysical-philosophical tone that Dickinson connects to the everyday.]

On the other hand, she brings Borges's words back to formulate a gender criticism, in which he would operate as a dictator or ruler who would mark the "territorio estético-retórico destinado a las mujeres" [the esthetic-rhetorical territory assigned to women] (16).

In Muschietti's argument readers can perceive an echo of her enlightening essay "Mujeres: feminismo y literatura," but perhaps in a less fortunate context. She fails to fully explore the notion that "[e]n la elección de Dickinson como corpus a traducir no se halla ausente una apuesta de género" (6) [in her selection of Dickinson one can find a commitment to gender]. Borges's gendered statements awaken an interest that Ocampo's translation examples do not satisfy and cause Muschietti to close too soon on Ocampo's approach. Thus we read the following baseless condemnation:

> En poesía no pudo abandonar al patrón Borges, y el canon domina su traducción de una poeta tan revulsiva como Dickinson, cada vez que aquieta las aguas del poema, atempera su tendencia a lo físico y a lo concreto, haciéndolo fugar hacia la emoción, cuando el texto de Dickinson se aparta expresamente de ese campo, para constituir otro. En el prólogo al libro de las traducciones de Ocampo, Borges vuelve a insistir en su prejuicio de género. (16–17)

> [In poetry she was unable to abandon the Borges pattern, and the canon dominates her translation of a poet as shocking as Dickinson. Every time she quiets the waters of a poem she tempers the tendency to the physical and the concrete, making it flee to emotion when Dickinson's text expressly moves away from that field in order to constitute another. In his prologue Borges insists on his gender prejudice.]

According to Muschietti, Ocampo would have been unable to ignore this mandate.

Translation: Prose and Other Poetry

Although poetry was the genre Ocampo translated most, it was not the only one. She first published a translation of Julien Green's novella, *Le voyageur sur la terre* (*El viajero sobre la tierra* [The Pilgrim on the Earth]). Published in *Cuadernos de la Quimera* in 1945, in its theme and argument it has a close relationship with Ocampo's novella, "El impostor." She also translated several chapters of De Quincey's autobiography with poet Patricio Canto, which appeared in *Sur* in 1944. Her translation of a theatrical play is essential in this enumeration:

her version of *Les Bonnes* (*Las criadas* [The Maids]) by Jean Genet was made in secret collaboration with her friend José Bianco. According to the curator of her archive, Ocampo left unpublished a translation of *Four Seasons* by Arnold Wesker and another of *JB*, a play by Archibald MacLeish. These two translations were made in response to a request by the director Cecilio Madanes and could be dated around the late 1950s and the early 1960s (Montequin, interview). These milestones not only show that translation became an early and constant practice for this writer, but also that it transcended the boundaries of genre.

Nevertheless it is true that poetry was the primary material that held Ocampo's interest as a translator. She worked on several poems by authors other than Dickinson. The volume *Poesía inédita y dispersa* includes two translations, one of Graham Greene and another of Verlaine. Some of her versions of Pope and Marvell were included in the anthology *Poetas líricos ingleses*, for which she wrote the introduction; she also participated in translating several English poets for the *Sur* magazine triple issue devoted to English literature (153–56, July–October, 1947).[7] Both projects predated the Dickinson translations, and Ocampo's participation is, somehow, more limited, due to the fact that these were assignments that responded to other people's selections. Nevertheless, Ocampo included her versions in her own poetry books: some would be part of the "Traducciones" section in her *Poemas de amor desesperado* (1949).[8] This practice of including poetic translations in her poetry volumes continued in *Lo amargo por dulce* (1962)[9] and *Amarillo celeste* (1972).[10] In neither of these two books is there a "Traducciones" section; rather, the translations are included among Ocampo's poems, each indicating their respective authors. About the same time that these few translations were published (the beginning of the 1970s), Ocampo began the Dickinson enterprise.

Among the many authors whose poems she translated, Ronsard occupies a privileged place, following Dickinson in importance. The author's preference

7   Poems translated for the triple issue of *Sur* were by A.E. Housman, Walter de la Mare, Vita Sackville West, Stephen Spender, Edith Sitwell, Edwin Muir, David Gascoyne, and Kathleen Raine. The *Poetas líricos* volume, with selection made by Ricardo Baeza, gathered two pre-existent translations: the first was published in *Sur* in 1945 and the second in *Los Anales de Buenos Aires*.

8   Besides the poems by Marvell and Pope included in *Poetas líricos ingleses*, translations included in this book are Horace's "Oda V" (published in *Los Anales de Buenos Aires* in 1946), Pierre de Ronsard's sonnets XII, LI, CLX, CLXXI, CLXXII, CCXV, and "A Casandra," together with poems by Gérard de Nerval and Charles Baudelaire.

9   Translations include poems by Jean-Paul Toulet, Gottfried Keller, John Donne, Charles Baudelaire, Paul Verlaine, and William Butler Yeats.

10   In this book, translations included are works by Lucilio de Samosata (for a comment on this "joke," which is not an actual translation but a heteronymic poem, see Paz Leston 318), Rupert Brooke, and Louise Labé.

is supported by the evidence of several unpublished translations of his poetry in the Ocampo archive, and is confirmed by Paz Leston: "Pienso que Ocampo buscó en Ronsard un modelo alternativo. Detestaba los sonetos de Quevedo, que le parecían muy duros, según me dijo una vez" (316) [I think that Ocampo looked to Ronsard as an alternative model. She detested Quevedo's sonnets; they seemed very hard, according to what she told me once]. Her first translations of Ronsard's poetry date back to the 1940s; in fact, she included seven of his sonnets in *Poemas de amor desesperado*. In 1963 she signed a contract with the Ministerio de Educación y Justicia de la Nación for a book of Ronsard's translations that was never published (Montequin, interview). The unpublished translations in Ocampo's archive would theoretically have been part of that volume.

Original Writing in Different Languages and Self-translation

Finally in this account we should consider the pieces Ocampo originally wrote in French and English. Here, as we have already seen, poetry prevails, but it is also not the only genre: Ocampo's memoir of Borges, "Images de Borges," published in an issue of *Cahiers de L'Herne* as a homage to the Argentine writer (1964), was written directly in French; in English she wrote a sort of authorial manifesto that is the "Author's Introduction" to *Leopoldina's Dream*, an anthology of her short stories translated by Daniel Balderston in 1984.

Her poetic work in French includes four published poems: "Rencontre de Narcisse" and "L'Adieu de Narcisse," published in 1942 in *Lettres Françaises*, the magazine Roger Caillois edited in Buenos Aires; and "L'Eau" ["The Water"] and "Poéme d'adulation du poéte aux lecteurs" ["Adulatory Poem from the Poet to the Readers"], published in *Disco* in 1946 and 1947, respectively. Both manuscripts bore the pseudonym of Anselme Ponsert. There are self-translations of the two first texts, into both Spanish and English, that merged in a single poem under the title of "Habla Narciso"/"Narcissus Speaks." These were published in 1987 in the catalog for an exhibition of Duilio Pierri's paintings on the Narcissus myth in the Galería Furlong, and the Spanish version was included in "Otros poemas no recogidos" in *Poesía completa*. A self-translation of the poem "L'Eau" remains unpublished (Montequin, interview; "Nota" 393).[11] In English, she wrote the poem "Dream of Death of a Harlot" and published it under the pseudonym George Selwyn; the second part of this essay is devoted

---

[11]   In an interview published in 1988, Ocampo explained that she wrote it first in English and later in Spanish, a process similar to that of "Dream of a Death of a Harlot." There are approximately thirty unpublished poems in the archive also written in English (Montequin, interview); researchers do not have access to this material.

to an analysis of this poem and its translation, "Sueña con su muerte una prostituta."

The Poem "Dream of Death of a Harlot"

In the sixth issue (1946) of *Disco* – Juan Rodolfo Wilcock's magazine – the poem "Dream of Death of a Harlot" appeared in English signed by George Selwyn. The same poem would be published again much later, on October 11, 1981, in the *Buenos Aires Herald*, accompanied by a note about the author that seems ambiguous and humorous. Selwyn is evoked, but the real identity of the poem's author is disclosed: Silvina Ocampo. This development is important because it reveals the long-lasting relationship between Ocampo and languages other than Spanish, and also because it reveals Ocampo's fidelity to a specific theme, topic, or text.

In 1984 the magazine founded and directed by Octavio Paz, *Vuelta*, published a Spanish version of this poem under the title "Sueña con su muerte una prostituta," attributed to Silvina Ocampo. With conspicuous differences, this poem consists of the English version rewritten in Spanish, and would later be included as part of her complete poetry. It is important to consider the context of both versions within Ocampo's poetic production, both in relation to her work as a poet and as a translator. The practice of rewriting was an intrinsic part of her poetic writing and one of its most singular sources of productivity. I argue that this poem and its development across time, languages, and genres offers an enlightening path for the exploration of zones of Ocampo's writing practice that have previously been consigned to oblivion.

The Texts

For this analysis, we have several versions of the poem. In English, there exists a typed version with handwritten notes by Ocampo and a marginal note by Jorge Luis Borges; the version printed in *Disco* contains profuse corrections and changes by the author, which no later version considers or includes; and there is a version published in the *Buenos Aires Herald* which, except for some minor corrections and alterations, reproduces the typed text from 1946 (words like "Ulysses" and "foreseen" are corrected; capital letters are added to "Italian" and "Lacedemonian"; the word "paths" is changed to "path" in line 67 and "like" is replaced by "as" in the following one). In Spanish, there is also a typed version (with the subtitle "Versión corregida"), the version published by Paz in 1984, and the one included in the *Poesía completa*, which reproduces the latter. Here we see the English poem as it appears in *Disco*:

DREAM OF DEATH OF A HARLOT

O rose that lies within my lonely hand
with sleep, lost, standing all around like sand!
O joy for ever ending on my breast,
we did not know this was my final rest!

I lied before, but now believe me please!
I have to sleep dressed in the shade of trees.
Forgotten wreaths upon my hair with lust
want still the worms to love them. In the dust

the ribbons of my dress with crimson red
remind sweet blood, as if I was not dead.
Long chosen flowers died by my side the day
I died. I heard the angels laugh and pray.

They were true angels, I could see their heads
disdainfully reclined. The words they said!
Ah from what abyss of delight they spoke,
with happiness of wings on a dark oak.

Hermaphrodites they seemed. They waked my fear.
Unladylike, they whispered in my ear.
"These are the bows they gave you; they are dead.
You have a withered wreath just round your head.

It is of paper, with a dreadful smell.
Is it that way that ladies dress in hell?
You could have died just like a saint for gold.
But you were rich. No, you were sad, and sold

your body to be pleased." O pray for me!
I was a siren distant from the sea,
Just like the ones Ulises saw with rings,
and I could change myself in other things:

I have been music, words I could not say,
I have been some one else a night of May,
a face reflected in a miniature
of some uplifted eye, with pain demure.

In a forgotten house, lost, strange and dark
with fotographs of angels, yes and larks,
I have been still as if I was of lead:
I have been death before I could be dead.

Some saints have looked like me, with praise, too soon,
their prayers like hands were sought beneath the moon
like mine. They had no hopes, no dress, no shoes,
their eyes were gems, they did not mind to lose,

their tresses, robes. O angels are you blind?
and because you are pure, you are not kind?
Is it because you are so near to god
that you don't know me yet it seems so odd

that I should still be waiting for your kiss
when there are other things that I should miss!
Like Eve, like a lacedemonian queen
my kindness was a gift but unforseen.

I am still modest like the quiet night
which in the brothel gave her precious light.
O take my rings, my festered wreaths, my gold,
I want again O angels to be sold

I want your faces like new gardens, skies
that shall be praising only all our sighs.
As in the Bible you are cross. I weep
as if this dream was true. I know the deep

resistance of your smile. You don't forgive
as lovers can forgive. O I could live
but not in Paradise where I will never
be sure to clasp you in my arms for ever.

In some italian garden, dressed in blue
I would have loved in summer to meet you.
We would have heard a distant piano play
or violins that unforgotten day

next to a deep and artificial lake
all words of tenderness we should forsake.
Newly made statues in the paths would seem
to smile between the leaves like in a dream

and when the rising moon would touch our hair
unheedingly we would ascend the stair...
amid the jessamine perfume, clad
in happiness, we would at last look sad.

GEORGE SELWYN

In the upper margin of the third page of the typed poem, these words in Borges's handwriting appear:

> ~~By a long~~ {chalk} the best English
>   {~~run~~ }
> Obviously
> poem ~~yet~~ <ever> written   J.L. Borges

This note should be considered within the context of the gregarious, exceedingly humorous atmosphere in which Ocampo, Borges, and Bioy Casares conceived "En la literatura hay que evitar" [In literature one must avoid], for example, an extended joke that is included in "Letras y amistad." Although published by Adolfo Bioy Casares, it is the result of a dialog among friends, as is indicated in the text itself. The note on the manuscript suggests a similar context in which the poem was written.

By the time of this publication in *Disco*, Ocampo had already published two books of poems: *Enumeración de la patria y otros poemas* (1942) and *Espacios métricos* (1945). Between 1945 and 1947 she published several translations in *Sur*, and in 1949 some of her translations appeared in her *Poemas de amor desesperado.* Therefore "Dream of Death of a Harlot" appeared simultaneously with her writing in Spanish as well as with her translations of poetry from English and Spanish. The themes are consistent with her work from this period: in particular, the relationship between death and sleep. The topic of sleep appears in "A una persona dormida" [To a sleeping person], "En busca del cielo" [In search of the sky], "Memoria irremisible" [Irretrievable memory], and "La abandonada" [The abandoned woman]. The connection between sleep and death, related or analogously presented, is explicit in "Epitafio de un náufrago" [Epitaph for a castaway] (all the poems of the "Epitafios" series, an important section in *Espacios métricos*, convey a deliberate attention to death). Other elements present here can be acknowledged as part of the still brief poetic path that preceded the poem: examples include the lake, the gardens, the trees, and, in particular, Hellenistic, scriptural, and religious references. These topics and references belong to the poetic universe Ocampo crafted through the 1940s.

The figure of the angel not only entails biblical references, but also introduces, within the poem, an external voice. Angels had appeared in "Memoria irremisible" and "Estrofas a la noche" [Verses to the night], but the enunciative intervention is articulated in the poem "Autobiografía de Irene." This device and the quotation marks that frame the angel's discourse in direct speech introduce an external voice which determines a dialogic situation. In "Dream," without being explicit, the angel – an hermaphrodite that in "Lot, los ángeles y la estatua" had been described as having an "afeminado perfil" [effeminate profile] – formulates a sort of condemnation or conviction about the life of the prostitute to whom it is talking and from whom it keeps an eloquent distance. Different from the angel in "Autobiografía de Irene," this one has no "pacífico lenguaje" [peaceful language]. On the contrary, it is marked by censure which refers to the past, to talents, and to the body.

With regard to the poem's form, if we consider the whole of Ocampo's work up to that date, it is a relatively exceptional structure, but not absolutely new: it has aspects in common with "A Francia en 1942" (where one can read the singular line, "tu idioma que no es enteramente el mío" [your language which is not entirely mine]). It is particularly similar to "Euterpe," a poem in three parts; the first has five stanzas and the other has two, seven in all. Each stanza has four lines, with rhyming couplets, and it includes various elements mentioned in "Dream," such as the rose, the gardens, and the angel.

Affinities can also be traced to the work of other poets. Dante Gabriel Rossetti's "The Blessed Damozel" was a poem highly esteemed in Ocampo's circle and it offers a similar enunciative situation to the one conceived in "Dream." In this same sense, the topic of sleep in poetry was repeated in some of Ocampo's readings, as her translation practice shows: it can be found in her translations of A.E. Housman's "My Dreams Are of a Field Afar," Walter De La Mare's "All that's Past," and Stephen Spender's "The Separation," among others. Similarly, the topic of death appears in various poems translated by Ocampo in those years, such as Edith Sitwell's "Colonel Fantock" and Kathleen Raine's "The Silver Stag." Both translations, included in *Poetas líricos ingleses*, are enlightening in this sense: topics of love and death are present in both Andrew Marvell's "To His Coy Mistress" and Alexander Pope's "Eloisa to Abelard." In the latter, besides angels and saints, we also find the source of the voice between quotation marks, this time attributed to "oscuros murmullos" [dark murmurs] which do not necessarily exclude religious and biblical allusions.

Finally, the English used by Ocampo to compose this poem does not correspond to a contemporary phase of her writing. On the contrary, she uses deliberately old-fashioned terms (such as "harlot" and "tresses"), and she also pursues a "delatinizing" effect with many of her lexical choices, mainly in the use of strong consonants, a preference for words of distinctly Germanic origin, and an abundance of monosyllabic or disyllabic words. These strange words lead to a precise moment of the English language – or, more precisely, of English literature – the beginning of the eighteenth century. Thus, she offers an encyclopedic repertoire similar to the one available to the Romantic poets.

This double shift, in language and in time, can also be connected to another particularity: Ocampo includes in this poem a character completely alien to her work up to this point (both in original poetry as well as in translations): the prostitute.[12] The inclusion of pariahs or outcasts is characteristic of the poetry Ocampo emulates with this poem. This would be the most significant thematic novelty to accompany the double shift of linguistic and temporal alienation, and we will see its parallel development in Spanish in her self-translation.

Here, then, is Ocampo's version of "Dream" in Spanish:

[Typed version]
SUEÑA CON SU MUERTE UNA PROSTITUTA
Versión corregida

Oh, solitaria rosa adentro de mi mano!
en mi sueño perdida y rodeada de arena
Oh alegría incesante que palpita en mi pecho
no sabías que este era mi descanso final.

Antes siempre mentía pero créanme ahora
yo tengo que dormir vestida por los árboles
Olvidadas coronas en mi peinado, lúbricas
quieren que los gusanos las amen. En el polvo

las cintas del vestido de un rojo de carmín
recuerdan el color de mi sangre feliz,
dilectas flores ávidas murieron en el día
de mi muerte. Los ángeles rezaban y cantaban,

ángeles verdaderos, veía sus cabezas
con desdén reclinadas las cosa que decían!
De qué abismos ocultos del deleite me hablaban
con dicha de alas tersas en la oscura caoba

Hermafroditas eran? Despertaban terror.
Mal educados, rígidos susurrando en mi oído:
"Estos serán los lazos que te atan están muertos.
"Tienes una corona marchita en tu cabeza

---

[12] The closest contemporary reference that can be found is the mention of a brothel in the poem "Inscripción para un cinematógrafo suburbano" [Inscription for a suburban cinema] (*Enumeración de la patria*), where prostitution is merely an ornamental geographic detail.

-2-

"es de papel y tiene adornos ~~miXXXXrosos~~ <luminosos>
"de ese modo se visten las damas del infierno?
"Podrías haber muerto como una pobre santa
pero eras rica. No. Eras triste y vendiste

"Tu cuerpo complacida". Ángel rece por mí
Yo he sido una sirena alejada de mar,
como aquellas que Ulises extasiado escuchó
Yo pude transformarse en muchas otras cosas

Fui una lejana música, palabras que no dije,
yo fui varias personas, una noche de mayo,
un rostro reflejado en una miniatura
con ojos elevados al cielo, recatada,

una olvidada casa, perdida, anfibia, oscura,
fotografías de ángeles y de alondras plateadas
Permanecí tan quieta como está quieto el plomo:
estaba muerta ya mucho antes de morir

Algunas santas me aman con párpados cerrados
manos como oraciones, bajo la luna, anhelos
sin ninguna esperanza, ni velo, ni zapatos,
ojos en vez de joyas que no temen perder

-3-

xxxx <extremadas> vestiduras. Oh ángel mío eres ciego?
<¿> Es porque eres tan puro que no tienes piedad?
<¿>Será porque xxx <pretendes ser idéntico a> Dios
que no me reconoces? Qué extraño me parece

que yo siga esperándote durante tanto tiempo
cuando otras cosas hay más buenas de esperar.
Como Eva o como una árida reina lacedemonia
mi bondad fue un presente sobrio o inadvertido

Yo suelo ser modesta a ejemplo de la noche
que en el burdel me dio su resignada luz
tomen mi aro y mi anillo mis marchitas guirnaldas
de nuevo yo quisiera, ángeles, que me vendan;

Quiero tus rostros nuevos con cielos dibujados
que alaban incesantes todos nuestros suspiros.
Como en la Biblia escucho tus amenazas. Lloro.
¿Este sueño tal vez será un sueño? conozco

tu severa sonrisa. Yo sé que no perdonas
como algunos amantes. Yo podría vivir
pero no en el Edén en donde no podré
estrecharte en mis brazos para siempre jamás

En un jardín de Italia, de azul toda vestida
yo quería en verano pluralmente encontrarte
hubiéramos oído un piano muy distante
o violines aquel inolvidable día.

-4-

En la orilla de un lago que alumbran las luciérnagas
toda palabra dulce de amor desecharíamos
Estatuas imitando al marmol llegarían
a sonreir entre hojas a un perdurable sueño

y cuando la alta luna fuera la única luz
quietos ascenderíamos con invisibles ruedas
entre perfumes lilas de jazmines reunidos
a tu éxtasis: podríamos por fin parecer tristes

Pero me han engañado. Yo sé que no son ángeles,
son diablos disfrazados. No todo es vestidura.
Crueldad del castigo que hasta en la muerte llega
queriendo seducir la seducción final.

No me amó ningún hombre. No me amó <a> ningún ángel
mi alma buscó el amor de alas artificiales,
sin querer, en la túnica, mentiras de un disfraz
Narciso devoró su imagen, yo mi sombra

<Silvina Ocampo>
<1981>

The first noteworthy detail is that the Spanish version is two stanzas longer.
New themes are included in these stanzas as well as a new, final move that
changes the significance of the poem's whole idea.

The rhyme scheme of the English original disappears in the Spanish version.[13] There are notable changes not only in grammatical structures but in the semantic shifts, such as, for example, in the second line the change from "like sand" to "rodeada de arena" [surrounded by sand]. Although most of the poem seems to retain a certain fidelity to the English version, there are some striking changes, more striking perhaps due to their scarcity. One example is the translation of "the ribbons of my dress with crimson red/ *remind sweet blood, as if I was not dead*" as "las cintas del vestido de un rojo de carmín/ *recuerdan en color de mi sangre feliz*" (ll. 9–10, my emphasis).[14] In Spanish, the hypothetical quote "as if I was not dead" disappears completely. Another, perhaps stranger, example arouses suspicion: "They were true angels, I could see their heads/ disdainfully reclined. The words they said!" In translating as "ángeles verdaderos, veía sus cabezas/ con desdén *reclinadas* las cosas que decían" (ll. 13–14, my emphasis), the adjective "reclinadas" has an ambiguous attribution: does it refer to the heads or to the things said? It is highly probable that this ambiguity was, as is typical in Ocampo, desirable, if not deliberately sought.

In the Spanish version, the English "we" turns into the second person singular (l. 4) and the imperative formulation, forcing a choice between singular and plural (which are undifferentiated in English); the latter prevails (l. 5). There are several changes in adjectives (and, to a lesser extent, in the adverbs), some of which are nuances and others substantive modifications of the sense of the phrase. It is also worth noticing that some syntactic changes in Spanish pursue the idea expressed in English rather than a parallel set of words. One example of this is how "I know the deep/ resistance of your smile" (ll. 56–7) becomes "Conozco/ tu severa sonrisa."

The added stanzas, mentioned above, would have been immediately evident to readers of *Vuelta* magazine, because the distribution of the two versions of the poem on the page clearly shows this increase and also because the introductory note describes the Spanish version as "corregida y aumentada" (22) [corrected

---

13 Tension between meaning and sound is part of Ocampo's concern in translating poetry. In a 1983 interview, she affirmed: "Lo ideal sería mantener, al traducirlo, la armonía de sonido y sentido que tenía en su idioma original. No desvirtuar el sentido de un poema puede ser importante, pero no lo es menos reproducir, en la medida de lo posible, sus valores acústicos, su musicalidad. A veces, una traducción mejora el verso original" ("Conversación" 297) [the ideal would be to maintain the harmony of the sound and meaning when translating. To avoid distorting the meaning is important, but no less so is to reproduce, as much as possible, its acoustic values, its musicality. Sometimes a translation improves the original].

14 This idea in the English version recurs in Ocampo: the closeness of death or its presence in a life that is not yet over. This theme appears in the above-mentioned poem "Colonel Fantock" and reappears in a much later letter to her personal doctor, Alejo Florín, to whom she writes: "Love and secrecy: Si fuera yo normal me suicidaría. ¿Sabés lo que significa morir sin morir?" [If I were normal I would kill myself. Do you know what it means to die without dying?]

and expanded]. In the added verses there exists an "unmasking" of the angels presented in the poem: they are "diablos disfrazados" [disguised demons]. This section, in turn, opens with the adversative connector "pero" [but] which repudiates the identity of the speaking angel and, in doing so, its whole enunciation. Lastly, the reference to Narciso in the final verse revisits a topic Ocampo had already developed in her poetry, in an eminently dialogic poem, "Diálogo de Narciso," in which the final verse closes, similarly to this one, with a reference to shadows.[15]

The Pseudonym

There are several sources that, like an echo, repeat Ocampo's claims to being unaware of the existence of a George Selwyn at the time of creating the name. In this case, the pseudonym can be considered a play on words related to her own name: Selwyn is a historical English form related to the Latin name Silvanus. The invention would have been motivated, then, by the search for a deliberate cipher, a name unknown in relation to a real historical character as an immediate referent. Nonetheless, Ocampo later discovered the existence of Selwyn in English history, and the most salient feature of his biography was his interest in public executions. The *Oxford Dictionary of National Biographies* provides this description:

> Less light-hearted was Selwyn's interest in executions, at which he was a regular attender. In 1757, for example, he went to Paris to watch the dismemberment of the would-be royal assassin Damiens. His fascination with the moment of death and the resultant corpse was widely commented on within his circle. "The next time Mr Selwyn calls show him up," commented Henry, first Baron Holland, on his deathbed: "if I am alive I shall be delighted to see him, and if I am dead he will be delighted to see me" (Jesse, 1.5). After his own death, Selwyn's peculiar pastime was vigorously debated by his friends in the *Gentleman's Magazine*; the biographer Philip Thicknesse, for instance, downplayed Selwyn's association with the macabre, which he attributed to gossip by Sir Charles Hanbury Williams and Lord Chesterfield (*GM* 299, 705). (Carter)

This peculiarity appears in the note that accompanies the English version of the poem published by the *Buenos Aires Herald* in 1981 and in the brief introduction to the bilingual version in *Vuelta* in 1984. Ocampo curiously revived

---

[15]   The last lines of "Diálogo de Narciso" are part of the last apparently dialogic intervention and reinforce the notion that ambiguity impregnates the idea of duality, allowing no easy resolution but instead insisting on ambiguity itself.

it in a prose narrative, titled "George Selwyn," included in her short story volume *Y así sucesivamente* (1987). This text begins with a biography of Selwyn, noting that he was born in 1719, and relates anecdotes about him. In the middle of this brief fictional narrative, one reads: "Hoy día en la Argentina, en 1945, se ha descubierto un poema en una revista literaria, atribuido a George Selwyn" (*Cuentos completos* II 202) [Today in Argentina, in 1945, a poem has been discovered in a literary magazine attributed to George Selwyn]. This piece of information is presented as enigmatic, as awakening general incredulity because of its deliberate anachronism. In describing the recently discovered poem, the narrative voice of the story characterizes it as removed from its era, pointing out that "pertenece más bien a la época pre-rafaelita" [it belongs rather to the pre-Raphaelite era]. After referring to Selwyn as "un fantasma que apareció en 1945" [a ghost who appeared in 1945], the text slides into an ambiguous and vague set of questions on historical time, authorship, and angels, and ends with a succinct reference to a portrait, attributed to a historic painter, Sir Joshua Reynolds, that "Tal vez nos ayude a conocerlo" (203) [might help us to know him].[16] This pseudonym, somehow a consequence of writing in English, was the genesis of a new short story. By developing a character out of this name, the creative process goes a step further.

Translation in Practice

In her well-known series of interviews with Noemí Ulla, Ocampo describes the creative practice as a circular process in which one inevitably repeats oneself with what she describes as an "involuntary fidelity" (*Encuentros* 14). The practice she details here deserves attention because it is key to Ocampo's poetics: creation as a circular process that never ceases is a concept which accompanies her production through time and in several genres and languages.[17] The matter of Ocampo's allegedly conflictive relationship with the Spanish language also deserves further comment: many times her words quoted in Ulla's unarguably essential book of interviews have been taken too literally by her critics. A letter

---

[16] In an interview by Mirta Arlt, in 1980, Ocampo responded to the question "¿Qué cuentista le hubiera gustado ser?" with a long and invented story about George Selwyn and quoted part of her own poem as if it were a short story written by Selwyn, entitled "Sueño de una cortesana" (interview reprinted in Ocampo, *Dibujo* 275).

[17] Examples abound to illustrate her remarks here: she translated her own poems, she rewrote poems in the same language, and published more than one version of a poem, such as "La abandonada" and "La abandonada. Segunda versión," "La eternidad" and "La eternidad. Segunda versión" (all included in *Espacios métricos*). She also wrote narrative versions of topics first approached in poetry, such as "Autobiografía de Irene" and "El diario de Porfiria," poems included in *Espacios métricos* in 1945.

that she wrote to Octavio Paz, in which she sent a clipping of the above-mentioned poem published in the *Buenos Aires Herald*, provides a different view. It reads:

> Te mando un recorte de un diario inglés donde comentaban el poema que publicaron y que te mandé. *Escribir en un idioma ajeno es incómodo* y por ese motivo cuando lo publiqué lo firmé con un seudónimo que inventé creyendo que ese nombre nunca había existido. ("Carta a Octavio Paz" 2, my emphasis)

> [I am sending you a clipping from an English newspaper where they commented on the poem they published and which I sent to you. *Writing in someone else's language is uncomfortable* so when I published it I signed it with a pseudonym that I invented thinking that name had never existed.]

Without contradicting her own prior statements, Ocampo reveals that English, in spite of how familiar it was for her, is nevertheless an alien language and that it produces uneasiness. From her referring to English in this manner, it is tempting to consider that Spanish, the language she uses to write most of her work, is after all the language that she holds as her own more than any other.

Eduardo Paz Leston comments on poetic translations by Ocampo in general and relates them to Ocampo's own poetry as possible influences on her tone (313–24). He pays attention to similarities between the work of translation and creation, especially in the connection between her translations of works by Ronsard, Pope, Marvell, and Baudelaire, on the one hand, and poems included in *Espacios métricos* and *Los nombres*, on the other. Paz Leston is the only critic to consider Ocampo's translations who seems more interested in the process rather than the result. According to him, her translations not only "le permitieron practicar su arte de manera constante, a la manera de un cuaderno de ejercicios" (315) [allowed her to practice her art with a degree of constancy similar to that of a book of exercises], but also "estos ejercicios de retórica que fueron sus primeras traducciones conocidas afinaron sin duda su destreza" [these rhetorical exercises which made up her first known translations without doubt refined her skill]. In the same vein, Montequin conceives translations as "una suerte de manifiesto poético por ejemplos" (interview) [a kind of poetic manifesto through examples]. Here Montequin precisely describes how translation works for Silvina Ocampo, clarifying a difference that Mackintosh had noticed regarding the work of translation done by her sister Victoria:[18]

---

[18] Mackintosh describes Silvina Ocampo's work as partial compared to her sister's ("A Happy Transmigration" 24) but does not contrast, as Montequin does, each sister's intention: Victoria as the founder of *Sur* was engaged in promoting pan-American and transatlantic cultural exchange, while Silvina's interest was more personal.

Al igual que sucede con Borges y Bioy, la traducción es para Silvina una práctica *estética*, no *cultural*. Es decir, no se traduce para difundir una obra que se considera valiosa por sí misma, sino aquélla que instala y refuerza *una* idea de la literatura... Silvina participaba, aunque con menor intensidad, en esa política literaria que buscaba crear un contexto de recepción, moldear un gusto en los hipotéticos lectores proporcionándoles traducciones que, más allá de su intrínseco valor literario, los acercara estéticamente a las propias obras de los traductores. (interview)

[Just as happens with Borges and Bioy, translation for Silvina is an *esthetic*, not a *cultural* practice. That is, one does not translate in order to promote a work considered valuable in itself, rather, one translates the work that establishes and reinforces *one* idea of literature... Silvina participated, to a minor degree, in that literary politics that sought to create a context of reception, to mold a taste in its hypothetical readers offering them translations that, more than their intrinsic literary value, would foster the works of the translators.]

Silvina Ocampo's relationship with languages is plural and complex, as we have seen by way of the several episodes described in the first part of this essay and through the analysis of the poem. Her own attitude toward some languages, her work as translator – both for publication and for private use – and her writings in English and French are diverse forms of this relationship.

Translation and its Relationship with the Literary System

In Ocampo's view, English and French are literary languages par excellence, not only in her personal imaginary but also in that of her immediate group of social and intellectual acquaintances.[19] Regarding this close relationship with languages – the metonymic identification of these two foreign languages with their literatures, and the inclusion of the translation practice as an intrinsic part of her literary activity – there are three conclusions that contextualize this aspect of her work.

First, these are not phenomena that the writers of *Sur* invented, but rather that they adapted from a solid precedent in *modernismo*. Latin American *modernistas* had an intense relationship with French literature and were prolific translators,

---

[19] As Montequin points out, "ambas lenguas, sobre todo el francés, estaban sobredeterminadas estéticamente; en ellas se habían escrito las 'obras clásicas' y las lecturas formativas, no en el doméstico y utilitario español" (interview) [both languages, especially French, were overdetermined aesthetically; the 'classic works' of formative reading had been written in them, and not in the domestic and utilitarian Spanish].

claiming the practice was more than a matter of linguistic transference. Indeed, they asserted that many French literary experiments of the period had a profound influence on them as writers, because, as Analía Costa states, "con la traducción se ponen de manifiesto las intensas relaciones interliterarias que tienen lugar entre la literatura receptora (en este caso latinoamericana) y la literatura traducida" [with translation the intense interliterary relations become evident between the receiving literature (in this case Latin American) and the translated (French) literature]. These relations, thus, have to do with the privileged position translation acquires in the literary system and how it enriches vernacular literary practices:

> El Modernismo literario latinoamericano había dado muestras claras del lugar que la traducción, como práctica discursiva, llegó a ocupar dentro del sistema literario latinoamericano, en la medida en que se constituyó en una de las *fuentes fundamentales de asimilación y apropiación de modelos europeos* (sobre todo provenientes de la literatura francesa, pero extensivo al ámbito de las literaturas anglófonas y alemanas). (Costa n.p., my emphasis)

> [Latin American literary *modernismo* had given clear signs of the place that translation, as a discursive practice, came to occupy within the Latin American literary system, inasmuch as it constituted one of the *fundamental sources of assimilation and appropriation of European models* (especially those coming from French literature, but extending to the realm of Anglo and German literatures).]

Secondly, a generation later the *Sur* group and the intellectuals related to them gave continuity to an integrative attitude as an inherent part of their active literary practices. Patricia Willson has focused on the importance and transcendence of translation for some members of this group, with particular attention to Victoria Ocampo, Jorge Luis Borges, and José Bianco. She views the translation operation as a key part of how a literary system is composed. Willson's theoretical perspective, stemming from translation studies, speaks of a "migración de temas, de variantes genéricas, de rasgos escriturarios" [migration of themes, variations of genre categories, of writing traits] as possibilities that translation opens. This group embraced translation, according to her, as a nuclear and crucial activity within the literary system, as "uno de los modos de elaborar un nuevo repertorio" [one of the ways to develop a new repertoire] (33). Ocampo's case, as we have analyzed here, would not be central to this process, though it is deeply intertwined with other writing practices and, because of that, remains completely indissoluble from them. Rather than thinking in terms of margin and center, I find it crucial to identify Ocampo's work with languages as an organic part of a complex exercise of literature in which her generation of *Sur* authors participated.

Lastly, it is worth commenting on a link with Modernism, understood in its English sense.[20] The close connection to English modernists is exemplified by the inclusion of a poem by Pound in the same issue of *Disco* in which Ocampo's poem and pseudonym appear. Translation practices are also common to that generation, as Steven G. Yao puts it:

> Within the context of these efforts and concerns, translation represented for Modernism much more than either just a minor mode of literary production or an exercise of apprenticeship, though for some writers it continued to fulfill such a traditional function. Rather, it constituted an integral part of the Modernist program of cultural renewal, a crucially important mode of writing distinct from, yet fundamentally interconnected with, the more traditionally esteemed modes of poetry and prose fiction. (6)

This idea of translation as an integral part of a broader literary program seems to be at work in all the examples presented in this essay, from promoting foreign writers in translation by magazines such as *Sur* and *Disco*, to projects such as Clásicos Jackson, and extends to translations developed by eminent writers and intellectuals such as José Bianco, Jorge Luis Borges, Ricardo Baeza, and Juan Rodolfo Wilcock as well as to Silvina Ocampo. Within Ocampo's personal literary project, translation was crucial to integrating her constant rewriting practices. In her poetics, translation had less to do with a faithful rendering of meaning than with a literary exercise of creative freedom.[21]

[20] Latin American *modernismo* was a poetic movement of the late nineteenth century (1880–1910); English modernism is associated with the generation of writers that followed, primarily from the 1920s. (editor's note)

[21] This essay owes a debt of gratitude to my friend Dr. Amy Romanowski. The intelligibility of this piece would have been impossible without her countless helpful comments and corrections. Anything that remains unclear is my responsibility. I thank Daniel Balderston for his encouragement and trust, Gayle Rogers for his careful reading and comments, and Ernesto Montequin for his knowledge and generosity.

9

The Gender-Bending Mother of "Santa Teodora"

Fernanda Zullo-Ruiz

In *What Does a Woman Want? Reading and Sexual Difference*, Shoshana Felman claims that "mothers live, as mothers, through and for the story of the Other. The story of the mother ... is precisely one of having *no autobiography*, no story of her own" (146–47). Many of Silvina Ocampo's texts bear witness to precisely that elimination or negation of the mother's story, yet one of her unique poems, "Santa Teodora" (which appeared in *Amarillo Celeste*, 1972, and later in *Breve Santoral*, 1984),[1] both supports and subverts this postulate. By blurring the distinctions between motherhood and fatherhood, woman and man, heterosexuality and homosexuality, this poem investigates these identities through the lens of sexuality, thus allowing Teodora's body to reveal her own story.

The poem emphasizes the centralizing force of sexuality in the construction of the mother position, so much so that it (con)fuses sexuality and motherhood: the speaker in the poem is a woman masquerading as a man who is then accused of raping and impregnating a young woman. A series of tensions between the seen and heard, fiction and reality, exterior and interior demonstrate the irony of the tenuously gendered position. Is "she" a transgender mother? Is "she" a father in drag? What role does sexuality "play" in this gendered farce? This poem alludes to "ever shifting realities" through the performative nature of gender that Judith Butler ponders and the alterability that Donna Haraway theorizes. Through the voice and situation of the main character a closer inspection of a particular maternal paradigm is possible; Teodora opens up the virginal, saintly, Madonna-like conceptualization of motherhood and simultaneously forces a re-evaluation of the conflictive paternal role vis-à-vis her very presence.

---

[1] For the latter, see Mackintosh and Quance's excellent article, "Speaking/Seeing Saints: Norah Borges and Silvina Ocampo Collaborate," which details the reimagining of the devotional tradition of santorales through the dialogue between Borges's images and Ocampo's texts.

5. Block print "Santa Teodora" by Norah Borges from *Breve santoral*, 1984.

The conventional form of the poem, a sonnet, tells the very unconventional story of the main character, Teodora, a woman who takes on the identity of a man.

Santa Teodora

> Os digo, que así habrá gozo en el cielo de un
> pecador que se enmienda, más que de noventa y
> nueve justos, que no han menester enmendarse.
> Lucas, XV, 7

Yo, disfrazada de hombre. Yo, Teodora
entro en un monasterio para expiar
mis culpas, más difícil es borrar
lo que ocurre en secreto, cada hora.

Dentro de mí la culpa ya no mora,
mas algo en la mirada como un mar,
en los labios un sello sin cesar
el semblante me da de pecadora.

De haber violado a una muchacha pura
me acusaron, mas yo con gran ternura
cuido al hijo del cual me creen el padre

como si fuera verdadera madre.
Revela Dios, sólo después de muerta
mi santidad como una abierta puerta.²

[Epigraph: In the same way, I tell you, there will be more rejoicing in heaven over one sinner who repents than over ninety-nine righteous people who have no need of repentance, Luke 15:7.

I, disguised as a man. I, Teodora
enter a monastery to atone for
my sins, yet it is more difficult to erase
what happens in secret, every hour.

Sins no longer dwell within me,
yet something in my gaze like a sea,

---

2   The 1972 version of this poem, found in *Amarillo Celeste*, has a slightly different first stanza: "Con disfraz de hombre, yo, Santa Teodora" [Wearing the disguise of a man, I, Santa Teodora]. This earlier version of the poem uses the noun "disfraz" instead of the adjective "disfrazada," but more importantly, the poetic voice in the poem affirms her status as a saint from the start. The later poem simply postpones the possibility of sainthood until the final verse and her future death. Another interesting change is that the poem from 1984 begins the first two declarations by Teodora with the pronoun "yo" in the first stanza; this repetition asserts Teodora's identity which, ironically, is sublimated in the story she recounts.

in my endlessly sealed lips
my face makes me look like a sinner.

Of violating a pure girl,
they accused me, but with great tenderness
I care for the son they believe me to have fathered

as if I were a real mother.
God will reveal, only after my death
my sainthood as an open door.]

On first reading, both the title and epigraph appear to complement each other and lead us to believe that some facet of the protagonist's life is being offered as an exemplum. Since the epigraph, which comes from the Gospel of Luke, explicitly details paradise's qualitative approach to redemption – that is, one repentant sinner is worth more than ninety-nine righteous people – we might assume that it appears before the text in order to solidify some redemptive episode that occurred in Teodora's life and elevated her status to that of saint. As the poem proceeds, it elicits exactly the opposite effect: implicitly, the epigraph infuses the poem with the same ironic indifference towards virtue as found in the biblical citation. The text, "Santa Teodora," has on some level betrayed us by building up our expectations through its tacit manipulation of conventional reading habits; the title of the poem, the epigraph, and the delayed climactic revelation foster a certain interpretation that unravels at the end. And thus begins the extended metaphor of the deceitful body: from the body of the text to the body of Teodora, and then from the body of the pure girl to the body of the infant, each body, or "text," has the capability of being deceitful, of "performing," and of being misinterpreted.

Of course, the deceitful body that facilitates the existence of all the other deceitful bodies belongs to Teodora: by means of her body we can explore the performative aspect of gender and its precarious role in motherhood. As she dramatically enters the poem, she establishes one of the main points of the text, the motif of gender-bending: "Yo, disfrazada de hombre. Yo, Teodora/ entro en un monasterio" [I, disguised as a man. I, Teodora/ enter a monastery]. With that entrance she also ushers in a chain of binary tensions that centers upon a strict division of interior spaces from exterior spaces, in turn producing a splitting of the seen from the heard, and of fiction from reality. Ocampo crafts a virtual Chinese box: the poem cloisters a monastery that cloisters Teodora who cloisters her secret identity in her body. Outside the walls of the monastery, public denunciations against her circulate wildly, claiming, "De haber violado a una muchacha pura/ me acusaron" [Of violating a pure girl,/ They accused me]. Her accusers, and obviously the pure young woman in question, condemn Teodora for the rape and subsequent pregnancy. Her appearance, her exterior, provides all the evidence her accusers require to determine her sinful demeanor: "Dentro de mí la culpa ya no mora,/ mas algo en la mirada como un mar,/ en los labios un sello sin cesar/ el semblante me da de pecadora" [Sins no longer dwell within me,/ yet something in my gaze like a sea,/ in my endlessly sealed lips/ my face makes me look like a sinner]. Her eyes, her lips, and her face betray her by exposing her to the world as a sinner – yet why does she choose to refer to herself with the feminine noun, "pecadora," since in society's eyes she is a man? Apparently she must, in part, still consider herself a woman despite the fact that she chooses to live her life as a man; this choice will not be addressed in the poem and her decision to adopt the male gender will remain an unresolved enigma.[3]

Again, we learn that Teodora actually is a woman because she specifies that she dresses as a man, in the appropriate "costume," and she refers to herself with the feminine form of a noun. The situation reaches absurd proportions when the outside world identifies her as a man and condemns "him" for violating a young woman whom they have defined as pure. Once more the division of exterior spaces from interior spaces plays with the concepts of fiction and reality: not only does Teodora's body contain the truth about her identity and her innocence in this crime but so, too, does the young woman's body enclose the secret of her sexual relationship with an unidentified man which produces a son; and the son's body is a testament to Teodora's innocence and to his mother's guilt for concealing such information. This omitted information, information that the three deceitful bodies and the deceitful body of the text contain and preserve, condemns Teodora to a life of fatherhood which she did not solicit and for which she has no practical experience.[4]

Yet, without rancor, Teodora affirms that "yo con gran ternura/ cuido al hijo del cual me creen el padre/ como si fuera verdadera madre" [with great tenderness/ I care for the son they believe me to have fathered/ as if I were a real mother]. Her acceptance and ostensibly genuine affection for the child allow us to examine the differences between the gendered positions of motherhood and fatherhood. Other than the biological realities of each position (which modern technological advances in reproduction have altered somewhat), what constitutes the difference between

3   According to Roman Catholic tradition, Saint Theodora of Alexandria or Saint Theodora the Penitent (feast day September 11) adopted a male identity in order to enter a monastery and do penance. *Breve santoral* includes an explanatory fragment from R.P. Jean-Etienne Grosesz's *El Diario de los Santos* (1828) [The Diary of the Saints], but the quote does not specify the sin for which Teodora does penance. Orthodox Churches, however, do define the sin as adultery. Ocampo ignores the motivation for cross-dressing, and unless the reader is familiar with this story, the poem purposefully plays with the lingering ambiguity.

4   This poem presents the bizarre societal demand that an alleged rapist assume his fatherly duties. The reader understands that Teodora could not have raped the young woman, but all the accusations that swirl around her reveal that, in that society, it is more disgraceful to have "fathered" a child out of wedlock rather than to have raped a woman. The poem highlights the disturbing treatment of sexual violence in a traditional society: the crime of sexual aggression against a woman will essentially be absolved if a man assumes his role as father.

fatherhood and motherhood? Can a woman assume the role of father? Can a man mother? These issues permeate the text in spite of its seeming disregard for such distinctions – perhaps this lack of insistence actually obliges us to divest the subject positions of mother and father of their gendered identities in order to evaluate the performative aspects of these "natural" states. The irony of Teodora's situation opens up the discussion since, as Donna Haraway asserts, "Irony is about contradictions that do not resolve into larger wholes, even dialectically, about the tension of holding incompatible things together because both or all are necessary and true. Irony is about humor and serious play" (65).

The humor and serious play of Teodora's ironic predicament foregrounds the dynamic possibility of gender-bending and its consequences in her life. By incorporating two supposedly incompatible discourses or roles, masculinity and femininity, in one person, Ocampo problematizes the presumed stability of meaning in gendered positions and in particular their maternal and paternal expressions. The subtle shifts in Teodora's perception of herself, a man to the world while still self-identifying as a woman, eloquently illustrate Haraway's notion of boundaries. Haraway calls "for *pleasure* in the confusion of boundaries and for *responsibility* in their construction" (66). Teodora incorporates both the confusion of gender boundaries and her own responsibility in their construction; however, the idea of pleasure, her pleasure, remains puzzling: does she experience pleasure as a man and a woman? I will postpone this issue in order to first examine the gendered positions of mother and father that Teodora incarnates.

By providing a character who brings together the disparate sites of motherhood and fatherhood without attempting to synthesize them, Ocampo opens up the various theoretical fields that have attempted to analyze these issues. In so doing, she enables us to examine gender in its function as the "center" of meaning, or as Slavoj Žižek calls that "center," the *point de caption*. He argues that,

> Ideological space is made of non-bound, non-tied elements, "floating signifiers," whose very identity is "open," overdetermined by their articulation in a chain with other elements ... The "quilting" performs the totalization by means of which this free floating of ideological elements is halted, fixed – that is to say, by means of which they become parts of the structured network of meaning. (87)

Žižek's exploration of the mechanisms at work in totalizing theories abets our inquiry into how gender operates in the production of meaning. The *point de caption* "is the point through which the subject is 'sewn' to the signifier, and at the same time the point which interpellates individual into subject by addressing it with the call of a master-signifier ... in a word, it is the point of the subjectivation of the signifier's chain" (101). Hence, Teodora's appearance as both man and woman, a dual subjectivity in many ways, destabilizes the concepts of masculinity and femininity and their manifestations as fatherhood and motherhood. These concepts, and the tensions that they play with, will split open and lend themselves to performance, parody, and misinterpretation, all of which will be made possible through the *point de caption* of the poem, Teodora.

One of the key models in Teodora's interpretation of motherhood springs from the masochistic maternal image of the Virgin Mary. According to Julia Kristeva, this impossible paradigm of motherhood suggests that the Madonna is

A Unique Woman: alone among women, alone among mothers, alone among humans since she is without sin. But the acknowledgement of a longing for uniqueness is immediately checked by the postulate according to which uniqueness is attained only through an exacerbated masochism: a concrete woman, worthy of the feminine ideal embodied by the Virgin as an inaccessible goal, could only be a nun, a martyr or, if she is married, one who leads a life that would remove her from the "earthly" condition and dedicate her to the highest sublimation alien to her body. (181)

Apparently, Teodora's bodily sublimation, like that of the Virgin Mary, is a prerequisite for the "virginal" birth that takes place. In a similar fashion to the redemption motif that pervades many of Ocampo's texts ("La furia" [The fury] is a prime example), the "sacrifice" that occurs in this poem will redeem only one person: Teodora. In this aspect she diverges from the Madonna paradigm since the Virgin provides humanity with a second opportunity when her body becomes the vessel that produces the Redeemer; Teodora's body, on the other hand, does not engender redemption for others, nor does it give birth to the child whom she mothers. Teodora ironically approximates the concept of a virginal birth: not having known man, at least not in this particular circumstance, she becomes a mother, "como si fuera verdadera madre" [as if I were a real mother].

Since she did not conceive the child, nor even *conceive of him* before the accusations – and she obviously could not have given birth to him – Teodora's relationship to the child is that of surrogate mother, if only because of her gender. But, as she has stated, her accusers see her as a father despite the fact that she is a woman and identifies as a mother. This conflict breaches the fixed interpretation of each position and provides a unique gender palimpsest where the overlapping features can be detected and studied. As Magdalene Redekop has elaborated regarding surrogacy, a "mock mother" can be a man or a woman, simply requiring someone to behave maternally.[5] Clearly, maternal behavior remains an ambiguous and debatable issue, but what emerges from Redekop's reasoning is the perception that the important skills in "mothering" can be performed by members of both sexes. This potential alterability of motherhood pries open that role to an infinite number of possible representations and to an equally infinite number of interpretations of these roles. Teodora, as a mother/father, undoubtedly complicates the traditional, patriarchal rendition of motherhood: her mere existence as such challenges the subject position of mother, since, after all, people read her as a man and her actions as "paternal" when she should be read as a woman and her actions as "maternal." If this perceived "natural" behavior can be interpreted as both paternal and maternal, how solid are the differences that patriarchy establishes between fatherhood and motherhood? Is gender the *point de caption* at the heart of the debate? If so, "misreadings" of gender must inevitably render the debate less meaningful or at least more problematic.

The misreading of Teodora as a man and subsequently as a father sheds some light on the issue of gender and performance. Judith Butler has argued that gender, masculinity and femininity, are two performances or signifying practices that (un)organize identity and hence have the potential to operate politically. For example, she concludes that "As the effects of a subtle and politically enforced performativity, gender is an 'act,' as it were, that is open to splittings, self-parody, self-criticism, and those hyperbolic exhibitions of 'the natural' that, in their very exaggeration, reveal its fundamentally phantasmatic status" (146–47). Butler's innovative approach to the parodic possibilities of gender fails when it attempts to discuss the interpretative process of these performances. Criticism of her theory focuses on her failure to problematize the variety of possible readings of performances: she only highlights the subversive element in parody and does not address the potential parody has to backfire and reinforce the very element to which the performance wishes to call attention. In other words, the "authorial" intention will not necessarily coincide with the reader's interpretation. In "Santa Teodora," the poetic voice draws attention to the locus of meaning and it centers heavily on the gender identity of Teodora. The text never reveals the reason she chose to live her life as a man, but we can be certain that the outcome of her "performance" was not the result she originally desired. She continues the charade, at least in part, because she feels she will receive compensation for her sacrifices in the

---

5   Hansen, in *Mother Without Child*, cites Redekop's definition of "mock mothers" as "stepmothers, foster mothers, adoptive mothers, child mothers, nurses, old maids, mothering husbands, sisters mothering each other, and numerous women and men behaving in ways that could be described as maternal" (14).

hereafter. As long as Teodora continues to perform as a man and as a father, the patriarchal system in which she lives remains "stable" as gender and gender-related activities appear to be what they are. Upon her death, when her true gender identity will be discovered, the entire system will be in a state of flux, for, as Butler states, "The loss of gender norms would have the effect of proliferating gender configurations, destabilizing substantive identity, and depriving the naturalizing narratives of compulsory heterosexuality of their central protagonists: 'man' and 'woman'" (146).

This brings us to the concept of compulsory heterosexuality, as Adrienne Rich defined our cultural bias towards male/female romantic relationships in her seminal essay, "Compulsory Heterosexuality and the Lesbian Experience." She questions "first, how and why women's choice of women as passionate comrades, life partners, co-workers, lovers, and community has been crushed, invalidated, forced into hiding and disguise; and second, the virtual or total neglect of lesbian existence in a wide range of writing" (312). By counterpointing the moments of suppression by the hegemonic powers with the moments of resistance to it, Rich stresses the peremptory nature of heterosexuality as an institution in modern society. Admittedly, Rich points out that within a heterosexist society there have existed "qualitative differences," but what has not existed is choice (325). In "Santa Teodora," her gender-bending contributes to the feeling that she lacks choices: why does Teodora initially dress as a man? Does that facilitate access to certain arenas that might otherwise be off limits to her as a woman? Is her sexuality one of the reasons why she feels compelled to masquerade as a man in a society marked by compulsory heterosexuality?

Teodora herself initiates the lesbian subtext in the poem. She establishes a contrast between her "sins" and her secret activities, recounting that "entro en un monasterio para *expiar/ mis culpas,* mas difícil es borrar/ *lo que ocurre en secreto,* cada hora" (emphasis added) [I, Teodora/ enter a monastery *to atone for/ my sins,* yet it is more difficult to erase/ *what happens in secret, every hour*]. As readers, we wonder what compels her to feel remorse. According to the people who observe her, she is guilty of the rape of a young woman, which leads to pregnancy, yet we know the absurdity of this claim. In her own defense, Teodora later asserts, "Dentro de mí la culpa ya no mora" [Sins no longer dwell within me] – so, from her perspective, what is she guilty of? What are those secret activities that occur every hour? The text is enigmatic enough to suggest but not confirm a lesbian reading of "Santa Teodora": we do not know if Teodora and the mother of her son marry and live together as a socially sanctioned "heterosexual" couple. She does, however, profess that she tends to this child as if she were his mother; if her relationship to the child is that of parent, what then is her relationship to the biological mother? Are they lesbian lovers? Or is

Teodora the sole source of lesbian desire in the text? Teodora's allusion to those secret activities is vague enough that, together with other aspects of her identity, all of the aforementioned possibilities are viable.

Now, if we accept the premise of a lesbian subtext, we must reinterpret the concept of motherhood through that filter and examine why a patriarchal system finds it menacing. As E. Ann Kaplan has suggested, "the lesbian mother challenges and explodes the mythic underpinnings of the patriarchal mother-construct," such as the maternal sacrifice paradigm and the phallic mother paradigm (193). These patriarchal mother-constructs ensure the perpetuation and maintenance of a male-centered and male-dominated culture: she secures the future of society through her reproductive capacities, her role as the backdrop for her child's subjectivity, and her subordinate position in patriarchy. Adrienne Rich confirms this view when she states that:

> When we look hard and clearly at the extent and elaboration of measures designed to keep women within a male sexual purlieu, it becomes an inescapable question whether the issue feminists have to address is not simple "gender inequality" nor the domination of culture by males nor mere "taboos against homosexuality," but the enforcement of heterosexuality for women as a means of assuring male right of physical, economic and emotional access. (316)

The lesbian in such a society necessarily threatens its very foundations, since her sexuality and her reproductive abilities cannot be harnessed by men; the potentially liberating aspects of this sexual orientation and its capacity for enacting other forms of resistance to the system destabilize the premise on which patriarchy rests: the phallus as the ultimate signifier.

The two areas that defy the phallus on various levels, and therefore require their reining in by society, are lesbian sexuality and motherhood. Rich identifies an affinity between the lesbian experience and that of mothers:

> I perceive the lesbian experience as being, like motherhood, a profoundly *female* experience, with particular oppressions, meanings, and potentialities we cannot comprehend as long as we simply bracket it with other sexually stigmatized existences. Just as the term parenting serves to conceal the particular and significant reality of being a parent who is actually a mother, the term *gay* may serve the purpose of blurring the very outlines we need to discern, which are of crucial value for feminism and for the freedom of women as a group. (318–19)

On defining motherhood, Rich and Redekop are somewhat at odds: while Rich sees motherhood as "a profoundly female experience," Redekop affirms that men or women can adopt that role as a "mock mother." The character of Santa Teodora embodies yet a further complication in defining motherhood because she *blurs the very outlines we need to discern* in lesbian mothering: we cannot affirm that she is a lesbian nor can we affirm that she is a mother. The only concrete details the text provides indicate that society finds her guilty of having raped and impregnated the biological mother of the child she cares for and that she cares for the child as if she were his mother. The outlines, indeterminate as they may be, do, however, cast some further doubts onto the presumably determinate field of motherhood and its relationship to sexuality and gender. For example, in a lesbian family setting, what happens to the Oedipal configuration? Do both women signify a lack for the child or does one of them embody the phallus that she plainly lacks? Will the phallus cease to be privileged in such an environment?

This virtually unexplored terrain, the "borders of motherhood" as Elaine Tuttle Hansen calls it, still warrants a thorough evaluation: Patrice DiQuinzio surmises that "Further analysis of mothering would benefit from a focus on nontraditional instances of mothering – for example, lesbian mothering or the mothering of women without custody of children" (qtd in Hansen, "Exclusion and Essentialism" 10). Our perceptions of motherhood and sexuality essentially will continue to appear restricted, incomplete, and skewed if we do not factor into the equation the lesbian component in both arenas. Interestingly, in spite of Teodora's somewhat unorthodox existence, the fact that she lives that way because of her persistent vigilance and secrecy suggests more about the limitations placed on personal choice rather than any radical upheaval of convention. Once more, Rich provides insight into this matter; as she puts it, "Within the institution [of heterosexuality] exist, of course, qualitative differences of experience; but the *absence of choice* remains the great unacknowledged reality" (325, emphasis added).

The question of choice punctuates every aspect of Teodora's existence – from her gender to her sexuality and parenthood – and highlights the very precarious state of her options. The only unequivocal decision she makes, to live as a man, invites us to speculate about the motives behind this choice: could it be that, in Teodora's opinion, certain options would become available to her if, and only if, she were a man? Indeed, certain arenas, which would otherwise remain off-limits to her, now form part of her domain, as do the privileges that come with that territory. Yet, ironically, in her attempt to overturn conventions and seize control of her life, she unwillingly initiates a virtual backlash of repression that truncates not only her possibilities as a man, but also as a lesbian, father, and mother. Through the competing forces of personal agency and societal repression, Ocampo neatly compresses some of the most volatile issues concerning gender, sexual orientation, and parenthood into the character of Teodora – and into the limits of the sonnet form – without engaging in a simplistic, one-dimensional analysis of them. By overlaying these identities – man and woman, father and mother, heterosexual and lesbian – she creates a matrix of conflicting desires, needs, and opportunities, in addition to the conflicting performances and interpretations that permit a more insightful reading than if she were to limit the scope to only one of those matters.

We witness the curtailing of Teodora's opportunities as a man when her accusers name her the father of the young woman's child. Fatherhood, in that sense, first becomes an imposition upon Teodora which later turns into a source of joy. Kaplan has highlighted that in various cultural texts "Fathering is not seen as part of any identity they [men] *need* assume ... fatherhood is chosen, not demanded, as motherhood is" (197).[6] Even though Kaplan's conclusion (that fatherhood is not an expectation as motherhood continues to be) may be true, Ocampo reveals a subversive power of female desire in this poem: despite all of patriarchy's overwhelming attempts to rein in female sexuality, the desire of the mother escapes its persistent policing. The poem sprinkles doubts and questions throughout: do the accusers name Teodora because the mother feels she needs to protect herself or another person? Is there a transgression or taboo that she must conceal? What was the relationship between the mother and Teodora before the accusations? This fundamental detail, the desire of the mother, does not escape Ocampo's scrutiny. In fact, by presenting the "demand" for fatherhood of a woman (Teodora), Ocampo traces the violation of Teodora's personal freedom and good name that such an ill-founded claim can enact; the fact that the designated father of the child is a woman heightens our awareness of the potential for abuse in such circumstances. More contentious still is the accusation of rape in the poem: here Ocampo presents a dangerous false charge of sexual abuse by presenting it through the perspective of an apparently innocent accused. This portrayal of rape and paternity does not minimize the many real-life situations or artistic depictions of them that have exposed the abuse and exploitation of women in patriarchy; on the contrary, it simply offers a more comprehensive look at a scenario of conflicting desires. Power, as Michel Foucault theorizes, is exercised from innumerable and mobile sites within relationship; no "binary and all-encompassing opposition between rulers and ruled" exists (94). Ocampo illustrates how power can be negotiated and exerted by those believed to be at the bottom of an established hierarchy as well as by those believed to be favored by it.

This problematization of power underscores the constant clipping of options, a clipping also visible in Teodora's clandestine existence as a woman. As noted

---

6   Although Kaplan is dealing here with the representation of fatherhood and motherhood in certain popular texts, her thesis concerning the assumed link between child-rearing and womanhood remains true of a plethora of cultural texts and discourses.

previously, her decision to live as a man must on some level imply that the opportunities available to her as a woman appear unsatisfactory. This lack of adequate alternatives becomes most apparent in two fundamental areas of Teodora's life: her sexuality and motherhood. Lesbianism continues to rock the foundation of patriarchy by assailing its principle of compulsory heterosexuality and overvalorization of the phallus. Perhaps Teodora's male public identity provides her with the opportunity to explore an alternative to the heterosexual dictate: the choice to live as a lesbian is facilitated if she can exist as a man. A further complication arises from the combination of motherhood and lesbianism, since patriarchy privileges the heterosexual couple in all aspects of parenting. Ocampo's portrayal compels us to examine a nontraditional form of mothering through lesbianism and a nontraditional life through her gendered identities. This focus reaffirms the precarious context in which she lives: motherhood becomes an unsolicited condition that defines a principal aspect of her self-identity. In the end, Teodora's performance causes her to lose control of her identity and autonomy since she cannot ward off the imposition of her maternal/ paternal status and the restriction of her sexuality.[7]

At the core of all these issues, whether it be parenthood, sexuality, performance, or opportunity, resides the conflicted notion of gender. Ocampo scrutinizes the centralizing force attributed to gender and how this feature not only produces "meaning" in a patriarchal society but also how it becomes the very locus of "meaning." Teodora manifests the tight grip patriarchy holds on the concepts of motherhood and fatherhood by cataloguing the gendered behavior of both: the maternal component is either masochistic or phallic and the paternal does not receive any limitations in its rendition. The phallus, of course, remains the determining signifier against which all texts – including gender – are read and develop meaning. In such a system, subjectivity itself attests to the scripting nature of the phallus: the Oedipal configuration bolsters the importance of the phallus for those who possess it (and fear losing it) and for those who do not, yet undoubtedly wish to possess it. The overvalorization of the phallus empowers a society to exist as a male-centered and male-dominated community where no blurring of roles, spheres, or attributes can be tolerated if it is to survive as such.

Teodora's mini-insurrection, albeit unwitnessed and confined, will only partly receive attention upon her death when her secret existence or identity will be discovered. In the meantime, she buttresses the infrastructure of a patriarchal society by "playing" her part as a man, a virile, aggressive man in fact, who

---

7   If Teodora were heterosexual, her masculine identity might be an obstacle in her attempts to conduct a traditional heterosexual relationship with men. Should she be a lesbian, her masculine identity might hinder a specific type of homosexual relationship with women. On the other hand, a more "masculine" lesbian identity might open up another set of opportunities.

forces himself on a pure, unmarried young woman, leaves her pregnant, and finally accepts his paternal duties to the child. Teodora's body becomes the key to the truth about the mother of the child, the child, and Teodora's identity: her body contains secrets that could upset the basic structure of meaning in patriarchy. Since Teodora identifies herself as a woman yet manages to fool everyone with her performance of masculinity – she is accused of rape, after all – what does that indicate about the stability of patriarchy's gendered roles, in particular motherhood and fatherhood? If such a society misreads her interpretation of motherhood, which they understand to be fatherhood, then these roles must not be forged from such solid attributes. On the contrary, the very concept of gender and the importance of the phallus falters. By utilizing Teodora's body as the nexus of the debate, Ocampo maneuvers deftly into the problematic realms of motherhood, fatherhood, sexuality, and gender, and reveals their contradictory characteristics. "Santa Teodora" obliges us to inspect what motherhood can mean in a lesbian context; it asks us to question what constitutes the difference between "mothering" and "fathering" and it makes us interrogate, if not mistrust, the possibilities that patriarchy authorizes for women.

10

Illicit Domains:
Homage to Silvina Ocampo in Alejandra Pizarnik's Works[*]

Daniel Balderston

This essay posits the hypothesis that in addition to personal affective ties, which were revealed with the publication of part of their correspondence,[1] there were also strong connections between the works of Alejandra Pizarnik and those of Silvina Ocampo. There are moments when that relationship is made explicit – a review, a title of a poem, a few dedications – but the homage to Ocampo in Pizarnik's work is also a blurry presence in other areas. It is useful to think of *La condesa sangrienta* not only in relation to Valentine Penrose's book, or to Borges's *Historia universal de la infamia* – two models that have garnered critical attention – but also to the stories from *La furia* (1959). It is useful to think of Pizarnik's poetic projects, quite different on the surface from those by Ocampo, in part as an homage to the poetry of her friend and precursor. And it is also useful to think of what Ocampo might represent for Pizarnik in the Argentine literary landscape – her differences from other women writers, the strangeness of her works – as something productive in her own creative processes.

The review Pizarnik wrote in 1967 (which was published the following year in *Sur*) of *El pecado mortal*, an anthology of Ocampo's short stories that the

---

[*]   This essay was originally presented as a paper at the Pizarnik colloquium organized by Adelaïde de Chatellus and Milagros Ezquerro at the Sorbonne in 2012, and was published in Spanish in the proceedings volume from that conference, *Alejandra Pizarnik: el lugar donde todo sucede*. I would like to dedicate it to the memory of Adelaïde de Chatellus, who died much too early in the summer of 2014.

[1]   Pizarnik's letters to Ocampo were published, at least in part, in *Correspondencia Pizarnik*, the volume compiled by Ivonne Bordelois in 1998. Bordelois notes: "De todas las cartas de este epistolario, éstas son las únicas donde la amistad rápidamente asciende a pasión y se enciende en ella" (190) [Of all the letters from this epistolary exchange, these are the only ones where friendship quickly ascends to passion and ignites]. The most notable letter is the last, dated January 31, 1972 (210–12). See also Piña's biography (especially 162–64). Regarding Pizarnik's sexuality, see Mariana Enriquez's note, "La poeta sangrienta."

publishing house Centro Editor de América Latina distributed with a prologue by José Bianco, is notable because it initiated (with Bianco's text) the serious study of Ocampo. Pizarnik's review, titled "Dominios ilícitos," speaks of the "extrema concentración" of Ocampo's stories, the "insumisión a los esquemas del relato," her "reserva delicada" and the use of ambiguity (Pizarnik, *Obras completas* 252) [extreme concentration ... rebellion against the short story schemas ... delicate reserve], as well as the "modo de hacer visibles las pasiones infantiles" (253) [manner of making visible infantile passions]. She mentions her delicate humor (255) and her preference for unexpected perspectives:

> Como puede comprobarse, la autora no intenta poner en tela de juicio la noción de realidad. Pero, por las dudas, prefiere que los hechos más normales sean transmitidos por "puntos de vista" de la estirpe de la enanita muerta de risa (de "El vestido de terciopelo"). (254)

> [As one can attest, the author does not try to question the notion of reality. But, just in case, she prefers that the most normal actions be transmitted through "points of view" like that of the laughing dwarf (in "El vestido de terciopelo").]

It is of special interest how Pizarnik discusses the "dialéctica del desamparo y del humor" [dialectic of helplessness and humor] in Ocampo (Evelyn Fishburn brilliantly comments on this aspect in Mackintosh and Posso 38), because that dialectic can be discovered in some areas of her own writing (I am thinking, for instance, of "La bucanera de Pernambuco o Hilda la polígrafa"). That is, she perceives in Ocampo's works something that also characterizes her – at least in part – as a writer. I do not believe that we are dealing here with an influence, since the review is rather late in her production, and this facet had been manifested already in its own form, but it is the recognition of an affinity with Ocampo's singular work.

There have been some interesting discussions in the last few years about self-writing and the many ways it is achieved. Clearly Pizarnik is a strong case of a writer who constructs a "figure of the author," to use one of the terms that has been introduced. The "figure" she invented was novel, and for that reason it caught the attention of many other writers and critics. In regard to models of self-fashioning, it is evident that Pizarnik forges an original figure, very different from some of the existing models (let us recall some figurations of the woman writer: Victoria Ocampo, Alfonsina Storni, Gabriela Mistral). It is here, I believe, that there is a possible hidden connection with Silvina Ocampo, another writer who invented a totally original form of self-writing for the time, even though critics have been late to recognize this (much later than in Pizarnik's case). That is, Pizarnik was one of the first to have recognized the uniqueness and originality of Ocampo's works.

A text that shows another side of Pizarnik's admiration for Ocampo's works is the poem "A un poema acerca del agua, de Silvina Ocampo" [On a poem about water by Silvina Ocampo]. It has a dedication "A Silvina y a la condesa de Trípoli" [To Silvina and the Countess of Tripoli] and an epigraph by Octavio Paz (from *Piedra del sol*): "que emana toda la noche profecías" [which emanates prophecies all night long].

> Tu modo de silenciarte en el poema.
> Me abrís como a una flor
> (sin duda una flor pobre, lamentable)
> que ya no esperaba la terrible delicadeza
> de la primavera. Me abrís, me abro,
> me vuelvo de agua en tu poema de agua
> que *emana toda la noche profecías*.
> (*Poesía completa* 356)

> [Your way of silencing yourself in the poem.
> You open me up like a flower
> (without a doubt a poor, lamentable flower)
> that no longer hoped for the terrible delicacy
> of spring. You open me up, I open up,
> I turn to water in your water poem
> that emanates prophesies all night long.]

This poem, unpublished during Pizarnik's lifetime, is printed in the Lumen edition with the following note by Ana Becciú: "Hojita mecanografiada y corregida por AP, sin fecha" [Page typed and corrected by AP, no date]. This text is intriguing for various reasons, as already noted by Susana Chávez Silverman (Mackintosh and Posso 17–19). First, it is difficult to know which of the many Silvina Ocampo poems about water this poem honors, especially since we don't know the date of Pizarnik's poem. The fact that the epigraph and the final verse belong to Octavio Paz and not Ocampo also does not help much in this respect. However, I have a good candidate: the poem "Para el agua" from *Amarillo celeste*, published in 1972, the year of Pizarnik's death. This poem was certainly written some time between the publication of *Lo amargo por dulce* in 1962 and *Amarillo celeste* ten years later, in other words, during the years of greatest intimacy between the two poets.[2] Ocampo's poem reads:

---

2   Another possible intertext is "Amar" from *Amarillo celeste*, which ends with these notable lines: "Ah, me hubiera gustado ser la helada/ agua tragando tu garganta ardiente/ como un ángel en furia, puramente./ ¡Heroica ambición de ser tragada!" [Ah, I would have liked to be the frozen/ water drinking your parched throat/ like an angel in fury, purely./ Heroic ambition to be swallowed!] (*Poesía completa* II 169).

Estoy hablando al agua que es espejo:
"Como a una madre yo amo al universo
que me hubiera abrazado al despertar,
que me trajera cestos de duraznos,
caminos y estaciones y abanicos.
Dentro de algunas piedras muy preciosas
veo brillar tus ínfimos paisajes,
tus personas que mueren o que nacen.
Hasta el crimen por eso me da lástima
y la insolencia misma me enternece.
Te contemplo alejándote en el río.
¡Y daría mi vida por la tuya
imaginando tu llegada al mar
desnuda, impersonal y aun tan mía
formando parte como yo del mundo!"

(*Poesía completa* II 194)

[I am speaking to the water that is a mirror:
"I love the universe like a mother
who would have embraced me upon wakening,
brought me baskets of peaches,
pathways and seasons and fans.
Inside some very precious stones I see your tiny landscapes shine,
your people who die or are born.
For that reason I feel pity even for crime
and insolence itself moves me.
I gaze at you as you sail away down the river.
And I would give my life for yours
imagining your arrival at the sea
nude, impersonal, and still so mine
forming part of this world as much as I!"]

If this is the poem Pizarnik glossed in her own, "Tu modo de silenciarte en el poema" [your way of silencing yourself in the poem] refers specifically to the manner in which Ocampo turns into a poetic voice whose words, cited in the last fourteen lines of the poem, have something impersonal and hieratic about them: in a certain way the poetic "I" of the poem is reduced to the voice of the first line, which says: "Estoy hablando al agua que es espejo" [I am speaking to the water that is a mirror]. At the same time, the splitting of the poetic "I" produces a strange splitting of the addressee, which is and is not the sea: there is a "you" in the last four lines which reaches the sea, and which is "desnuda, impersonal y aun tan mía" [nude, impersonal, and still so mine]. That nudity ("desnudez") and that impersonality are also in Pizarnik's poem, where the poetic voice opens "como una flor/ (sin duda una flor pobre, lamentable)" [like a flower/ (without a doubt a poor, lamentable flower)] and then repeats "Me abrís, me abro" [You open me up, I open up]: that is, the nude "I" is poor and lamentable, opened up by another, but at the same time, opens up herself. The sexual act is also suggested in the penultimate line, "me vuelvo de agua en tu poema de agua" [I turn to water in your water poem], which suggests that the poetic "I" recognizes herself in the "you" of Ocampo's poem.

The epigraph and the Paz quote are intriguing. We know that Paz greatly admired Ocampo as well as Pizarnik, and that both of them admired him, but these flowery gestures (even if they are poor and lamentable) in the form of quoting him do not cease to be strange. Even stranger is the fact that the quotation is wrong: Paz says "mana," and not "emana." The first stanza of his famous long poem reads:

> un sauce de cristal, un chopo de agua,
> un alto surtidor que el viento arquea,
> un árbol bien plantado más danzante,
> un caminar de río que se curva,
> avanza, retrocede, da un rodeo
> y llega siempre: un caminar tranquilo
> de estrella o primavera sin premura,
> agua que con los párpados cerrados
> mana toda la noche profecías,
> unánime presencia en oleaje,
> ola tras ola hasta cubrirlo todo,
> verde soberanía sin ocaso
> como el deslumbramiento de las alas
> cuando se abren en mitad del cielo
>
> (*Poemas* 259–60)

> [a crystal willow, a poplar of water,
> a tall fountain the wind arches over,
> a tree deep-rooted yet dancing still,
> a course of a river that turns, moves on,
> doubles back, and comes full circle,
> forever arriving: the calm course
> of the stars or an unhurried spring,
> water with eyes closed welling over
> with oracles all night long,
> a single presence in a surge of waves,
> wave after wave till it covers all,
> a reign of green that knows no decline,
> like the flash of wings unfolding in the sky][3]

·3   Translation by Eliot Weinberger. (translator's note)

That is, this stanza from Paz's poem is also a poem about water and an opening that is produced in water. The "profecías" in the tenth line can be linked to Pizarnik's poem in her way of making her own Paz's and Ocampo's verses, while also converting them into something new. Pizarnik's error in quoting Paz not only adds an additional syllable to Paz's hendecasyllable line but also alters its meaning: *"manar"* [to well or to overflow] suggests a spontaneous action, whereas *"emanar"* [to emanate], especially when it is linked to *"profecías"* [prophecies or oracles], implies communication. I believe that is why Pizarnik mistakes or alters the line: she is using Paz's verse to *interpellate* Ocampo's poem (and perhaps its author). The intertextual game is delicate and complex, with that "terrible delicadeza/ de la primavera" [terrible delicateness/ of spring] from Pizarnik's poem, violent and sudden.

Another poem by Pizarnik that she dedicated to Ocampo has the title "... Al alba venid ..." [Come at daybreak], with an ellipsis before and after the three words of the title. The quote is from an anonymous villancico:

> Al alba venid, buen amigo,
> al alba venid.
> Amigo el que yo más quería,
> venid al alba del día.
> Amigo el que yo más amaba,
> venid a la luz del alba.
> Venid a la luz del día,
> non traigáis compañía.
> Venid a la luz del alba,
> non traigáis gran compaña.

> [Come at daybreak, sweet friend,
> come at daybreak.
> Friend whom I love the best,
> come at the dawn of day.
> Friend whom I love above all,
> come at the break of dawn.
> Come at the break of day,
> but bring no company.
> Come at the dawn of day,
> bring little company.][4]

This Spanish poem is related to the Galician-Portuguese tradition of the *cantigas de amigo* [songs of friends and of love], and to the Mozarabic jarchas; it is thought to date from the fifteenth century. Pizarnik's version has a dedication "A Silvina Ocampo," and later says:

---

[4]   Translation by Gerald Brenan. (translator's note)

al viento no lo escuchéis,
al viento.
   toco la noche,
a la noche no la toquéis,
al alba,
   voy a partir,
al alba no partáis, al alba
voy a partir.   (*Poesía completa* 443)

[do not listen to the wind,
to the wind.
   I touch the night,
do not touch the night,
at daybreak,
   I will go,
do not go at daybreak, at daybreak
I will go.]

Once again, here we see complex work with an intertext, since instead of coming at dawn, the poetic voice declares her intention of leaving at daybreak. The repetitions in the anonymous villancico echo in Pizarnik's poem, while the use of "vosotros," in the title as much as in the poem, inscribes the peninsular tradition of the jarchas and *cantigas* in the poem. At the same time, it radically transforms the medieval poem, converting it from a lover's monologue into a possible dialogue. One could rewrite it as follows:

A: al viento no lo escuchéis,
B: al viento,
   toco la noche,
A: a la noche no la toquéis,
B: al alba,
   voy a partir,
A: al alba no partáis,
B: al alba
   voy a partir.

[A: do not listen to the wind
B: to the wind.
   I touch the night
A: do not touch the night
B: at daybreak,
   I will go
A: do not go at daybreak
B: at daybreak
   I will go.]

This transforms the discursive situation from the *cantigas de amigo*, monologues that invite the reader/listener to imagine the object of desire and noted for their gender-sexual ambiguity, a theme explored by the Mexican poet Abigael Bohórquez in his modern *cantigas* with a homoerotic theme, as I have commented elsewhere.[5]

In the Pizarnik archives at Princeton there is a typed version of this poem, with another title and with some minimal but important differences in terms of the division of the lines that, as I indicated before, can be read as a dialogue. The title is "Simple comme una phrase musicale," and the same dedication appears (but in lower case, "a Silvina Ocampo"). This version reads as follows:

> al viento no lo escuchéis
> al viento
>   toco la noche
> a la noche no la toquéis
>   al alba
> no partáis
>   al alba
> voy a partir

> [do not listen to the wind
> to the wind
>   I touch the night
> do not touch the night
>   at daybreak
> do not go
>   at daybreak
> I will go]

The title could refer to the musicalized version of the anonymous villancico, but the reason as to why it is written in French is unclear to me. What is noticeable is that the text included in *Textos de sombra* alters the place where the first iteration of "al alba" [at daybreak] appears and it adds the phrase "voy a partir" [I will go] which is repeated once more at the end.[6]

Pizarnik, therefore, establishes a dialogue with Ocampo at different moments in her work, and I imagine that there must be many more examples that are not as explicit as those which I mention here. At any rate, what draws our attention is the power Ocampo represents for Pizarnik as a model for a woman writer. In Pizarnik's chaotic papers in Princeton there are other remains of their

5   See "Never Say I," 337–9. (translator's note)
6   Since *Textos de sombra* is a posthumous book, published in 1982, I do not know if the editors consulted another version of the poem, handwritten or typed, or if the differences are due to errors of transcription.

relationship. To conclude, I will cite a fragment from a letter from Severo Sarduy to Pizarnik, dated November 24, 1969. Sarduy tells her, undoubtedly commenting on something Pizarnik had mentioned in an earlier letter:

Ah, conocía y *admiraba* ya la obra de Silvina O. Sin duda fuerte, bien imbricada y con algo de cáustico, de agresivo solapadamente, de agujita metida en curare ... sí: su escritura es una araña pollito por dentro de una caja inglesa (decorada por Gainsborough, of course) de chocolatines, algo así. Me gusta, suscita mi complicidad, en estos tiempos de littérature au ventre, de tripitas expuestas, de agresividad sin freno, esa "elegancia," o casi diría, si la palabra no estuviera tan desvalorizada, ese pudor. Ahora, el problema es radical: no hay nada que hacer en el mundo editorial parisino, o al menos en el que está a mi alcance, por un libro de cuentos (me parece que S.O. es una autora de cuentos), no hay transposición editorial con ese género en París: sabrás por experiencia que aquí un libro de poemas, o uno de cuentos, por buenos que sean, están condenados a la gaveta. No obstante, con la ayuda de Alberto Manguel, que también disfruta de lo que hace S. vamos a emprender una pequeña cruzada, más bien del lado de Nadeau, etc. Veremos ...

[Ah, I was familiar with and already *admired* Silvina O.'s work. Without a doubt strong, very imbricated and somewhat caustic, covertly aggressive, like a needle dipped in curare ... yes: her writing is a tarantula inside an English chocolate box (decorated by Gainsborough, of course), something like that. I like it, it elicits my complicity, in these times of *littérature au ventre*, of exposed innards, of unchecked aggressiveness, that "elegance," or I would almost say, if that word were not so devalued, that modesty. Now, the problem is radical: there is nothing to be done with the Parisian publishing world, or at least with the one that is within my reach, with a book of short stories (I think S.O. is an author of short stories), there is no publishing transposition with that genre in Paris: you must know from experience that here a book of poems, or one of stories, as good as they may be, are condemned to the drawer. Nevertheless, with the help of Alberto Manuel, who also enjoys what S. does, we are about to embark on a small crusade, but rather on the side of Nadeau, etc. We shall see ...]

That "small crusade" would be successful: *Faits divers de la terre et du ciel*, an anthology of Ocampo's stories in French translation, was subsequently published by Gallimard, but only in 1974, two years after Pizarnik's death, and with the help of Héctor Bianciotti, not Sarduy.[7] It is a pleasure to see that she modestly contributed to Ocampo's fame, even though the first glimpses of that

7   I thank Silvia Baron Supervielle for clarification regarding this detail.

fame arrived too late for her to know that her efforts had not been in vain.

In the 2003 edition of Pizarnik's diary, there are many annotations about Ocampo, some enthusiastic, "Es la única persona de Argentina que me inspira confianza" (428) [She is the only person in Argentina who inspires my confidence], others less so, "pacto a lo Sade-Masoch pero tácito" (429) [a pact like that of Sade-Masoch, but tacit]. On many occasions she compares herself to Ocampo, at times with her husband, such as when she considers them "representantes de la literatura tradicional" (464) [representatives of traditional literature] or when she says: "S. estará en mis funerales. Por eso no logro evitar, a veces, el sentirme más vieja y –¿cómo decirlo?– más experimentada que ella" (429) [S. will be at my funeral. That's why I cannot avoid, sometimes, feeling older and – how can I put it? – more experienced than she]. As Suzanne Chávez Silverman notes, in the diaries at Princeton there is an entry on January 2, 1970 where she retracts the praise she published in "Dominios ilícitos" in *Sur* (Mackintosh and Posso 9), an entry that is transcribed in the expanded 2013 edition on pages 924–5. At any rate, it is still significant that the 1971 diary ends thus: "Alegría al recibir los cuadernos que me regaló Silvina" (498) [Happy to have received the notebooks that Silvina sent me].

Translated by Fernanda Zullo-Ruiz

Afterword

Reflections on Silvina Ocampo

MARJORIE AGOSÍN

Silvina silent silhouette. Distracted you cross your city, always Buenos Aires.
You know it from dreams, you imagine it in all your waking hours and in all
your nightfalls. From its domes, its enormous avenues tapestried with autumn
leaves and stories. You write and you dream, you dream and write as if from
your hands stories flowed. Everything in you Silvina reminds me of a time
without time or maybe the time of magic encrusted with sequins of mystery.

I hold your words in my hands, I caress them and enter. I enter your spell,
into the unfolding of your days wild with stories. More than anything I lose
myself in your city as if it were the most exquisite labyrinth of your desires.
But suddenly, I know that that city is an open book where your readers accompany
you. Do you want to play with us Silvina or do you want to play at imagining
bewilderment? Moments where the magic blends with illusion, where your
words mix with other words, the invisible, the imagined, those that play with
the unsaid of the said.

Buenos Aires is your city and that of Bioy and of Borges but as with everything
yours is more than a city. It is a labyrinth of unlimited spaces for the coming of
sleep and wakefulness, of fantasy and reality. You appear in it as if everything were
someone's story and where spaces are borders; where the imagination and the
strangeness of reality wander together; where the beginning of the story is inverted
with its ending; where awe and discomfort are united in a single voice.

Silvina, your writing always recognizes only itself and therein lies the power
we find in it. Its autonomy, its inexorable beauty, its rain of images and its poetry.
I always felt that your words were rain. Rain that illuminates us, that came to
us from the space of mystery that has always been your literature. Better than
saying that you belong to the group that practices the art of fantastic literature,
I only know that you are a maker of words. That you allow the rain to fall at
last on your eyelids and when you set out to write you enter beyond the space
of magic. You enter the story of a dream and beyond the dream, the words, and

6. Image of Silvina Ocampo's handwriting:
fragment of a letter to José Bianco written June 5, 1949.

beyond the words to what they hide on their reverse, in their interior, as if each one of them might be a magical sign waiting to be discovered. Waiting to awaken through the reader who finds it.

I always read you Silvina to later dream about you, or I dream about you in order to later read you. The balance between the story you tell and the images that inhabit them is mysterious, like a magic pendulum able to interpret reality. Your stories are like that, grand master of prose. They are stories contained in themselves and where one universe revolves around another. And, that universe is formed by details: velvet dresses, sugar houses, country dwellers, and urbanites, intrepid women as well as the timid.

Poetry is the zone of your mysteries, where few dared to enter, where only those with the desire to brave the art of the soul enter. Because reading you is just that, an adventure of a playful soul, a restless soul who feels and thinks.

It is impossible to catalog your stories, to situate these characters because they flow from a zone where strangeness mixes with innocence, where the perturbing is always such a part of you. And it is perturbing in an almost intangible sense as if to perturb were a perfect fusion in the anomaly of things.

I read your anthologies, your stories and poems. I cannot pause for just one of them because your writing is a delicate thread like your rumpled hair that looks like the color of the moon, between blue and moon colored. Everything in you is an organic combination of poetry that describes and narrates and of the mystery of words beyond themselves, as if each one had folds, imperfections, and invisible stitches.

You narrate like no one else Silvina. You are the only one who can tell things this way, who can imagine, and this is your value, that you are like no one and no one like you. You shift from the everyday detail to the essence of things, to the strange intelligence of events. Within this space you narrate, dream, and the fantastic literature that you weave is born of that center so much your own and no one else's.

They say you prefer times of solitude. That you flee from power and fame. That the presence of your sister Victoria and your husband Bioy overshadowed you. But it is not true. You chose to live like that and within the stories you invented. Stories of dark rooms, of innocent labyrinths and an enormous cruelty. Cruelty Silvina, violence was so often the warp that you wove and unwove. And we your readers didn't know if you were writing for children or for old people or for perverts or innocents, if you invented fairy tales or horror stories or tales of terror.

Your "Autobiografía de Irene" is perhaps the best evidence of this liminal zone where the wondrous and anomalous confront mystery. Where the ordinary is ambiguous, at times perverse and where what does not exist, like a painting that appears in *La torre sin fin* or a flying horse, conjure the magic and wonder of our days. Or the restless animals that you invent while naming yourself. To read you it is necessary to be fearless before the unknown, the unseen, the dream of what lies beyond the imagination.

Subversive and dreamy. Ancient and modern. Conjuror of the living and the dead. You are always Silvina, the one who wrote incessantly and found in the strangest places readers who loved the extraordinary surprise of the everyday, the subversive, the unexpected and anomalous. You were writing for the subversives, for invisible women and those characters submerged in the transitory, in the transformation and the unbounded imagination. You never feared them. You must have been comfortable between sleep and wakefulness, crossing these intertwining zones.

Here we celebrate you with the certainty of your brilliance and of the extraordinary inheritance that you knew to leave us. Thank you Silvina for the alchemy of your writing, for your humility and your magical pathways.

May these words be just the entrance into the blue space of your dreams where words alone celebrate your days and your nights, that this entrance may be the opening to a profound silence dressed in luminous words!

Translated by Patricia N. Klingenberg

Bibliography

Works by Silvina Ocampo

Viaje olvidado [Forgotten Journey]. Buenos Aires: Sur, 1937.
Antología de la literatura fantástica. (with Jorge Luis Borges and Adolfo Bioy Casares) Buenos Aires: Sudamericana, 1940.
Antología poética argentina. Buenos Aires: Sudamericana, 1941.
Enumeración de la patria [Enumeration of My Country]. Buenos Aires: Sur, 1942.
Espacios métricos [Metered Spaces]. Buenos Aires: Sur, 1945.
Los sonetos del jardín [Sonnets from the Garden]. Buenos Aires: Sur, 1946.
Los que aman odian [Those Who Love, Hate]. (with Adolfo Bioy Casares) Buenos Aires: Emecé, 1946.
"Dream of Death of a Harlot." *Disco* 6 (1946): 3–6.
Autobiografía de Irene. Buenos Aires: Sur, 1948.
Poemas de amor desesperado [Poems of Desperate Love]. Buenos Aires: Sudamericana, 1949.
Los nombres [Names]. Buenos Aires: Emecé, 1953.
Los traidores [The Traitors]. (with Juan Rodolfo Wilcock) Buenos Aires: Losange, 1956.
La furia y otros cuentos [The Fury and Other Stories]. Buenos Aires: Sur, 1959.
Las invitadas [The Guests]. Buenos Aires: Losada, 1961.
Lo amargo por dulce [The Bitter for Sweet]. Buenos Aires: Emecé, 1962.
"Images de Borges." *L'Herne* (1964): 26–30.
El pecado mortal [The Mortal Sin]. Ed. José Bianco. Buenos Aires: Eudeba, 1966.
Informe del cielo y del infierno [Report from Heaven and Hell]. Ed. Edgardo Cozarinsky. Caracas: Monte Ávila, 1970.
Los días de la noche [Days of the Night]. Buenos Aires: Sudamericana, 1970.
Amarillo celeste [Sky-Blue Yellow]. Buenos Aires: Losada, 1972.
El caballo alado [The Winged Horse]. Buenos Aires: Ediciones de la Flor, 1972.
Faits Divers de la terre et du ciel. Trans. François-Marie Rosset. Preface Jorge Luis Borges. Intro. Italo Calvino. Paris: Gallimard, 1974.
El cofre volante [The Flying Trunk]. Buenos Aires: Ediciones de la Flor, 1974.
El tobogán. Buenos Aires: Estrada, 1975.
La naranja maravillosa: Cuentos para chicos grandes y grandes chicos. [The Magic Orange: Stories for Children Young and Old]. Buenos Aires: Sudamericana, 1977.
"Tres poemas de Emily Dickinson." *La Prensa*, 19 February 1978.
Canto escolar [School Song]. Buenos Aires: Fraterna, 1979

Árboles de Buenos Aires [The Trees of Buenos Aires]. Photographs by Aldo Sessa. Prolog Manuel Mujica Láinez. Buenos Aires: Crea, 1979.

La continuación y otras páginas. Ed. Noemí Ulla. Buenos Aires: Centro Editor de América Latina, 1981.

"Dream of Death of a Harlot." *Buenos Aires Herald*, 11 October 1981.

Páginas de Silvina Ocampo, seleccionadas por la autora. Ed. Enrique Pezzoni. Buenos Aires: Celtia, 1984.

"Sueña con su muerte una prostituta." *Vuelta* 8.95 (1984): 22–3.

Breve Santoral. Con dibujos de Norah Borges [Brief Devotional. With drawings by ...]. Prolog Jorge Luis Borges. Buenos Aires: Gaglianone, 1984.

Narciso/Narcissus. [Catálogo de la exposición de Duilio Pierri]. Buenos Aires: Alejandro Furlong, 1987.

Y así sucesivamente [And So Forth]. Barcelona: Tusquets, 1987.

Cornelia frente al espejo [Cornelia Before the Mirror]. Barcelona: Tusquets, 1988.

Leopoldina's Dream. Trans. Daniel Balderston. Ontario: Penguin Canada, 1988.

Las reglas del secreto. Ed. Matilde Sánchez. México: Fondo de Cultura Económica, 1991.

"Palinurus Sleeps." Trans. Timothy Adès. *Classical Association News* 7: 12.

La Pluie de feu. Trans. Silvia Baron Supervielle. Bobigny: C. Bourgois, 1997.

Cuentos completos. 2 vols. Buenos Aires: Emecé, 1999.

Poesía inédita y dispersa. Ed. Noemí Ulla. Buenos Aires: Emecé, 2001.

Antología esencial. Ed. Mercedes Güiraldes and Daniel Gigena. Buenos Aires: Emecé, 2001.

"¿Qué quedará de nosotros?" and "Imágenes de Borges." *Cuadernos Hispanoamericanos* 622 (2002): 7–16.

Poesía completa. 2 vols. Ed. Sara Luisa Carril and Mercedes Rubio de Zocchi with Daniel Gigena. Buenos Aires: Emecé, 2002–03.

Cuentos difíciles: Antología. Ed. Raquel Prestigiacomo. Buenos Aires: Colihue, 2005.

Las repeticiones y otros relatos inéditos [Repetitions and Other Unpublished Stories]. Ed. Ernesto Montequin. Buenos Aires: Sudamericana, 2006.

Invenciones del recuerdo [Inventions of Memory]. Ed. Ernesto Montequin. Buenos Aires: Sudamericana, 2006.

Ejércitos de la oscuridad [Armies of Darkness]. Ed. Ernesto Montequin. Buenos Aires: Sudamericana, 2008.

La promesa [The Promise]. Ed. Ernesto Montequin. Buenos Aires: Sudamericana, 2011.

Antología: Cuentos de la "nena terrible." Ed. Patricia N. Klingenberg. Doral, FL: Stockcero, 2013.

El dibujo del tiempo: Recuerdos, prólogos, entrevistas [The Sketch of Time: Memoirs, Prologs and Interviews]. Ed. Ernesto Montequin. Buenos Aires: Sudamericana, 2014.

Thus Were Their Faces. Trans. Daniel Balderston. New York: New York Review Books, 2015.

Silvina Ocampo. Trans. Jason Weiss. New York: New York Review Books, 2015.

Works Cited

Aarne, Antii, and Stith Thompson. *The Types of the Folktales: A Classification and Bibliography.* Helsinki: Academia Scientiarum Fennica, 1973.

Agosín, Marjorie. "Mujer, espacio e imaginación en Latinoamérica: dos cuentos de María Luisa Bombal y Silvina Ocampo." *Revista Interamericana de Bibliografía* 41.4 (1991): 627–42.

Aldarondo, Hiram. *El humor en la cuentística de Silvina Ocampo.* Madrid: Pliegos, 2004.

——. "Barbarrossa enfrenta a Barbazul: Debate paródico entre Charles Perrault, Silvina Ocampo y Luisa Valenzuela." *Bulletin of Spanish Studies* 80.6 (2003): 729–42.

Alonso, Amado. "Aparición de una novelista." Introduction. *La última niebla* by María Luisa Bombal. 2nd ed. Santiago: Nascimento, 1941. 7–34.

Álvarez Morán, María Consuelo, and Rosa María Iglesias Montiel, eds. *Contemporaneidad de los clásicos en el umbral del tercer milenio: actas del congreso internacional de los clásicos. La tradición grecolatina ante el siglo XXI.* Murcia: Universidad de Murcia, 1999.

Amícola, José. "Silvina Ocampo y la *malseánce.*" Domínguez and Mancini 129–38.

Andersen, Hans Christian. *Fairy Tales.* Ed. Stend Larsen. Trans. R.P. Keigwin. Odense: Flensted, 1953. 2 vols.

Aponte, Barbara A. "The Initiation Archetype in Arguedas, Roa Bastos, and Ocampo." *Latin American Literary Review* 11.21 (1982): 45–56.

Araújo, Helena. "Ejemplos de la niña impura en Silvina Ocampo y Alba Lucía Angel." *Hispamérica* 13.38 (1984): 27–35.

Ariosto, Ludovico. *Orlando Furioso.* Ed. Cesare Segre. Milano: Mondadori, 1976.

Arlt, Mirta. "El cuentista y su mundo." *La Nación*, June 8, 1980. Rpt. in Ocampo, *El dibujo del tiempo* 273–7.

Assis de Rojo, M. Estela, and Nilda M. Flawia de Fernández. "Del Lacio a las pampas argentinas: itinerario de relaciones internacionales." Alvarez Morán and Iglesias Montiel 481–5.

Astutti, Adriana. *Andares clancos: Fábulas del menor en Osvaldo Lamborghini, J.C. Onetti, Rubén Darío, J.L. Borges, Silvina Ocampo y Manuel Puig.* Rosario, Argentina: Beatriz Viterbo, 2001.

Aulnoy, Madame de (Marie Catherine le Jumel de Barneville). "L'oiseau bleu." *Les cabinet des fées.* Ed. Elisabeth Lemirre. Arles: Philippe Picquier, 2000: 31–54.

Badano, Valeria. "Silvina Ocampo y las visiones del mundo." *Alba de América: Revista Literaria* 30.57–58 (2011): 537–47.

Baeza, Ricardo, ed. *Poetas líricos ingleses.* "Estudio preliminar" by Silvina Ocampo. Buenos Aires: W.M. Jackson, 1949. IX–XLIV

Balbi, María Noemí. "Silvina Ocampo y sus niñas inquietantes." *CLIJ: Cuadernos de Literatura Infantil y Juvenil* 21.217 (2008): 28–36.

Balderston, Daniel. "Los cuentos crueles de Silvina Ocampo y Juan Rodolfo Wilcock." *Revista Iberoamericana* 49 (1983): 743–52.

——. "Silvina y lo religioso." Domínguez and Mancini 81–7.

——. "'Never Say I:' Inscriptions and Erasures of the Self in Queer Poetry in Spanish and Portuguese." *A Contracorriente* 9.1 (2011): 336–47.

——. "Dominios ilícitos: homenaje a Silvina Ocampo." *Alejandra Pizarnik: el lugar donde todo sucede.* Ed. Adelaïde de Chatellus and Milagros Esquerro. Paris: L'Harmattan, 2013. 197–205.

Bastos, María Luisa. "Dos líneas testimoniales: *Sur*, los escritos de Victoria Ocampo." *Sur* 348 (1981): 9–23.

——. *Borges ante la crítica argentina, 1923–1960*. Buenos Aires: Hispamérica, 1974.

Beaumont, Madame de (Jeanne Marie Leprince de Beaumont). *Le Magasin des enfants. La Belle et la Bête et autres counte*. Arles: Philippe Picquier, 1995.

Beccacece, Hugo. "Los Bioy: La guardiana de los secretos." *Suplemento Cultura La Nación* (Buenos Aires), 23 June 2002.

Bello, Andrés. *Silvas americanas y otros poemas*. 1823. Rpt. Barcelona: Ramón Sopena, 1978.

Bermúdez-Arceo, Viviana. "Las venganzas de la infancia." *El cuento: Homenaje a María Teresa Maiorana*. Ed. Martha Vanbiesen de Burbridge. Buenos Aires: Fundación María Teresa Maiorana, 1995. 283–7.

Bettelheim, Bruno. *The Uses of Enchantment: The Meaning and Importance of Fairy Tales*. New York: Knopf, 1976.

Bialowas Pobutsky, Aldona. "¡A festejar! Fiestas mórbidas en algunos cuentos de Silvina Ocampo." *Texto Crítico* 8.16 (2005): 79–95.

Bioy Casares, Adolfo. "En memoria de Paulina." *La trama celeste*. Buenos Aires: Sur, 1948.

——. "La fiesta del monstruo." See Borges, *Obras completas en colaboración*.

——. "Letras y amistad." *La otra aventura*. Buenos Aires: Emecé, 1968. 169–75.

——. *Memorias*. Barcelona: Tusquets, 1994.

——. *En viaje, 1967*. Ed. Daniel Martino. Bogotá: Norma, 1996.

——. *Borges*. Ed. Daniel Martino. Buenos Aires: Destino, 2006.

Bloom, Harold. *The Anxiety of Influence: A Theory of Poetry*. Oxford: Oxford UP, 1973.

Bombal, María Luisa. *La última niebla*. 1935. 2nd ed. Santiago: Nascimento, 1941.

Borges, Jorge Luis. *Historia universal de la infamia*. Buenos Aires: Tor, 1935.

——. Rev. of *Enumeración de la patria* by Silvina Ocampo. *Sur* 101 (1943): 64–7.

——. *Obras completas*. Buenos Aires: Emecé, 1974.

——, and Bioy Casares. "La fiesta del monstruo" [co-authored under the pseudonym Bustos Domecq in 1949]. *Obras completas en colaboración*. Madrid: Alianza, 1981. 392–402.

Bradford, Lisa Rose. "La visión de las versiones: Un estudio de diferencias/resistencias en Emily Dickinson." *Celehis: Revista del Centro de Letras Hispanoamericanas* 4.4–5 (1995): 117–32.

Brenan, Gerald. "Come at Daybreak." *The Literature of the Spanish People: From Roman Times to the Present Day*. Cambridge: Cambridge UP, 1976. 124.

Brescia, Pablo. "A 'Superior Magic:' Literary Politics and the Rise of the Fantastic in Latin American Fiction." *Forum for Modern Language Studies* 44.4 (2008): 379–93.

Browning, Richard L. *Childhood and the Nation in Latin American Literature: Allende, Reinaldo Arenas, Bosch, Bryce Echenique, Cortázar, Manuel Galván, Federico Gamboa, S. Ocampo, Peri Rossi, Salarrué*. New York: Peter Lang, 2001.

Butler, Judith. *Gender Trouble: Feminism and the Subversion of Identity*. New York: Routledge, 1990.

Calafell Sala, Nuria. "Para-textos corporales: Sobre los cuentos de Silvina Ocampo." *Cuadernos de ALEPH* 2 (2007): 63–72.

Calvino, Italo. ed. *Fiabe italiane*. vol I. Milano: Mondadori, 1979. 246–58.

Campra, Rosalba. "Sobre *La furia*, otros cuentos y las sorpresas de lo previsible." *América. Cahiers du CRICCAL* 17 (1997): 189–97.

Campuzano, Luisa. "Tradición clásica en la literatura latinoamericana contemporánea de autoría femenina: meditación en el umbral." Alvarez Morán and Iglesias Montiel 323–8.

Carrizo, Juan Alfonso. *Antecedentes hispano-medievales de la poesía tradicional argentina.* Buenos Aires: Estudios Hispánicos, 1945.

Carter, Angela. *The Bloody Chamber and Other Stories.* New York: Penguin, 1981.

Carter, Philip. "Selwyn, George Augustus (1719–1791)." *Oxford Dictionary of National Biography.* Oxford: Oxford UP, 2004. http://www.oxforddnb.com.pitt.idm.oclc.org/view/article/25065. Web.

Castellanos, Rosario. "Silvina Ocampo y el más acá." *Mujer que sabe latín.* México: SepSetentas, 1973. 149–64.

Castillo, Abelardo. "La furia y otros cuentos." *El grillo de papel* 4 (June–July 1960): 17.

Castillo de Berchenko, Adriana. "Imágenes y contra-imágenes: *La furia y otros cuentos* de Silvina Ocampo." *América. Cahiers du CRICCAL* 17 (1997): 177–88.

Chacel, Rosa. Rev. of *Los que aman odian* by Silvina Ocampo and Adolfo Bioy Casares. *Sur* 143 (1946): 75–81.

La ciénaga. Dir. Lucrecia Martel. 2000. Film.

Clark, Maria B. "Feminization as an Experience of Limits." *Inti* 40–41 (1994–95): 249–68.

Corbacho, Belinda. *Le monde féminin dans l'oeuvre narrative de Silvina Ocampo.* Paris: L'Harmattan, 1998.

——. "El personaje femenino y su identificación con el espacio en la narrativa de Silvina Ocampo: análisis de 'La escalera' y de 'El sótano.'" Ulla, *Una escritora oculta* 16–30.

Cornelia frente al espejo. Dir. Daniel Rosenfeld. 2012. Film.

Cortamosondulamos. By Inés Saavedra. La Maravillosa, Buenos Aires. 2002. Performance.

Cortázar, Julio. "No se culpe a nadie." *Final del juego.* Ed. Jaime Alazraki. Madrid: Anaya, 1995. 25–29.

Costa, Analía. "Tradición y traducción en el Modernismo hispanoamericano." *Revista de Historia de la Traducción* 5. http://www.traduccionliteraria.org/1611/art/costa.htm. Web.

Costa, Walter Carlos. "Las traducciones de la *Antología de la literatura fantástica* de Borges, Bioy Casares y Silvina Ocampo." *Cuadernos Americanos* 23.3 (2009): 159–67.

Cox, Fiona. *Sibylline Sisters: Virgil's Presence in Contemporary Women's Writing.* Oxford: Oxford UP, 2011.

Cozarinsky, Edgardo. "Introducción." *Informe del cielo y del infierno.* Caracas: Monte Ávila, 1970. 7–13.

——. *Borges y el cine.* Buenos Aires: Sur, 1974.

——. *Blues.* Buenos Aires: Adriana Hidalgo, 2010.

Dahlgren, Marta. "'Preciser What We Are': Emily Dickinson's Poems in Translation. A Study in Literary Pragmatics." *Journal of Pragmatics* 37 (2005): 1081–1107.

Darío, Rubén. *Canto a la Argentina y otros poemas.* Madrid: Biblioteca Corona, 1914.

Las dependencias. Dir. Lucrecia Martel. 1999. Film.

Derrida, Jacques. *Writing and Difference.* Trans. Alan Bass. Chicago: U of Chicago P, 1978. [*L'écriture et la différence.* Paris: Seuil, 1967.]

——. "Signature Event Context." Trans. Alan Bass. *Derrida Reader: Between the Blinds.* Ed. Peggy Kamuf. New York: Columbia UP, 1991. 83–111. ["Signature, événement, contexte." *Marges de la philosophie.* Paris: Les Éditions de Minuit, 1972. 365–93.]

———. *Chaque fois unique, la fin du monde*. Paris: Galilée, 2003.

Díaz, Roberto Ignacio. *Unhomely Rooms: Foreign Tongues and Spanish American Literature*. Lewisburg, PA: Bucknell UP, 2002.

Díaz, Valentín. "Como el agua en el agua: formas del no-saber y la influencia en Silvina Ocampo." Domínguez and Mancini 91–105.

Dickinson, Emily. *The Complete Poems*. Ed. Thomas H. Johnson. Boston: Little, Brown, 1952.

———. *Poemas de Emily Dickinson*. Trans. Silvina Ocampo. Prolog Jorge Luis Borges. Barcelona: Tusquets, 1985.

Dirán que fue la noche. By Alfredo Martín. La Scala de San Telmo, Buenos Aires. 2013. Performance.

Divagaciones. By María Marta Guitart and Inés Saavedra. La Maravillosa, Buenos Aires. 2004. Performance.

Domínguez, Nora, and Adriana Mancini, eds. *La ronda y el antifaz: Lecturas críticas sobre Silvina Ocampo*. Buenos Aires: Facultad de Filosofía y Letras, Universidad de Buenos Aires, 2009.

Duncan, Cynthia. "Double or Nothing? The Fantastic Element in Silvina Ocampo's 'La casa de azúcar'." *Chasqui* 20.2 (1991): 64–72.

———. "An Eye for an I: Women Writers and the Fantastic." *Inti* 40–41 (1994–95): 233–46.

———. *Unraveling the Real: The Fantastic in Spanish-American Ficciones*. Philadelphia, PA: Temple UP, 2010.

Eloy Martínez, Tomás. "Silvina Ocampo: la crueldad, la pasión." Suplemento Literario de *La Nación*, 10 January 1960: 25.

"Emily Dickinson por Silvina Ocampo." Rev. of *Poemas de Emily Dickinson* by Silvina Ocampo. *La Razón*, 23 March 1986: 6–7.

Enriquez, Mariana. "La poeta sangrienta." *Suplemento Soy*, 28 September 2012. http://www.pagina12.com.ar/diario/suplementos/soy/1-2635-2012-09-28.html. Web.

———. *La hermana menor: Un retrato de Silvina Ocampo*. Santiago, Chile: Universidad Diego Portales, 2014.

Escari, Raúl. *Actos en palabras*. Buenos Aires: Mansalva, 2007.

Espinoza-Vera, Marcia. *La poética de lo incierto en los cuentos de Silvina Ocampo*. Madrid: Pliegos, 2003.

———. "Unsubordinated Women: Modernist Fantasies of Liberation in Silvina Ocampo's Short Stories." *Hecate: An Interdisciplinary Journal* 35.1/2 (2009): 219–27.

Ezquerro, Milagros. "Apuntes para una poética del relato fantástico." Ulla, *Una escritora oculta* 9–15.

———. "Barba Azul en el jardín de invierno." *Cuadernos Hispanoamericanos* 622 (2002): 39–48.

Feldherr, Andrew. "Metamorphosis in the *Metamorphoses*." *Cambridge Companion to Ovid*. Ed. Philip Hardie. Cambridge: Cambridge UP, 2002. 163–79.

Felman, Shoshana. *What Does a Woman Want? Reading and Sexual Difference*. Baltimore, MD: Johns Hopkins UP, 1993.

Filer, Malva E. "The Ambivalence of the Hand in Cortázar's Fiction." *Books Abroad* 50.3 (1976): 595–99.

Fishburn, Evelyn, ed. *Short Fiction by Spanish-American Women*. Manchester: Manchester UP, 1998.

Flaubert, Gustave. *Madame Bovary*. 1857. Ed. Jacques Neefs. Paris: Livre de Poche, 1999.

Foucault, Michel. *The History of Sexuality: An Introduction*. Trans. R. Hurley. New York: Vintage, 1990.

Francomano, Emily. "Escaping by a Hair: Silvina Ocampo Rereads, Rewrites, and Re-Members 'Porphyria's Lover.'" *Letras Femeninas* 25.1–2 (1999): 65–77.

Galeota Cajati, Adele. *Le regole dell'enigma. La narrativa di Silvina Ocampo*. Rome: Aracne, 1997.

Gamerro, Carlos. *Ficciones barrocas: Una lectura de Borges, Bioy Casares, Silvina Ocampo, Cortázar, Onetti, Felisberto Hernández*. Buenos Aires: Eterna Cadencia, 2010.

García, Mariano. "Pasiones metamórficas: La transformación en algunos relatos inéditos de Silvina Ocampo." *RILCE: Revista de Filología Hispánica* 24.2 (2008): 306–22.

Ginastera, Alberto. *Las horas de una estancia*. Buenos Aires: Argentina de la Música, c.1945. Score.

González Espitia, Juan Carlos. *On the Dark Side of the Archive: Nation and Literature in Spanish America at the Turn of the Century*. Lewisburg, PA: Bucknell UP, 2010.

González Lanuza, Eduardo. Rev. of *Autobiografía de Irene*. *Sur* 175 (1949): 56–58.

Gramuglio, María Teresa. "*Sur*, una minoría cosmopolita en la periferia occidental." *Historia de los intelectuales en América Latina*. Ed. Carlos Altamirano. Buenos Aires: Katz, 2010. 192–209.

Graña, María Cecilia. "La asimetría entre la voz y la escritura: 'Autobiografía de Irene' de Silvina Ocampo." *Semiosis: Seminario de Semiótica, Teoría, Análisis* 2.4 (2006): 71–85.

Green, Mandy. *Milton's Ovidian Eve*. Aldershot: Ashgate, 2009.

Guasta, Eugenio, and Mario A. Lancelloti. "Dos juicios sobre *La furia*." Rev. of *La furia y otros cuentos* by Silvina Ocampo. *Sur* 264 (1960): 62–66.

Habra, Hedy. "Escisión y liberación en 'La casa de azúcar' de Silvina Ocampo." *Hispanófila* 145 (2005): 47–59.

Hamon, Philippe. *Introducción al análisis de lo descriptivo*. Buenos Aires: Edicial, 1991.

Hansen, Elaine Tuttle. "Exclusion and Essentialism." *Hypatia* 8.3 (1993): 12.

——. *Mother Without Child: Contemporary Fiction and the Crisis of Motherhood*. Berkeley, CA: U of California P, 1997.

Haraway, Donna. "A Manifesto for Cyborgs: Science, Technology, and Socialist Feminism and the 1980s." *Socialist Review* 15 (1985): 65–102.

Harris, Daniel. "Cuteness." *Salmagundi* 96 (1992): 177–86.

Heker, Liliana. "Silvina Ocampo y Victoria Ocampo: la hermana pequeña y la hermana mayor." *Mujeres argentinas: El lado femenino de nuestra historia*. Ed. Graciela Batticuore. Buenos Aires: Alfaguara, 1998. 191–233.

Herlinghaus, Hermann. *Narcoepics: A Global Aesthetics of Sobriety*. New York: Bloomsbury, 2013.

Hernández, Juan José. "Conversación con Silvina Ocampo sobre los sonetos de Marguerite Yourcenar." *La Gaceta de Tucumán*, 11 September 1983. Rpt. in Ocampo, *El dibujo del tiempo* 295–97.

——. "La obra de teatro que escribimos con Silvina Ocampo." *La Nación*, August 5, 1999. http://www.lanacion.com.ar/214576-la-obra-de-teatro-que-escribimos-con-silvina-ocampo. Web.

Hinds, Stephen. *Allusion and Intertext: Dynamics of Appropriation in Roman Poetry*. Cambridge: Cambridge UP, 1998.

El impostor. Dir. Alejandro Maci. 1997. Film.

Invenciones. By Alejandro Maci. Teatro Presidente Alvear, Buenos Aires. 2009. Performance.

Iglesias, Jovita, and Silvia Renée Arias. *Los Bioy*. Buenos Aires: Tusquets, 2001.

Kaplan, E. Ann. *Motherhood and Representation: The Mother in Popular Culture and Melodrama*. London: Routledge, 1992.

Katzenstein, Inés, ed. *Listen, Here, Now!: Argentine Art of the 1960s: Writings of the Avant Garde*. New York: MoMA, 2004.

Keizman, Betina. "Ficción de autor: Las adivinas en Silvina Ocampo." *Actas del XVI Congreso de la Asociación Internacional de Hispanistas: Nuevos caminos del hispanismo... París, del 9 al 13 de julio de 2007*. Madrid: Iberoamericana, 2010.

———. "Visionnaires et créatrices dans l'oeuvre de Silvina Ocampo." *Lectures du Genre* 3 (2008): n.p. Web.

King, John. *Sur: A Study of the Argentine Literary Journal and its Role in the Development of a Culture 1931–1970*. Cambridge: Cambridge UP, 1988.

———. "Victoria Ocampo (1890–1979): Precursor." *Knives and Angels: Women Writers in Latin America*. Ed. Susan Bassnett. London: Zed, 1990. 9–25.

Klingenberg, Patricia N. "The Grotesque in the Short Stories of Silvina Ocampo." *Letras Femeninas* 8 (1984): 49–52.

———. "The Twisted Mirror: The Fantastic in the Short Stories of Silvina Ocampo." *Letras Femeninas* 13 (1987): 67–78.

———. "Portrait of the Writer as Artist: Silvina Ocampo." *Perspectives in Contemporary Literature: Literature and the Other Arts* 13 (1987): 58–64.

———. "The Mad Double in the Short Stories of Silvina Ocampo." *Latin American Literary Review* 16.2 (1988): 29–40.

———. "The Feminine 'I:' Silvina Ocampo's Fantasies of the Subject." *Romance Languages Annual* 1 (1989): 488–94.

———. "Silvina Ocampo frente al espejo." *Inti* 40–41 (1994–95): 271–86.

———. *Fantasies of the Feminine. The Short Stories of Silvina Ocampo*. Lewisburg, PA: Bucknell UP, 1999.

———. "A Life in Letters: Notes Toward a Biography of Silvina Ocampo." *Hispanófila* 139 (2003): 111–32.

———. "'Literatura como pintura': Images, Narrative and Autobiography in Silvina Ocampo," *Letras Femeninas* 32.1 (2006): 251–76.

Kristeva, Julia. "Stabat Mater." Trans. León S. Roudiez. *The Kristeva Reader*. Ed. Toril Moi. New York: Columbia UP, 1986.

Lagmanovich, David. "Un relato de Silvina Ocampo." *Espéculo: Revista de Estudios Literarios* 29 (March –June 2005): n.p. Electronic publication.

Lancelloti, Mario. Rev. of *Las invitadas* by Silvina Ocampo. *Sur* 278 (1962): 74–6.

Larrieu, Gérald. "Las travesuras pelirrosas: por una lectura de 'Las vestiduras peligrosas' de Silvina Ocampo." *Lectures du Genre* 1 (2007): n.p. Electronic publication.

Le fantastique argentin: Silvina Ocampo, Julio Cortázar. Centre de recherches interuniversitaire sur les champs culturells en Amérique latine. Paris: Presses de la Sorbonne-nouvelle, 1997.

Libertella, Mauro. "La biblioteca de tres maestros, en 400 cajas y en un depósito de alquiler." *Clarín*, September 14, 2014. http://www.revistaenie.clarin.com/literatura/ biblioteca-maestros-cajas-deposito-alquiler_0_1212479151.html. Web.

Lispector, Clarice. *Laços de familia*. Rio de Janeiro: Francisco Alves, 1960.

López-Luaces, Marta. *That Strange Territory: The Representation of Childhood in Texts of Three Latin American Women Writers.* Newark, DE: Juan de la Cuesta-Hispanic Monographs, 2004.

Louis, Annick. "Definiendo un género: La *Antología de la literatura fantástica* de Silvina Ocampo, Adolfo Bioy Casares y Jorge Luis Borges." *Nueva Revista de Filología Hispánica* 49.2 (2001): 409–37.

Lozano de la Pola, Ana. "Viajes de escritura y lectura en los cuentos de Silvina Ocampo." *El viaje en la literatura hispanoamericana: El espíritu colombino.* Madrid/Frankfurt: Iberoamericana/Vervuert, 2008. 843–51.

Mackintosh, Fiona J. "'El impostor:' From *cuento* to filmscript." *An Argentine Passion: María Luisa Bemberg and her Films.* Ed. John King, Sheila Whitaker, and Rosa Bosch. London: Verso, 2000. 193–215.

——. *Childhood in the Works of Silvina Ocampo and Alejandra Pizarnik.* Woodbridge: Tamesis, 2003.

——. "'My Dreams Are of a Field Afar' or Sonnets from the English: Silvina Ocampo's Relationship to British Poetry." *Symbiosis: A Journal of Anglo-American Literary Relations* 8.1 (2004): 3–23.

——. "A Happy Transmigration? Silvina Ocampo Translates Emily Dickinson." *Babel-AFIAL* (University of Vigo) 14 (2005): 23–41.

——. "Beyond Borders: Silvina Ocampo's Relationship to France." *Antes y después del Quijote.* Valencia: Biblioteca Valenciana, 2005. 309–19.

——. "'Tales eran sus rostros': Silvina Ocampo and Norah Borges." *Romance Studies* 27.1 (2009): 59–71.

——. "Bioy, Ocampo and the Photographic Image." *Adolfo Bioy Casares: Borges, Fiction and Art.* Ed. Karl Posso. Cardiff: U of Wales P, 2012. 143–61.

——. "Silvina Ocampo (1903–1993)." *A Companion to Latin American Women Writers.* Ed. Brígida M. Pastor and Lloyd Hughes Davies. Woodbridge: Tamesis, 2012. 83–94.

——, and Roberta Quance. "Speaking/Seeing Saints: Norah Borges and Silvina Ocampo Collaborate." *Romance Studies* 22.2 (2004): 149–63.

——, and Karl Posso, eds. *Arbol de Alejandra: Pizarnik Reassessed.* London: Tamesis, 2007.

Mancini, Adriana. "Amo y esclavo: una relación eficaz: Silvina Ocampo y Jean Genet." *Cuadernos Hispanoamericanos* 575 (1998): 73–86.

——. "Desvíos y pasiones: 'La paciente y el médico' de Silvina Ocampo." Ulla, *Una escritora oculta* 33–48.

——. *Silvina Ocampo: Escalas de pasión.* Buenos Aires: Norma, 2003.

Mangin, Annick. *Temps et écriture dans l'oeuvre narrative de Silvina Ocampo.* Toulouse: Presses Universitaires du Mirail, 1996.

——. "'El castigo' de Silvina Ocampo: Parole et châtiment." *Cahiers du Monde Hispanique et Luso-Brésilien/Caravelle* 66 (1996): 113–20.

——. "Fotos de familia." Ulla, *Una escritora oculta* 49–60.

——. "L'air du temps dans un conte de Silvina Ocampo." *Cahiers du Monde Hispanique Et Luso-Brésilien/Caravelle* 76–77 (2001): 559–68.

Mansau, Andrée. "Silvina Ocampo, du vert paradis à la pluie de feu." *L'Esprit et les Lettres.* Toulouse: Presses Universitaires du Mirail (1999). 321–7.

Martínez, Carlos Dámaso. "Apuntes sobre dos libros de Silvina Ocampo." *La seducción del relato. Escritos sobre literatura.* Córdoba: Alción (2002). 155–9.

Martínez Cabrera, Erika. "Silvina Ocampo, fantástica criminal." *Miradas oblicuas en la narrativa latinoamericana contemporánea: límites de lo real, fronteras de lo fantástico.* Ed. Jesús Montoya Juárez and Ángel Esteban. Madrid: Iberoamericana, 2009. 129–39.

Martínez de Richter, Marily. "Triángulo de tigres: Borges, Bioy Casares, Silvina Ocampo." Ulla, *Una escritora oculta* 61–85.

Matamoro, Blas. "La nena terrible." *Oligarquía y literatura.* Buenos Aires: Sol, 1975. 193–221.

Mattalia, Sonia. "Silvina, Angélica, Cristina: Viaje sin equipaje." *El viaje en la literatura hispanoamericana: El espíritu colombino.* Madrid: Iberoamericana, 2008. 833–41.

Meehan, Thomas C. "Los niños perversos en los cuentos de Silvina Ocampo." *Essays on Argentine Narrators.* Valencia: Albatros, 1978. 31–44.

Molloy, Sylvia. "Silvina Ocampo: La exageración como lenguaje." *Sur* 320 (1969): 15–24.

——. "La simplicidad inquietante en los relatos de Silvina Ocampo." *Lexis* 2.2 (1978): 241–51.

——. *Las letras de Borges.* Buenos Aires: Sudamericana, 1979.

——. *Desarticulaciones.* Buenos Aires: Eterna Cadencia, 2010.

Monteleone, Jorge. "La máscara sigilosa de Silvina Ocampo." *La Nación: Cultura,* October 6, 2002: 1–2.

Montequin, Ernesto. "Nota al texto." Ocampo, *El dibujo del tiempo* 375–94.

Morello, Lilian. "El vestido de terciopelo/ La Robe de velours." *Cinémas d'Amérique Latine* 12 (2004): 178–85.

La mujer sin cabeza. Dir. Lucrecia Martel. 2007. Film.

Mujeres terribles. By Marisé Monteiro and Virginia Uriarte. Teatro San Martín, Buenos Aires. 2010. Performance.

Mullaly, Laurence. "Silvina en el espejo de Lucrecia: Ocampo-Martel, regards croisés entre cinéma et littérature." Université Paris-Sorbonne, Les Ateliers du SAL. 2006. October 13, 2014. http://www.crimic.paris-sorbonne.fr/actes/tl2/mullaly.pdf.

Muschietti, Delfina. "Mujeres: feminismo y literatura." *Historia social de la literatura argentina* VII. *Yrigoyen entre Borges y Arlt (1916–1930).* Ed. David Viñas. Buenos Aires: Contrapunto, 1989. 129–60.

——. "Traducción de poesía: forma, repetición y fantasma en el estudio comparado de traducciones de Emily Dickinson (Silvina Ocampo, Amelia Rosselli)." *Orbis Tertius* 11.12 (2006): 1–24.

Neruda, Pablo. *Residencia en la tierra II.* Madrid: Cruz y Raya, 1935.

Ngai, Sianne. "The Cuteness of the Avant-Garde." *Critical Inquiry* 31.4 (2005): 811–47.

Nietzsche, Friedrich. *Beyond Good and Evil: Prelude to a Philosophy of the Future.* Cambridge: Cambridge UP, 2002.

La niña santa. Dir. Lucrecia Martel. 2004. Film.

Ocampo, Victoria. Rev. of *Viaje olvidado* by Silvina Ocampo. *Sur* 35 (1937): 118–21.

Orecchia Havas, Teresa. "Silvina Ocampo: los lazos de la escritura." *Actas del XIII Congreso Internacional AIH Madrid 1998.* Ed. Florencio Sevilla and Carlos Alvar. Madrid: Castalia, 2000: 320–8.

Ostrov, Andrea. "Vestidura/escritura/sepultura en la narrativa de Silvina Ocampo." *Hispamérica: Revista de Literatura* 25.74 (1996): 21–8.

——. "Género, tela y texto en la escritura de Silvina Ocampo." *América: Cahiers du CRICCAL (Le fantastique argentin: Silvina Ocampo, Julio Cortázar)* 17 (1997): 301–8.

——. *El género al bies: Cuerpo, género y escritura en cinco narradoras latinoamericanas.* Córdoba, Argentina: Alción, 2004.

Ovejero, José. *La ética de la crueldad*. Barcelona: Anagrama, 2012.

Ovid. *Fasti*. http://www.thelatinlibrary.com/ovid.htmlhttp://www.thelatinlibrary.com/ovid.html. Web.

——. *Metamorphoses*. http://www.thelatinlibrary.com/ovid.html. Web.

——. *Metamorphoses*. Trans. Anthony S. Kline (2000). http://ovid.lib.virginia.edu/trans/Ovhome.htm. Web.

——. *Metamorphoses*. Trans. A.D. Melville. Oxford: Oxford UP, 2008.

Páez Lotero, Claudia Marcela. "Mito y rito en el poema largo de Silvina Ocampo." *Alba de América: Revista Literaria* 32.60–61 (2012): 409–27.

Payró, Julio E. "La escuela de París." *Sur* 71 (1940): 80–5.

Paz, Octavio. "Arcos." *Libertad bajo palabra*. México: Fondo de Cultura Económica, 1960. 62.

——. *Poemas (1935–1975)*. Barcelona: Seix Barral, 1979.

——. "Piedra de sol." Trans. Eliot Weinberger. *World Poetry: An Anthology of Verse from Antiquity to Our Time*. Ed. Katharine Washburn, John S. Major, and Clifton Fadiman. New York: W.W. Norton, 2000. 3.

Paz Leston, Eduardo. "Las traducciones de poesía." Domínguez and Mancini 313–19.

Penrose, Valentine. *Erzsébet Báthory la comtesse sanglante*. Paris: Gallimard, 1962.

Percas, Helena. "La original expresión poética de Silvina Ocampo." *Revista Iberoamericana* 19.38 (1954): 283–98.

——. *La poesía femenina argentina (1810–1950)*. Madrid: Cultura Hispánica, 1958.

Perdomo Orellana, Jose Luis "Dos amigos, dos poemas." *La Nación* Suplemento literario, April 17, 1994: 3.

Pérez, Agueda. "La identidad genérica como sitio de conflicto en dos cuentos de Silvina Ocampo." *Ciberletras* 11 (2004): n.p. Web.

Pérez, Ashley Hope. "Translating María Luisa Bombal's *Última niebla*." *Translation Review* 75 (2008): 21–6.

Perrault, Charles. *Contes*. Ed. G. Rouger. Paris: Garnier, 1967.

Pezzoni, Enrique. "Aproximación al último libro de Borges." *Sur* 217–18 (1952): 101–23.

——. "Silvina Ocampo." *Enciclopedia de la literatura argentina*. Ed. Pedro Orgambide and Roberto Yanui. Buenos Aires: Sudamericana, 1970. 473–7.

Phelan, James. *Living to Tell About It: A Rhetoric and Ethics of Character Narration*. Ithaca, NY: Cornell UP, 2005.

Pichon Rivière, Marcelo. "Así es Silvina Ocampo." *Panorama*, November 19, 1974. Rpt. in Ocampo, *El dibujo del tiempo* 194–200.

Piña, Cristina. *Alejandra Pizarnik: Una biografiá*. Buenos Aires: Corregidor, 1999.

Pizarnik, Alejandra. "Dominios ilícitos." Rev. of *El pecado mortal* by Silvina Ocampo. *Sur* 311 (1968): 91–5.

——. *Obras completas. Poesía completa y prosa selecta*. Buenos Aires: Corregidor, 1993.

——. *Correspondencia Pizarnik*. Ed. Ivonne Bordelois. Buenos Aires: Seix Barral, 1998.

——. *Poesía completa*. Ed Ana Becciú. Barcelona, Lumen, 2001.

——. *Prosa completa*. Ed Ana Becciú. Barcelona, Lumen, 2002.

——. *Diarios*. Ed. Ana Becciú. Barcelona: Lumen, 2003.

——. *Diarios: Nueva Edición*. Ed. Ana Becciú. Barcelona: Lumen, 2013.

Pobutsky, Aldona. "¡A festejar! Fiestas mórbidas en algunos cuentos de Silvina Ocampo." *Texto Crítico* 8.16 (2005): 79–97.

Podlubne, Judith. "El recuerdo del cuento infantil." *Cuadernos Hispanoamericanos* 622 (2002): 29–38.

———. *Escritores de Sur: Los inicios literarios de José Bianco y Silvina Ocampo*. Rosario, Argentina: Beatriz Viterbo, 2011.

———. "*Sur* en los 60: Hacia una nueva sensibilidad crítica." *Badebec: Revista del Centro de Estudios de Teoría y Crítica Literaria* 1.2 (2012): 44–60.

———. "Desvío y debilitamiento en la búsqueda narrativa de Silvina Ocampo." *Anales de Literatura Hispanoamericana* 41 (2012): 213–29.

Poggi, Giulia. "'Las vestiduras peligrosas' di Silvina Ocampo: Analisi di un'antifiaba." *Studi Ispanici* 3 (1978): 145–62.

———. "Dalla parte delle bambine: Il giro di vite di Henry James in due racconti di Silvina Ocampo." *Letterature d'America* 22.90 (2002): 91–117.

Prieto, Adolfo. *Borges y la nueva generación*. Buenos Aires: Letras Universitarias, 1954.

Prieto, Martín. "Poeta en busca de su patria." *Clarín: Suplemento Cultura y Nación*, 16 November 2002. Web.

Princeton University Library. Rare Books and Special Collections. Manuscripts Division. José Bianco Papers: CO 681, folder 3. Elena Garro Papers, CO 827, Box 1: folders 20–22. Fraga and Peña Collection: CO 783, Box 1: folders 23–25; Box 3: folder 11. Manuel Mujica Láinez Papers: CO 819, Box 3: folder 50. Alejandra Pizarnik Papers: CO 395. Silvina Ocampo Papers: CO 973.

Propp, Vladimir J. *Morfología del cuento*. Madrid: Akal, 1998.

Quiñones, Michelle. "La muerte violenta: Una perspectiva infantil en dos cuentos de Silvina Ocampo." *Hispanet Journal* 6 (2013): 1–15.

Rabinowitz, Peter J. *Before Reading: Narrative Conventions and the Politics of Interpretation*. Ithaca, NY: Cornell UP, 1987.

Rancière, Jacques. "Las desventuras del pensamiento crítico." *El espectador emancipado*. Buenos Aires: Manantial, 2008: 29–52.

Reliquia. By Julia Nardozza, Carlos Peláez, and Valeria Pierabella. Pan y Arte Teatro, Buenos Aires. 2013. Performance.

Rich, Adrienne. "Compulsory Heterosexuality and Lesbian Experience." *Feminism in Our Time: Essential Writings, World War II to the Present*. Ed. Miriam Schneir. New York: Vintage, 1994.

Roffé, Reina. "Sabia locura." *Cuadernos Hispanoamericanos* 622 (2002): 17–20.

Romera Rozas, Ricardo. "Aspectos esotéricos en *La furia y otros cuentos* by Silvina Ocampo." *América. Cahiers du CRICCAL* 17 (1997): 309–18.

Ruskin, John. "Of the Pathetic Fallacy." *Modern Painters* 3. London: George Allen, 1904.

Sabatés, Paula. "Ocampo, ese material de dramaturgia." *Página 12*, May 12, 2013. http://www.paginal2.com.ar/diario/suplementos/espectaculos/10-28627-2013-05-12.html. Web.

Sánchez, Brenda. "Resonancias de las Erinias esquíleas en 'La furia' de Silvina Ocampo." *Espéculo: Revista de Estudios Literarios* 22 (2002). http://www.ucm.es/info/especulo/numero22/erinias.html. Web.

Sánchez Sorondo, Fernando. "No hay cómo saber qué fue sueño y qué realidad." *La Prensa* Buenos Aires, January 10, 1988. Rpt. in Ocampo, *El dibujo del tiempo* 350–4.

Santos-Phillips, Eva. "La representación femenina en la narrativa de Silvina Ocampo." Diss. U of California, Davis, 1995.

———. "Questioning and Transgressing in the Representations of Silvina Ocampo and Remedios Varo." *Hispanic Journal* 25.1–2 (2004): 155–70.

Sartre, Jean-Paul. "Why Write?" *"What Is Literature?" and Other Essays*. Trans. Bernard Frechtman. Cambridge, MA: Harvard UP, 1988. 48–69.

Selnes, Gisle. "The Feminine (Ob)Scene of Cruelty." *Orbis Litterarum* 63.6 (2008): 510–28.

"Silvina Ocampo traduce a Emily Dickinson." Rev. of *Poemas de Emily Dickinson* by Silvina Ocampo. *La Capital*, April 6, 1986.

Speranza, Graciela. "La voz del otro: Bioy Casares y Silvina Ocampo." *Homenaje a Adolfo Bioy Casares: Una retrospectiva de su obra.* Ed. Alfonso de Toro and Susanna Regazzoni. Madrid: Iberoamericana, 2002.

Stavans, Ilan, ed. *Prospero's Mirror: A Translators' Portfolio of Latin American Short Fiction.* Williamantic, CN: Curbstone, 1998.

Swahn, Jan Öjivond. *The Tale of Cupid and Psyche (Aarne-Thompson 425§428).* Lund: Gleerup, 1966.

Terán, Oscar. *Nuestros años sesenta.* Buenos Aires: Puntosur, 1991.

Todo disfraz repugna a quien lo lleva. By Alfredo Martín and Grupo Hipocampo. Teatro del Borde, Buenos Aires. 2013. Performance.

Tomassini, Graciela. "La paradoja de la escritura: los dos últimos libros de Silvina Ocampo." *Anales de Literatura Hispanoamericana* 21 (1992): 377–86.

——. *El espejo de Cornelia: La obra cuentística de Silvina Ocampo.* Buenos Aires: Plus Ultra, 1995.

——. "Menos que un puñado de polvo ... Acerca de 'Fragmentos del libro invisible'." Domínguez and Mancini 171–84.

Torres, Isabel, ed. *Rewriting Classical Mythology in the Hispanic Baroque.* Woodbridge: Tamesis, 2007.

——. *Love Poetry in the Spanish Golden Age: Eros, Eris and Empire.* Woodbridge, Tamesis, 2013.

Tryphonopoulos, Demetres P., and Stephen J. Adams, eds. *The Ezra Pound Encyclopedia.* Westport, CT: Greenwood, 2005.

Ulla, Noemí. *Tango, rebelión y nostalgia.* 1967. Buenos Aires: Centro Editor de América Latina, 1982.

——. *Encuentros con Silvina Ocampo.* 1982. Buenos Aires: Leviatán, 2003.

——. *Ciudades.* 1983. Trans. Ascensión Berthelot. Toulouse: Ombre, 1994.

——. *El ramito y otros cuentos.* 1990. Buenos Aires: Proa, 2001.

——. *Invenciones a dos voces: Ficción y poesía en Silvina Ocampo.* Buenos Aires: Torres Agüero, 1992.

——. *La insurrección literaria.* Buenos Aires: Torres Agüero, 1996.

——. "Huellas de una poética en los cuentos-carta de *La furia.*" *Co-Textes* 33 (1997): 107–15.

——. "La música y la plástica en la literatura de Silvina Ocampo." *Segundas Jornadas Internacionales de Literatura Argentina/Comparatística: Actas.* Ed. Daniel Altamiranda. Buenos Aires: Universidad de Buenos Aires, 1997. 408–16.

——, ed. *Silvina Ocampo: Una escritora oculta.* Hipótesis y Discusiones #18. Buenos Aires: Facultad de Filosofía y Letras de la Universidad de Buenos Aires, 1999.

——. "Construcción de una poética en la exaltación de la patria: Sara de Ibáñez y Silvina Ocampo." *La mujer en la república de las letras.* Ed. Maryse Renaud. Poitiers: Centre de Recherches Latino-Américaines/Archivos, Université de Poitiers, 2001. 197–203.

——. *Silvina Ocampo: Poesía inédita y dispersa.* Buenos Aires: Emecé, 2001.

——. "Los Bioy." *Cuadernos Hispanoamericanos* 609 (2001): 53–5.

——. "En memoria de Silvina." *Cuadernos Hispanoamericanos* 622 (2002): 21–8.

——. *Variaciones rioplatenses.* Buenos Aires: Simurg, 2007.

Vargas Llosa, Mario. "Prólogo." *El verdadero Barba Azul: La tragedia de Gilles de Rais.* Barcelona: Tusquets, 1972.

El vestido de terciopelo. Dir. Lilián Morello. 2001. Film.

Walas, Guillermina. "La mirada en la escritura: Identidades femeninas en *Personas en la sala* de Norah Lange y 'El diario de Porfiria Bernal' de Silvina Ocampo." *Cuadernos para Investigación de la Literatura Hispánica* 21 (1996): 159–80.

Warner, Marina. *From the Beast to the Blonde: On Fairy Tales and their Tellers.* London: Chatto and Windus, 1994.

Whitman, Walt. *Leaves of Grass.* www.whitmanarchive.org. Web.

Wilcock, Juan Rodolfo. *Sexto.* 1953. Buenos Aires: Emecé, 1999.

——. *El caos.* Buenos Aires: Sudamericana, 1974.

Willson, Patricia. *La constelación del sur: Traductores y traducciones en la literatura argentina del siglo XX.* Buenos Aires: Siglo Veintiuno, 2004.

Yao, Steven G. *Translation and the Languages of Modernism: Gender, Politics, Language.* New York: Palgrave Macmillan, 2002.

Yelin, Julieta. "Kafka en Argentina." *Hispanic Review* 78.2 (2010): 251–73.

Zapata, Mónica. "Rire: Entre le plaisir et l'horreur: Les récits courts de Silvina Ocampo." *Études littéraires* 28.1 (1995): 9–19.

——. "'El castigo' de Silvina Ocampo: Parole et pouvoir." *Co-Textes* 33 (1997): 81–90.

——. "Entre niños y adultos, entre risa y horror: dos cuentos de Silvina Ocampo." *América. Cahiers du CRICCAL* 17 (1997): 345–61.

——. *Silvina Ocampo: Récits d'horreur et d'humour.* Paris: L'Harmattan, 2009.

Žižek, Slavoj. *The Sublime Object of Ideology.* London: Verso, 1989.

Zullo-Ruiz, Fernanda. "The Spatial Organization of Rape in Silvina Ocampo's 'El pecado mortal'." *Latin American Literary Review* 33.65 (2005): 88–108.

Index

CPSIA information can be obtained
at www.ICGtesting.com
Printed in the USA
BVOW03*0508091216

470238BV00008B/51/P